SAVE YOURSELF BEFORE NORMAL KILLS YOU

ASCENSION IN THE AGE OF CHAOS

MICHELLE CRENSHAW

A DIVISION OF HAY HOUSE

Balboa Press books may be ordered through booksellers or by contacting:

Balboa Press
A Division of Hay House
1663 Liberty Drive
Bloomington, IN 47403
www.balboapress.com
1 (877) 407-4847

All Scripture quotations are taken from the King James Version.

Print information available on the last page.

ISBN: 978-1-9822-3022-7 (sc)
ISBN: 978-1-9822-3023-4 (e)

Balboa Press rev. date: 10/03/2019

For Carl
Carl Kenneybrew Jr.
July 2, 1961 to July 26, 2016

CONTENTS

INTRODUCTION

This book beckons you to question everything you currently view as normal. It also challenges you to think with new ideas, see with new vision, and, act with more freedom and purpose. That process begins with questioning everything you think, believe, and "know" to be right, wrong, good, bad, and yes "normal. For it is "normal" for wars and rumors of wars to loom over our global community. It is "normal" for food to be "modified" so it lasts on the shelves for weeks and months and years instead of days. It is "normal" for our children and elderly to be misused as human "guinea pigs" as they are injected with synthetic vaccines and prescribed medications full of side effects that manifest defects, disabilities, terminal illnesses, and dependence on medications for a lifetime. It is "normal" to drive, and drive, and drive, headed nowhere fast as we deplete natural resources for the sake of faster, better, and more powerful. It is even "normal" to die trying to collect pieces of paper with White men's faces on them, just so we can buy possessions we believe will make us more influential and more relevant than our neighbors. Yes, it is normal that somewhere in the world, someone(s) will die because we need what we need and want what we want; even at the expense or demise of another. This is the normal world we now live in. And, this "normal" world is killing us all roughly and swiftly. ...whether we realize it or not.

This book is also about letting go. It is about letting go of past beliefs, behaviors, and thinking that have been with you all your life. Most of these thoughts, values, and belief systems were deposited in you long ago without your awareness or consent. Yes, we are all the target of a diabolical mind control system that has now been in place for centuries. To make matters even more disturbing, the book emphasizes that this mind control paradigm we all live in is as "normal: as baseball and hotdogs, pizza and beer, politics and election primaries. Simultaneously, this is a book about self-love, personal empowerment, and spiritual ascension. For it is my contention and experience that when you love yourself and others enough, you are empowered to replace destructive norms with a new paradigm full of possibilities, creativity and divine purpose. But first, you must wake up and recognize the effect that this mind control project is having on your current life paradigm.

Are you happy with your life? Is money making you happy? Are your spouse and friends making you happy? Is your job, your checkbook, your smart phone, your GMO food, your 2" eyelashes or your monthly rent payment making you happy? And exactly whose responsibility is it to "make" you happy anyway? Furthermore, how can you expect or rely upon the designers of this mind control project to tell you the truth about anything? And, why would you even have such an expectation in the first place? For each of us was given a mind to think for ourselves, a spirit to guide us divinely, and a will to do whatever we choose to do. These endowments have empowered us to be the keepers of our souls and the masters of our destiny.

This book teaches that you are the one who is responsible for your happiness. You are the one who must discern and choose what you will believe and think, as well as how you will behave in the world. Ultimately, therefore, this book is about spiritual ascension. For I believe once you tap into your divine awareness and power, you can and will let go of the "normal" way of seeing the world around you and the people in it. I believe, as you connect with the inner wisdom of your divine Self, you will know and inner-stand the interconnectivity of all living things, all joy, all peace and yes, all love. Thus, this book beckons you to let go of just about everything that limits your capacity to love in the fullness of collective divinity and identity. For we are all spirit beings are we not? We are all energy are we not? And we are all made in the divine image of creative love. If not...from whence does our divine life light originate?

Save Yourself Before Normal Kills You is a wakeup call for mankind. It is an alarm sounded for those who know "something just isn't right" about our current world condition. Ultimately, it is about cracking open a new way of knowing, thinking, and behaving; a revelation that has the power to shift our current global trajectory away from destruction and toward a new direction of wellness, awareness, clarity and universal harmony, purpose and cooperation. I pray, therefore, that this book is the light switch that activates complete, constructive change, transformation, and spiritual ascension in this Age of Chaos. I am certain you will look at the world differently after you read this book. May that different view lead you to more self-awareness, more self-love, and more divine humanity; which seeks truth, embraces change, and empowers you to save yourself (and others) before normal kills you. Together, we can think for ourselves and live free!

Peace & Blessings!
Michelle "Mama" Crenshaw

CHAPTER ONE

What Kind of Life Am I Living Anyway?

> *"Who Are You?"*
> ***The Cheshire Cat*** (from the **Walt Disney** animated film: **Alice In Wonderland**, 1951, **Dir.** Wilfred Jackson, Clyde Geronimi, Hamilton Luske)

Introduction:

I believe that eventually every person comes to a place in life where they seriously ask themselves the question, "what kind of life am I living anyway?" Sometimes the question arises after a catastrophic life event like the death of a spouse or loss of a career. Sometimes the question comes up as we take note of the disparaging conditions of society, or after some spiritual epiphany or awakening. Since you're reading this book, I'm certain you've already asked yourself this question more than once. In search of the answer, you have probably already given yourself over to the arduous process of reinventing "You" many times over; struggling to keep up with the everchanging world calling you to be everything you can be. But the truth is, this pursuit of the success-driven lifestyle most often leads us on a path to nowhere.

Like a frantic hamster on his wheel, our effort is aggressive yet forever stagnant. We recognize we are going nowhere, still, we rarely question the logic of a world system where only a few achieve the dream they seek to attain. We tell ourselves that the path to success is clear and attainable: obey your parents, excel in school, get a degree or two, compete against your colleagues, work harder, and by any means necessary...win. Our intelligent mind tells us that everyone cannot win in the current world paradigm. But even though our incessant pursuit of winning seems in vain, we press on. For we expect this pursuit will bring us money, possessions, status, comforts, and the high esteem of others; all symbols of so-called success. These symbols, however, most often fail to bring us the happiness, joy, peace or contentment we seek. So, despite our best efforts, success continues to elude us as we become increasingly weary and disenchanted with the entire process, as well as, the outcomes of all our efforts.

With such an existence, it is inevitable that we eventually come to a crossroads where we wonder whether the energy we expend is manifesting the outcomes that we seek. Once those questions take root, we begin to challenge the very thought processes and social systems that steered us toward these beliefs, which we know as true and constant, in the first place. In so doing, we must take into consideration that our parents, home environments, schools, social institutions, laws, and religious affiliations, as well as our perceptions of right, wrong, past, present and future events, all play a key role in shaping who we are, what we think, which goals we set for ourselves, and how we will strive to achieve them in our everyday lives.

In school, for example, we learned the laws of mathematics so we expect that 2+2 will always equal 4. We assumed from an early age that all the laws of the world system, like the laws of mathematics, would remain constant and predictable. However, the school of life teaches us that life is indeed very unpredictable it seems. In fact, we usually come to realize that life is chock full of unexpected roadblocks, mountains, valleys, floods, droughts and detours with enough blessings and achievements thrown in to keep most of us motivated. With time however, we often lose that wide-eyed sense of expectation we once had as awe-filled hope for the future dims in the afterglow of life's disappointments.

Yes, as children we were creative, imaginative, and full of expectation. But now the adult world finds us boxed-in, stagnant, disillusioned and inflexible with a never-ending list of reasons why we cannot seem to define or achieve our personal goals for success as we once envisioned them. Eventually, perhaps as we are breaking a proverbial sweat on the great hamster wheel of life, we hear that inner voice faintly calling out to us and begging the question *what kind of life am I living anyway?* In this chapter we will examine this question as the first step in our journey toward ascension.

As I recall the evolution of my own *"save yourself"* experience, I realize that putting this question first was what positioned me for my initial awakening. Why? Because at this starting place I was compelled to face the reality that my life, even with all its blessings, was out of control, no longer manageable and clearly self-destructive in nature. When I say out of control I specifically mean out of my control. For the agenda of the world around me, an agenda which I was subconsciously participating in, was clearly driving me to place the pursuit of money at the top of my life priorities. So work was my slave-driver and I, its loyal slave. I did not have pie in the sky dreams of being a millionaire nor was I the materialistic type. I just wanted what I think most want; a safe and comfortable home for my family, nutritious food, good health, quality education, and a home with a picket fence, 2.5 children and all that the American Dream had to offer. But the truth I had to face was that this pursuit, sincere and noble though it was, was, in truth, killing me, very slowly.

On top of that I had to face the fact that the very system I had trusted, followed, and believed in was fundamentally flawed. A more accurate term would be that the system itself is a well-constructed and quite diabolical, out and out lie designed to control the beliefs and actions of the masses. I admit, the idea that you are a victim of a global mind control project is a rather big pill to swallow at first, so I have devoted an entire chapter to that subject later in the book. The point here is that realizing the truth prompted me to take a full inventory of the values, beliefs, motivations, choices, issues, baggage, skeletons and decisions which I made along the way in order to arrive at this impasse of self-discovery.

In asking the question again and again, examining it under the scrutiny of mind, body, soul and spirit, I began to transform my thinking and my belief systems. In doing so, I found more personal truth, more freedom and more focused purpose for my life. It is my hope, therefore, that once you jump off your proverbial hamster wheel and embrace the **Ascending Mind** process, you too will catch your breath and slowly separate yourself from the repetitive assumptions and behaviors that keep your mind and your life stuck in stagnation. As your auto-pilot existence comes to a halt, you can finally be still. It is in the stillness, that the true spiritual work begins to unfold before you. In the quietness, your creativity is awakened, your energy is ignited, and your spirit journey of ascension begins.

With the truth uncovered, you will come to understand that the world, as you have come to know it, is an illusionary construct devised to form a collective consciousness that keeps you trapped in ignorance, fear, and repetition. But in the stillness of mind, body and spirit, you will find your way back to your forgotten self; the true you who knows who you are, where you came from, and where you are going. At this place of acute personal awareness, you will discover a healing path of truth and freedom which leads to peace, contentment, fearlessness, abundance and a whole new world of possibilities.

REFLECTIONS ON ASCENSION
STOP! I WANT TO GET OFF

Probably one of the hardest things for a hamster to do is to stop. I remember being fascinated with hamsters and gerbils as a child. My mother indulged my interest in them and so over the years, my bedroom was always emitting the annoying squeak of numerous pet hamsters running on their wheels. Every night, for a large portion of the night it seemed, my family had to endure the incessant rattle until the dear little creatures finally tuckered themselves out and went back to sleep.

Yes, a hamster on a wheel was a sight to behold as I'd sit there frozen; watching them run like hell to nowhere. The tenacity with which they were going nowhere fast was astounding to say the least. It amused me. Finally, modern technology improved and someone invented a little ball that allows the dear thing the chance to at least have the illusion of freedom as he runs inside the ball almost as feverishly as he ran on the wheel (as he runs in the ball, the ball rolls across the floor). So, run they did night after night. In fact, they say the wheel is an absolute necessity for a hamster cage and without it, the hamster will die earlier than his normally short little lifespan of 2 years.

But as I reflected on that, I suddenly realized that maybe the wheel is why hamsters' lives are so short lived. Maybe they just run themselves ragged until they burn out and croak. They are after all, trapped in a cage while in the care of humans, instead of running free in nature. I have never observed hamsters in a free environment. But the reality is that in the wild, hamsters dwell mostly underground and run mostly to avoid predators, gather food and in some breeds, travel, as far as a mile, to find a mate. Now that's a drastic contrast to the life of hamsters in captivity because in the wild, the running is a function of life rather than a byproduct of limitation. Thus, hamsters in captivity can be likened to inmates in prison who spend most of their time buffing up since opportunities to live creatively and free are not an option.

But we can only speculate as to whether the hamster is happier in a cage or roaming free in its natural state. I can only assume that all living creatures born free in nature are happier in their natural state, as was originally intended by the Creator. Most likely, this theory is, also applicable to humankind, even though the modern world system would probably disagree. For according to the Tell-Lie-Vision we are all happier with our modern conveniences, are we not? But the bigger question for us is: Do we truly believe that we are happier than our ancestors were without them? Afterall, we have all the conveniences we need to be comfortable, right? Homes made of brick, heat generated by natural gas, manufactured cars powered by fossil fuels and food grown with lots of pesticides and genetic modifications to make them last in the fridge for weeks without spoiling! Who wouldn't want to live this way?

WHAT DOES IT MEAN TO BE FREE?

Have you ever considered what it would be like to be truly free? Would the hamster's life be any longer or more fulfilling in the wild? For that matter, would your lifespan or quality of life improve if you lived a truly free existence? The reality of the hamster in captivity is that all these dear little creatures do is...

Sleep, eat, run Sleep, eat, run Sleep, eat, run until they die! The saddest thing about having pet hamsters is that every hamster I ever had died suddenly, without any indication of a previous illness. I concluded they just ran themselves to death. Sound familiar?

I remember crying about it as a child; that is, until I lived through the third or fourth hamster death. After a few years of hamster funerals, I simply accepted that at any time I might wake to find one of my furry friends turned feet up in the cage. Now, as an adult, the metaphor of the hamster wheel makes an emphatic point about the meaning of life and the current human condition; creating a strong argument for the need to STOP and assess one's life if one plans or aspires to experience true freedom, happiness, and spiritual ascension.

STOP: AN INTRODUCTION TO MIND CLEARING

When I learned to drive, my instructor used to make a joke that made STOP an acronym for: **S**pin **T**ires **on** **P**avement. At 15, it was a corny joke intended to help me relax as I was learning the very dangerous skill and art of driving. Unfortunately, most people spin their proverbial tires on the pavement of life and never realize that the stop signs of our journey are life-saving moments needed to bring balance, peace, clarity and purpose into our lives. Likewise, when it comes to saving yourself and activating your journey of spiritual ascension, the need to come to a full STOP is imperative if you want to change the trajectory of your life path. For in stopping the sleep, eat, run cycle, you create space in your life, mind, heart, and spirit to begin an assessment of your thoughts, perceptions, beliefs, hurts, disappointments and choices; past and present.

I believe that taking the time to stop is probably the most essential element of the ascension process. For how can you save yourself if you don't stop to realize that you need saving? Is that not what occurs when people *get saved* in church? For first, they must acknowledge that their soul needs saving. When I was a Christian minister, we always allowed time in the service for this type of reflection.

Accordingly, to save yourself, you will have to acknowledge the truth...that it is your "normal" life, rather than your eternal soul, that needs saving. Furthermore, if you really want to live a free, loving and contented life, you must etch out your own personal pathway to it. Afterall, when you're on a road trip and realize you're going the wrong way, don't you stop to look at the map and re-chart a course toward the desired destination? Likewise, how can you get to the right spiritual destination if you don't stop to assess the past beliefs, choices, decisions, and circumstances that got you lost in the first place. If you don't want to take the wrong path again and again, you must stop and assess your past so you can learn from it and make new choices to manifest a better, freer future.

Thus, the skill of Mind Clearing must be perfected and applied often on the journey to spiritual inner-standing and ascension. For you cannot learn the skill and art of ascension if you cannot even allow time to stop, look, listen, meditate, plan, adjust, heal, unlearn, learn anew, and analyze all the information, changes and transformations that go along with the process of being and becoming an ascending soul.

Going through life without this ongoing process is an invitation for spiritual disaster. Truth is, you'll never really be in the moments of life if you're too busy running through them. Instead you will find yourself forever living a life where the moment is lost to an imaginary future that is neither promised nor real. This is a common mistake most make while navigating through The System. For most of us exist on a predestined course designed to ensure that we achieve all the goals and desires the System has subliminally groomed and systematically trained us to pursue. Like the hamster, most of us live in a cage; longing to experience the joy that comes from living a life of freedom and spiritual inner-standing. We will revisit this topic as the book progresses.

ASCENDING MIND CHALLENGE #1
The 10 Minute Moment

It is important to accept, at this very moment therefore, that STOP means STOP, in the most literal sense. STOP, as in cease to engage in any and all events, actions, or processes you are currently participating in. As your Thought Train is currently saying to you, *when in the world will I ever have time to do that* or *that's ridiculous, you can't just stop doing everything* or *I can't just stop!*, it is probably the perfect time for you to actually prove your thoughts wrong and just STOP, right now. Find a quiet place, close your eyes, and take about 10 minutes to DO NOTHING. This is a skill you will cultivate as you work through this book and apply it to your daily life practices. Please pause now and set the timer on your cell phone for 10 minutes to prepare yourself for this exercise.

I hope you realize that by choosing to "stop, right now", you are immediately dispelling the failure messages from your Thought Train which may be telling you that you can't stop right now. But the truth is, if you can train yourself to stop right now for 10 minutes, with practice, you will eventually learn to stop for 60 minutes, or longer. This is where real spiritual work can be achieved...in the still silence of your spiritual ether. In the silence of infinite possibilities!

INTRODUCTION TO MIND CLEARING
The 10 Minute Moment

Find a quiet place in your home. For the purposes of this exercise, do not sit in nature or anywhere where even subtle sounds can be a distraction. Make sure your seat is comfortable. You may also choose to lay down if you wish.

Now...be still and breathe deeply for a few moments. When you feel yourself start to relax, start the timer and take a deep breath, exhale and say softly to yourself:

I can stop, I will stop, I am stopping

Repeat this to yourself until you feel your body relax and all urgency dissipates. Once you have brought your mind to accept where you're going, you will gradually arrive at a place where you can just STOP. As you repeat these words, breathe deeply and dismiss every thought that does not agree with your desire to be still, to be quiet, and to be at peace. As the clutter of your mind dims, breathe deeply and in your mind, quietly repeat the words:

I am stopping, I am stopping, I am stopping

The repetition establishes your desire to reprogram your conscious Self (heart, mind, soul, will). As you inform your conscious Self of your intention, your subconscious mind responds by slowing down the background chatter of the conscious mind. For our beliefs are established by what we hear, see, and entertain. In this process, audible self-talk is the creative energy force that instructs the mind of our purposeful intentions. Through repetition, we give the mind time to process new information and in turn, set a course for a change in our conscious and subconscious thoughts. That's why affirmations are such a valuable tool in the pursuit of mental reprogramming and spiritual ascension.

Remember, it might take you five minutes or more just to reach a place of stillness where you are experiencing the truth of the words *I am stopping.* That experience is to be expected so no worries. In fact, if it takes 20 minutes to get there, it's totally okay. This exercise is not a race. Likewise, if your failure thoughts come back, LET THEM GO and gently invite them to return to the Thought Train from whence they came! Eventually, in the quiet stillness, you will discover a place of solitude, peace and mindful stillness. Do not be afraid to be still. As ancient, holy texts remind us, *"be still, and know that I am"* (**Psalms 46.10**). So, if you want to connect with the god who lives within you and is expressed as you, you must teach yourself to be still.

BENEFITS OF THIS EXERCISE:

If you practice mind clearing for just 10 minutes a day, you will slowly train yourself to stop and clear the mind of thoughts that do not contribute to your ascension. For clearing the mind empowers you to recognize, isolate and address the thoughts and feelings that cause dis-ease, anxiety and confusion. With practice, thoughts of low self-worth, failure, unworthiness, guilt, envy, and selfishness, just to name a few, dissipate as your ability to still the mind becomes easier and stronger.

I will emphasize the usefulness of this practice again and again throughout the book in order to help you cultivate and master the skill and art of mind clearing. With time you will find this an extremely useful practice in your always ascending journey. For now, please close the book, find a quiet place and allow stillness. It's only 10 minutes. No background noise, no prayers, no self-talk, no music, no meditation tapes, etc. Just you and the Divine Spirit within you... for 10 minutes... in silence and peace.

PLEASE PAUSE FOR YOUR 10 MINUTE MOMENT

THE 10 MINUTE MOMENT-FOLLOW-UP

I hope you did not ignore the 10 Minute Moment you were just introduced to in the previous section. I know for a fact that someone reading this book did NOT STOP. I am, laughing out loud as I write this. Unfortunately, systemic programming tells us we don't have time for ourselves. And yet there is so much healing in a 10 Minute Moment, if well planned and executed. It requires intention for a person to use it; intention, discipline and trust. The first two requirements are understood, I think, however; the issue of trust is another matter altogether. Trust in what? Trust in who? To which I would insist...trust in...YOU.

It takes a lot of courage to take 10 minutes alone with yourself and even more to take 30 minutes or longer. Remember, I emphasized no music, no recitation, no chanting, no rituals, props, talisman, etc. Just you, yourself, and you, clearing your mind by purposefully slowing down your mental activity to a point where you can disconnect your mind and emotions from your inner Thought Train.

That is the true purpose of this practice. If you find it difficult at first, no worries. You may have to attempt many 10-minute moments before you even realize you're having a ***Conscious Observer*** experience. With practice, however, you will start to experience your thoughts as an intangible component of your tangible brain activity.

Thus, with practice, the 10-Minute Moment exercise trains and empowers you to:

1. identify thoughts and emotions that may no longer serve you and
2. remove those unproductive mental catalysts from your boxcar of beliefs

Ultimately, the goal is to reach a state where you simply have no thoughts at all. That is the ultimate mind clearing achievement! Some say that ancient shaman often used the practice of mind clearing to reach altered states of consciousness that opened a spiritual portal to the Mind of God. I would affirm such experiences are possible and I must admit that many in-depth mind clearing experiences I've had have been uniquely epic and life changing.

Personal Observations:

1. Did you find it easy or difficult to settle into your 10 Minute Moment? Why or why not?

   ____

   ____

   ____

2. How long did it take to calm your thoughts and experience some degree of stillness of mind, body and/or emotion? What challenges did you face to find stillness?

____

____

____

3. What changes (if any) did you notice in your mental, physical or emotional state during this quiet moment?

____

____

____

4. Which statement below best describes your 10 Minute Moment experience? (*choose all that apply*)
   a. I found myself thinking about the time.
   b. I reached a point where my mind was very still
   c. I found the experience awkward.
   d. My mind wasn't completely clear, but my thought-clutter diminished somewhat.
   e. Though I struggled at first, I finally settled down and became still and quiet.
   f. I felt more relaxed afterwards.
   g. I can see how practicing this activity might be helpful to me.
   h. It was a total waste of 10 minutes.

5. PERSONAL NOTES:

____

____

____

LIFE LESSONS ON ASCENSION:
Letting Go of Thoughts and Things

Ultimately, the 10 Minute Moment is an introduction to the concept of ***Letting Go***.

When Carl and I first let go of our systemic lifestyle, we had no roadmap or instruction manual on what the process would entail. What we did know was if we could just get our lives to a point where stopping was even remotely possible, we would at least be moving in the right direction. Soon, we began to visualize and brainstorm what bringing our daily grind of life to a screeching halt would look like, be like. Honestly, we had no idea what was going to happen but we both felt that the life we envisioned would manifest if we continued with intention and discipline. Months before we decided to move from the house we were renting, we started purging our belongings. I would spontaneously have yard sales, not for the money, but for the clearing. I started reading books that were collecting dust on the shelf, then giving them to the Goodwill. We were fortunate because we lived across the street from a Goodwill drop-off center. And piece by piece, box by box, drawer by drawer, we began to let go of our stuff.

Carefully discarding our stuff was a daunting and arduous task at first. I was so afraid of discarding some item of importance that had helped me connect to the many tender moments and memories of my life; believing that these things gave my life meaning. Certainly, those old boxes filled with mementos did produce some long, lost treasures that I had forgotten about. And as I examined all the miscellaneous pieces of paper and memorabilia along the way, I will admit, I sometimes found it hard to throw many belongings away. But since we had already decided that when we finally let go, most of these items could not go with us, I simply accepted that truth. So, item by item, paper by paper, piece by piece I asked myself...*is this necessary moving forward?*

For the truth is, material things are just that...things. They are merely the representation of memory patterns that your brain synapses retain, if you revisit them often enough. It is the thing that helps you recall that this memory has merely been deeply stored away. As I moved forward with my personal purge, I found so many treasures. But I was committed to the process and so, I savored every recollection and every emotion that these relatively insignificant items triggered. They were all there, trinkets from elementary and high school, years of birthday and Mother's Day cards; some from people I barely remembered but most from dear loved ones living and deceased. There were papers from past jobs, job descriptions, project portfolios I had created for employers and clients, and so many random ideas scribbled on post-it notes that I had to laugh at my past with a warm and endearing shaking of the head for keeping such things. It seemed I had saved everything. Nevertheless, with each new discovery, I reminded myself of the goal. Purge and let go.

The process was neither easy, nor was it simple. I'd be lying if I told you it was. But it was necessary. Slowly, library shelves full of books became one box of books. Numerous file cabinets full of my life's work became one box of important archival papers. Boxes and boxes of old greeting cards dwindled down to one 9 by 12 envelope of only the most important ones. In a nutshell, we took our time to relish the past and let it go; to cry and laugh and reminisce sentiments long forgotten. With each purge, I reminded my mind to remember these important elements that made my life what it had been. I gave thanks for all the love I'd shared, relished all the accomplishments that were documented, and rested in the assurance that none of these moments would ever be truly lost. For I believed they were a part of me and that they would continue to be with me, always.

After several months of purging, as Carl and I sat at our desks discussing what the future without all our stuff would be like, I suddenly said out loud, *I'm giving the landlord notice to move...it's time*!! Without hesitation Carl agreed. We had exactly 31 days to let go of the rest of our stuff and our way of life. That's when it got crazy and the awakening of letting go of stuff was truly realized.

I immediately decided it was time for a final yard sale. First, I separated the heirloom items I wanted to give to my three adult children. I put in a call to the two who were already on their own and told them we were moving in 30 days and if they wanted anything from the house they should come and get first pick of what was going out for the yard sale. They all showed up and added to the piles I had already made for them; some furniture, crystal, appliances, electronics, art, family heirlooms, and household items. Once that was over, we started setting things out for the sale.

Now this is where it gets interesting. A few weeks before, we saw a video in which the owner of a shoe repair and accessories store gave his customers the choice to pay any amount within the range of his wholesale cost and the retail price of the item. All the merchandise was labeled with both prices and the decision was completely up to the customer. Talk about an inspiring video! Some people chose the lowest price of course, even some for whom the higher cost was clearly within their price range. Some of them paid the full price, and others paid somewhere in between. But the odd part of this story was that most of the customers were completely befuddled by the choice! When the customer couldn't decide on his/her own, the owner replied, *"what does your heart tell you?"*

Well, we decided this was how we would start. So out the furnishings and trinkets went and along came the yard sale customers. One by one when asked, how much, we replied, *what does your heart tell you* to give.? It was an amazing day. Some of the shoppers were so confused by this approach that they lingered for hours, making small talk, and trying to get me to decide for them what to give. I refused and, simply laughed it off and replied, *what does your heart tell you?*

The entire day became an exercise in human behavioral psychology as people came and went, came and stayed a while (I made coffee) or came and gave much more and much less than the items were worth.

I vividly remember the story of one sale we made that day of an authentically hand-carved painting from Africa. I explained to the shopper that the gentlemen that made it had died and that this piece was the last of its kind. The woman lingered a while and I went back into the house. Finally, Carl came in the house and said: *the lady decided to take the painting from Africa.* Then he handed me $6.00. Well my face must have told on me because Carl burst into laughter and said, *that is what's in her heart dear.*

Well, I could, of course, do nothing but laugh too. What a day of learning that was! The next few days of the yard sale quickly became a yard giveaway and day by day, as we watched our things leave the front yard, we realized our emotional baggage was leaving with them. It was one of the most freeing experiences of my life and many people were blessed. In the end, we reduced the contents of a 3-bedroom home and garage down to a 5X5 storage unit.

It was a grandiose feat to say the least. But the entire experience proved to me that I could in fact let go of my things and remain emotionally and spiritually intact. I realized I was still me, but me with the lightest load I had carried in decades. And the experience created and established a true paradigm shift in my relationship with things forever. In truth, I almost felt my very soul lift a few feet off the proverbial ground! With so little baggage, I could think more clearly, see more vividly and most importantly, STOP.

This was the goal of letting go: to be able to stop and think. Best of all, without all our stuff, and without the stress and grind of a $2300 rent payment, I experienced true freedom. For a great weight had been lifted, enabling us to evaluate our next moves in peace. What a gift! Asé

Journal Reflection: August 2, 2014

Well, we did it. We REALLY let go. I guess the reality of all that set in today for sure. When we were driving, looking for a place to bed down for a couple of nights. We are both very tired physically, yet with an air of relief.

We are rethinking our packing since some important things were inadvertently stored. The kitchen tub with all the cooking supplies. I also stored the medicinals (vitamins mostly…and my pain medicine) which I wish I had today because my body is telling me I've pushed too hard. My calves hurt, shoulder and neck & upper back. My knees hurt because I fell today at the wedding we sang at in Santa Barbara. Oh, and yes, I have 3 enormous boils ON MY STOMACH!!??? I guess that's my body "letting go". So sleeping was not great because I couldn't get in a comfortable position.

Journal Reflection: August 3, 2014 (excerpt)

Yes, sleep was difficult last night. The beds here are small. Full size. Carl eventually got up and laid in the 2nd bed. Oh, last night, Carl went into a slight depressed mode; but I was like, "Hey, we're free"! He said, "I let you down". But I don't feel that way. I KNEW this part of the letting go process would be challenging. It's all NEW, DIFFERENT, etc. because all (most) variables are unknown. But like the man they call Jesus said: "TAKE NO THOUGHT" (**Matthew 6:25**) *for the basic needs… clothes, food, shelter. BUT SEEK FIRST the Kingdom of God. Which is…RIGHTEOUSNESS, PEACE AND JOY in the Holy Spirit. With all that said, I am oddly at peace. I AM ascending. I AM confident that all of this is necessary for me. That's the point. IT IS NECESSARY. The journey to Letting Go is underway. I AM (we are) learning every day to let go and let the Creator (within my Self) unfold my experiences as I AM desiring them to be. TODAY I AM. And all that IS, is good* *and desirable. No undesirable circumstance will become my reality. Even in my body, I refuse to accept this pain having final reality. I will rest and wait and renew my strength today. And I will experience my wholeness because I AM WELL…BODY, MIND & SPIRIT. Glory Hallelujah!*

CHAPTER TWO

Wake Up!

> *"You must unlearn what you have learned"* **Yoda**
> (from the film **Star Wars;** Dir. **George Lucas**)

INTRODUCTION: Code Red

I once had the great honor of serving on the board of directors of the largest urban recreational center in the country. The chairman of that board always used the expression *"the patient is bleeding profusely"* whenever he wanted to drive home the urgent need for all board members to quickly and effectively find a solution to the problem on the table. Though I always found the wording a bit extreme and slightly amusing, I knew that whenever he used the expression, it was time for all of us to roll up our sleeves and get to work saving the patient from imminent death.

Likewise, I am using this expression here in order to impress upon you the sense of urgency you need to have when you begin any journey of self-assessment and discovery. In this metaphor, you, and not some external problem from which you can detach yourself, are the patient lying on the operating table bleeding out and facing your own imminent demise. And you, more than anyone else, understand the severity of the conditions that ail you, and, the deep wounds and pains you have endured. Only you know how urgent the situation is so don't expect anyone but you to roll up their sleeves and get busy addressing what ails you. Ultimately you are the only one qualified to diagnose your condition, operate, and save your life!

The good news is...it's not your fault. Though you are culpable in your own self-destructive beliefs and lifestyle, there is also another factor that has wielded its assault on your mind, heart, spirit, soul, body, peace, freedom, understanding and awareness. That factor, pervasive and invasive as it is, is ironically, the very societal system that contextualizes your day to day experiences and destroys the core components that make you who you are in the first place. For though you have many demands entangling you with thoughts and things that make you feel trapped, the truth is that, ironically, you were created free.

Yes! In the beginning, you were free of emotional hang-ups, doubts and unbelief. You were born free; free of mental health syndromes like low self-esteem, self-hate and self-sabotage. Yes, you were born free and illuminated, free and full of love, free and without fear. But along the way, the thought processes that keep you in a perpetual experiential loop were installed in your mind like a computer virus. This virus was designed to obliterate your original birthright as a free, transcendent spirit-soul. Believe it or not, as a singular expression of an infinite totality (I AM), you began this creation journey through time and space with a blank canvas.

Yes, your creation story begins full of infinite possibilities! But as your life evolves through matter, time and space, the innate freedom to create, choose, love, and so on, was replaced with a holographic, mental Trojan virus chock full of lies and processes that reprogram you into a mere remnant of your original self. Selah! (*pause and think about it*).

THE MAKINGS OF YOU

> *"Almost impossible to do…describing the makings of you"* **Curtis Mayfield**

In studying the physiology of the human brain, we learn that at birth it functions very much like a brand-new computer hard drive. Beginning with an estimated 100 billion neurons each capable of making as many as 10,000 synaptic connections to other neurons, the brain can be compared to the equivalent of a computer with a 1 trillion bit per second processor. What an amazing natural wonder! At conception, these neurons begin the process of creating synaptic connections that respond to internal and external stimuli from our individual and cumulative human experiences. As this human hard drive begins to respond to physiological and experiential stimuli, our brain is programmed to interpret, repeat, and even anticipate the synaptic patterns that our life experiences record.

As we know and learned in school, the involuntary functions of the body, (such as blood pumping through the heart or maintaining physical pain and pleasure receptors), establish their synaptic firing patterns soon after conception. But what many do not consider is that this human mainframe is recording each experiential event, whether constructive or destructive, within the intangible, Unseen Mind of the person. I will refer to this unseen, formless, intangible recording function as The Ethereal Processor or EP. Thus, these two processing partners, the brain and the mind, work together to form the person's being.

When a fetus, for example, is exposed to calming music while in a gentle peaceful environment, neurotransmitters in the fetus' brain record the energy vibrations into its synaptic memory. Simultaneously, the experiential sensations attached to these energy vibrations are also stored within the child as emotions and feelings in its own, personal EP. Since everyone experiences life in a unique way, it is easy to see how two people can have completely different inner-standings about the meaning of love, happiness, good, bad, and the like.

In addition, the mother's mental and emotional energy is also transmitted to the fetus and recorded; adding another layer of experience and interpretation to be processed & stored. In fact, many studies demonstrate how the emotional state of the mother (cause) directly correlates (effect) to the emotional state of the fetus. As the fetus grows, these synaptic and ethereal events take root in the Unseen Heart (Inner Self). Once born, the child begins to express emotions and behaviors which are an amalgamation of all the messages processed in the womb and in the world. Consequently, these perinatal EP experiences, manifest as beliefs and behaviors as the child grows from infancy to adulthood; regardless of whether that behavior is perceived as right or wrong. The more consistently or frequently an experience is recorded, the more the Self is established and the more the normality of that Self is reinforced.

With each moment, therefore, one's personal EP, instantly establishes and integrates our synaptic and ethereal mental impressions into a cumulative database of memories, feelings, beliefs, values, etc. Thus, the blank slate we receive at conception quickly forms into an intricately designed human software program, unique to the individual. No wonder we need 100 billion neurons, and, an infinite ethereal storage drive in which to house all this information!

The problem we face in the current "normal" paradigm, however, is that a barrage of subliminal, and often overt messages, are being downloaded into our personal EP without our conscious awareness or consent. Because these messages, masked with deceptive double-speak woven through all areas of life, e.g. school, work, church, news, politics, advertising, etc., most of us have been unable to avoid their influence upon our world view and our Selves. Since these messages debilitate our ability to think independently, the unfortunate outcome is the pervasive de-evolution of our collective social and spiritual condition.

As we download a daily dose of fear, anxiety, complacency, apathy, ignorance, intolerance, aggression and hate, most of us are simply unaware we have done so. More disturbing is the fact that this global mind-ware has been created by and for the benefit of an elite community of beings whose minds and morals are, unfortunately, completely and utterly corrupt. In this paradigm, this mind control project touches almost all people in almost every part of the world. In this paradigm, the needs of the few, clearly outweigh the needs of All and The One. And that, my friends, also seems perfectly normal to most.

Since you're reading this book, you probably already realize that the current "normal" is anything but normal. You are also probably aware that your thinking is being manipulated; at least to some degree. At minimum, almost everyone is familiar with the New World Order global agenda of recent times. Surely you know that the designers of this world order possess the tools and the intention to control the thoughts, experiences, and behaviors of billions of people over many generations. You know this much even if you pride yourself on being too spiritual to pay attention.

Finally, you must surely know that we have become a global community of spirit-souls who have lost our deductive reasoning skills, our ability to think independently, our intelligence, our creativity, intuition, and collective divinity. It's okay if you don't know these things because you will know by the time you finish this book!

Therefore, if you truly wish to save yourself from an imprisoned mind, you must *"unlearn what you have learned"*. For according to the man called the Prophet Isaiah, *"All we like sheep have gone astray; we have turned every one to his own way"* (**Isaiah 53.6**). As such, we have surely only learned whatever the System operators want us to learn and little else. As generations pass, our collective and singular minds' ability to unlearn lies and relearn ancient inner-standings, becomes more and more daunting and less and less attainable.

As a global community, we are surely in very dire straits, as is evidenced by our current world condition. The pervasiveness of man's inhumanity to humankind is the definitive proof. For thousands of years of false programming has apparently prevented us from waking up and saving ourselves from imminent moral and material destruction. For this reason, I believe all organized religious institutions have an obligation, to facilitate quantifiable acts of peace, global unity, equity, self-love, self-esteem, appreciation of all difference, and recognition of the shared divinity of all humanity; and nothing else. For there is no need to evangelize, proselytize, or convert masses of followers to one belief system or another because ultimately, we are One Humanity and One Spirit. To date, however, most organized religious institutions still preach their religious principles in a vacuum of sameness of belief, repetitive ritual, and isolated exclusion from opposing doctrines.

Many of the religious elite are experts at beguiling their constituents with slogans, rituals, generational traditions, doctrines, and other group mind control tactics. These strategies insulate individual and institutional communities from their connection to the greater global condition. The outsiders are called sinners, heathens, infidels, unclean, or lost. If we are "really" religious, we go somewhere, sometime and pray that the world will miraculously become a better place. Then, we turn around and send our sons and daughters off to war to destroy entire countries around the world in the name of religious and political freedom. In this manner, religion has surely failed its commission to bring peace, wisdom, truth, love, unity, spirituality, and harmony to humanity. The reality is that the

"Holy" Wars changed the course of history for the entire world and turned out to be most unholy, to this day, for the global family.

No. Organized religion, as it has existed for thousands of years, cannot save you! For according to the Catholic News Agency, approximately 84% of the world population identified with some religious group as of 2012. The breakdown includes 3.3 billion Christians, 1.6 billion Muslims, 1 billion Hindus, almost 500 million Buddhists and 14 million Jews. Now, wouldn't you think that the world would be a much more peaceful place with nearly 84% of the global population practicing some form of spirituality? Though these religions purport to promulgate peace, unity and righteousness, the condition of the world, filled with bloodshed and chaos, is the undeniable evidence of man's propensity for hatred and self-destruction. Thus, people against people, and nation against nation, war, slavery, and oppression upon oppression continues as the perpetual "normal" paradigm for the modern world.

THIS PATIENT NEEDS A "MIND" TRANSPLANT!

If you are serious about your spiritual ascension, you must wake up now because it's you, unconscious on the operating table "*bleeding profusely*" and in desperate need of a mind transplant!

If you're waiting on someone else to come and save you be clear... it's not happening. Why do you think the person they call Jesus said?...

> *"Verily, I say unto you, He that believeth on me, the works that I do shall he do also; and greater works than these shall he do. Because I go unto my Father"* **John 14:12**

Here, this message is clearly telling us that we will do the same works (teaching, healing, blessing, forgiving, etc.) as the one who is speaking. He also says we will do "greater works" (miracles) than he did! Now if the man they call Jesus raised Lazarus and himself from the dead, what greater miracles could we possibly perform? Right? Yet, I believe this teaching was to let us know that we may have an equal or perhaps, even greater calling than the teacher! Therefore, I am asking you to, at the least, consider that maybe, just possibly… "*no one is coming to save you*"; except maybe, YOU! I realize the notion that you must "*save yourself*" is a big pill. But, as you read on, I believe you can swallow it. When you do, I am also confident that you will come to enjoy a greater freedom than you ever knew was possible.

THE OUTER AND INNER WORLD

As civilization grows older, our understanding of abstract concepts such as the meaning of life, freedom, joy, peace, spirit and truth has also been severely altered and compromised. When we consider the brain's capacity to process hundreds of trillions of life events, we realize that the overstimulating influence of the outer world overwhelms us and thus, cripples our ability to think independently, in our own best interests, and outside of the realm of pervasive, external, systemic programming limitations. In other words, the outer world is smothering the inner world and the result is a humanity lacking in spirit-infused intuition, wisdom, collective identity and personal esteem and empowerment. Instead, these qualities have been replaced with an overabundance of bad habits & lifestyles, as well as, pre-programmed beliefs and biases, which find us lacking in, and longing for, peace and inner-standing. That is why we have such a difficult time with awakening ourselves and saving the patient. But once we realize that, for the most part, our thoughts and beliefs are not our own, we can begin to recognize the urgent need to wake up and save the trauma patient before it is too late. Now, let's get back to the patient.

DOCTOR YOU, PAGING DOCTOR YOU!

Let's begin the awakening process by understanding that the bleeding patient is you. I reiterate...You are the patient lying on the table bleeding out. You are the one who needs emergency surgery and for you, this surgery is a matter of life or death. If you are not fed up enough with your illusionary life to accept this first step, you are probably still very much asleep and finding this first call to awakening extremely difficult to accept.

Moreover, those who are still asleep usually embrace the belief that someone or something else is coming to save them, i.e. the government, money, another person or even God perhaps. So, to make matters even more complicated, I am asking you to accept that you are also the surgeon, the nurse, the anesthetist, and the surgical technician who is monitoring your own vital signs. That's the real kicker for most because one of the basic truths of ascension applies here. That is: "**No One Is Coming to Save You**". I didn't make that one up. It's a quote from a well- respected change analyst and public speaker named Robert Ian. Carl and I listened to him on a show called Gold Seek Radio and we were profoundly impacted the day he spoke on this subject.

Since that time, the far-reaching meaning of those words has expanded in my consciousness one thousand-fold. I will expound on this in the following chapter. But for now, I am asking that you just go with me; proceeding with the understanding that for this exercise in awakening and ascension, you and only you can stop the bleeding, assess the level of damage, treat the wounds, and ultimately revive the dying patient! By now you realize that you must WAKE UP! Now, let's get to work!

LIFE LESSONS ON ASCENSION:
Question Everything

> *"I was looking for an answer. It's the question that drives us Neo. It's the question that brought you here. You know the question, just as I did".*
>
> **Trinity**-from the film: **The Matrix;** Dir. **Lana Wachowski, Andy Wachowski**

Once upon a time, there was a little girl who asked many questions about the world around her. Yet it seemed that no one could ever satisfy that hunger with answers that made sense to her. The little girl had many questions about God and religion, racism and prejudice, love and hate, happiness, and the meaning of life. As she pondered these questions and listened to the myriad of people around her struggle to answer them, she realized that she must set out to satisfy her own curiosity and find the answers to these questions, and many more, for herself.

For she realized that to do anything else would mean seeing the world around her through the eyes of others instead of her own. This made the little girl a very determined individual; one whom others viewed as curious, yes, and sometimes even strange. Strange because the more questions she asked, the more she realized the answers she received depended more on who she was asking, rather than objective facts. Her curiosity, therefore, was rarely satisfied when she depended on others to reveal the mysteries of life that she most needed to solve.

If she asked her classmates who God was, for example, she got answers like, "that's a stupid question…God is…well…God!" If she asked her father, what is racism, she was sure to get a long, and heartfelt explanation of African history along with a referral to read an impressive list of books on his bookshelf that would stimulate her intellect and imagination. But when researching history for herself, she discovered many discrepancies in facts, as well as, large gaps in tangible evidence to substantiate historical, anthropological, archeological and scientific theories on how the world began and evolved to become what it is today.

When she asked her teachers about paths of life that might be valuable for her to pursue, she was simply told: "*You can be anything you want to be as long as you study hard*". As the list of questions became more and more daunting over the years, the little girl, who was now a college student, was more confused than ever about the meaning of life and her purpose in it. That little girl was me.

Now I do not exactly know when I decided to become a life-time learner and researcher on the mysteries of life, but I do remember that at the ripe age of 12, I decided that believing in "God" was simply a path that I could not participate in. Upon telling my two, rather unreligious parents that I did not believe in God, I was informed that I would be baptized immediately. Yet, long after this family hysteria wore off, I found myself right back where I started; christened and Christ-less.

By age 17 I had become quite the skeptic on matters of religion, politics, economics, civil rights, racism and the American Dream. I had come to the early conclusion that nothing which had been laid out for me, in the form of explanations, personal opinions, textbooks, or social commentaries, seemed to connect much with the reality I was living day to day. I was told if I worked harder than my peers, I would achieve promotions and more status. Likewise, if I followed the status quo, I would go far in life. Moreover, I was assured that if I followed the rules and did not buck the system, I would excel in all my endeavors and become the person I was destined to become.

But none of these "ifs" seemed to pan out in the realities of my day to day life. I studied and worked harder, but my career path did not seem to bring success. I applied my skills, gifts and talents to many artistic endeavors and was often told I should pursue a field of work that was more reliable or prestigious. But when I pursued these worldly goals... money, money and more money, I was deeply dissatisfied within. Finally, the little girl who was so inquisitive rose again to the surface begging the question why?; at every turn. Why do we all have to live the same way? Why do we all have to take the same nuts and bolts approaches to success? What is success, really? Why is no one encouraging me to create my own path? And why are so many people still so unhappy with their lives if this System, which has been laid out to me, is so effective and predictable?

For it wasn't just questions of religion that frustrated me. It was all the little questions that only served to expose the greatest question of all within me which was... Who is making all these rules that dictate how we must live, treat one another, define happiness and success and so on? Who is it that decides how the masses must think, feel, respond, obey, grow, change, or remain the same and on and on? Is there one all-powerful entity making these decisions for all of us? And as we used to say as a child, who made you (whoever you are) the boss of me!?

Finally, the most important question of all rose to the surface as I grew older, which was...Am I compelled to adhere to these musts in order to become the fulfilled person whom I desire to be? Ultimately, I learned that the process of ascension requires one to let go of all these musts and embrace a lifestyle that uniquely expresses all Spirit in this world as one's authentically divine and creative Self.

FACTS, FICTION, REALITY AND QUESTIONS

I believe one of the most beneficial aspects of my personality has been my enthusiastic curiosity about life, nature, science, anthropology, psychology, logic, philosophy, spirituality, metaphysics and the supernatural. I was always inquisitive; entering the world with observations and questions about everything. Like most mothers, mine did a really good job of entertaining my curiosity with answers that sometimes met with my satisfaction but often, did not. Like my teacher, my mom taught me that if I worked hard, I could be whatever I wanted to be.

These words of encouragement, however, were always seen through the eyes of the parameters of the world system (I don't blame her of course). Ideas that fell outside of these norms were not even brought up in the discussion. You can be whatever you want to be really meant, you can have whatever kind of job or career you want to have. But the solution to BE whatever I wanted to be was not the answer to the question I was asking. Because the question I was really asking was "*who am I?*" or even "*what am I?*" As I grew older the question became "*why am I?*" followed closely by "*what am I supposed to be doing?*" and ultimately "*what is my purpose here?*"; all questions, I realized in later years, that had nothing to do with a career or job, and all questions that only I, alone, could answer.

REFLECTIONS ON ASCENSION
AM I AN ALIEN?

My first attempt to break the cycle of avoiding the questions "who am I" and "what am I" arose when I became a mother myself. One day, after a rough day at school, my oldest son, who was about six years old asked,

"Mommy am I an alien".

I admit, the question caught me off guard. In an instant, all the questions I had tried to verbalize to my mother as a child filled my mind!

In that instant I realized…that this was the question I'd struggled to frame properly and, moreover, this was the feeling I had been experiencing since childhood. That is, the feeling that I somehow did not belong in this superficial world in which I was submerged. So, as I contemplated his question, I realized the word "alien" suddenly described me! And here I was, at 32 hearing the question I had been asking, flowing from the lips of my first-born child! I pondered the question silently for a moment. Finally, he asked again…

"Mommy am I an alien?"

Well as most parents learn, we can often see the truth more clearly through the wonderment of the minds of our children. So, I gave him the only answer I could give, knowing my child, knowing his struggles with fitting in at school, knowing his gifts and talents and knowing the beauty and purity of his inner soul.

"Yes,"** I said softly. **Yes baby, you are."

"I knew it!"** he said with excitement. **"Oh mommy!"

Then he gave me a big hug and asked curiously,

"So…are you an alien too?"

***"Yes"** I laughed. He relaxed in my arms, clearly relieved.*

"And Daddy,"** he asked. **"Is he an alien too?"

***"Yes"** I replied with a smile.*

***"I knew it!"** he said again with even more exuberance.*

He continued inquiring about the origins of the grandparents and siblings and family friends. In most cases I answered yes or explained that the person was an alien but didn't know it yet. We laughed and hugged and comforted each other. And it was on that day that I decided to start seeing myself the same way I had been seeing my children since they were born; as heavenly beings sent to this world to make a difference. I heard the Spirit tell me this with each birth and I believed it. And now at the age of 32, I finally began to see myself as a spirit being human, rather than a human being searching for a spiritual experience.

The irony of this epiphany in my life was that at the time, I was an actively ordained Christian minister. Intellectually, I knew I was a Spirit, possessing a soul, and housed in a physical body. I had taught this concept to others many times. But here, in this moment, it clicked. Here, in this moment of genuine curiosity, I finally realized that I am <u>not</u> a product of this worldly, physical matter. Instead, I AM the living evidence of an unseen yet, ever-present, Creating Spirit who is, I AM.

So, yes, I AM an alien to the world of physical and mental limitation. Like all the collective hosts of Spirits being human; I AM evidence of the divine Christ-spark that is the entire life-force of a living universe! Not Christ the "savior of the world" as taught in religious doctrine, but Christ, that divine energy that is life itself and animates all living things. And this is the life: love, truth, wisdom, light, peace, joy, compassion, grace, forgiveness and faith! Yes, I AM faith, the divine spark of the creative mind, the substance of what is hoped for yet, unseen. Yes, I AM the physical manifestation of the will of the self-aware universe. Asé

I could not put all these truths into words back then. But I realized that day, that Harrison's question was the best way to describe how I had been feeling most of my life. And I understood, unlike so many, that I was one of the few who had escaped through the cracks of the system. Therefore, I was blessed to realize that being "different" was, in this case, a good thing. And yes, quite normal. That's because I am a part of something much greater than the limitations of this physical, man-made, collective consciousness called "reality". One who began a journey of discovery by having the courage to "Question Everything". And that journey opened a doorway to truth, freedom and ultimately, my own personal journey of self-discovery and personal ascension.

CHAPTER THREE

Everything You Know Is Wrong

...or Escape from Disneyland

> *"Toto, I have a feeling we're not in Kansas anymore."*
> **Dorothy** from **The Wizard of Oz** by L. Frank Baum

INTRODUCTION

I once met a man who lived in Los Angeles all his life, but, he had never been to Disneyland. I began to describe all the attractions; the light shows, virtual reality experiences, music, rides, and the other wonderful enchantments of "the happiest place on earth". As I spoke, his face lit up with wonderment. It was then that I realized he surely couldn't possibly imagine the magic of Disneyland, no matter how thoroughly I expounded on the subject. For everything at Disneyland is designed to stimulate your imagination, sense of wonder and surprise, and yes, even hope. Because the world has become a much smaller place over the decades, we have all become interconnected global citizens with a common goal of love, joy, and peace on earth... Right? Everyone who has been there knows you've got to see it to believe it. So, at that point I summed up my Disneyland pitch by saying... *"well, you just have to see it to believe it!"* Then I politely excused myself out of the conversation.

You see, I realized he could never have the perspective that I have because he had not seen what I have seen; neither had he experienced what I have experienced. So, before we proceed on this journey of awakening and ascension, please note the following acknowledgement:

This book is based purely upon my opinions; formed by the personal journey of discovery gained from experience, life lessons, education, and extensive research. Therefore, if you really want to know the truth and live free of ignorance and insanity you must teach yourself to...

THINK FOR YOURSELF

Let it be known. I search for truth, not the verification of my own predisposed beliefs. I look at all the facts; not just those facts that I can stomach. Ultimately, it is truth that perpetually sets me free mentally, spiritually and emotionally on this awakening journey. I have taught myself to accept the very hard truth about many things; sometimes with great trepidation and sorrow. But I had to let go of the bondage that systemic ignorance creates. I had to do it in order to be free. So, if you wish to save yourself from the systemic fantasy-reality you've been operating in since conception, you will have to let go of many beliefs, truths, values, traditions, rituals, habits and mis-understandings that you currently have.

The facts presented in this chapter will probably jolt or conflict with many existing beliefs you have and values you hold dear. But this journey of illusion vs reality, truth vs lie, normality vs insanity, must begin with dispelling many so-called truth's and givens that you have been operating with for most of your life. If you're like most people, you have heard many conspiracy theories that you easily dismissed because they sounded so farfetched. Perhaps they are farfetched simply because you didn't take the time to do your own research and think for yourself. Therefore, the thematic mantra I wish you to speak to yourself, as often as possible, will be: Think for Yourself (*insert your name here*).

Whenever you hear new information you find uncomfortable or hard to swallow...say it. When I make you angry because I negate or dismiss or expose the truth about something you hold sacred... Just STOP... and remind yourself that you must think for yourself if you truly want to be and live free. I want that for you so much. That is why I wrote this book. Not to prove myself right on the subjects and situations cited in the book. No. But rather, that you would begin to question everything you think you know is true. Just to open yourself up to the possibility that some of the things you "know" are not based in fact. If you can accept the possibility that you have been misled or influenced with biased or convoluted information, I am now asking you to take an objective look at everything you think you know; so that you may discover a whole new approach to "being".

I am praying for you now because I know the book is moving toward a new direction in thinking. I am honored to be here with you as we proceed. Keep reading and open your mind! It is, as you know, as limitless as the universe!

NEW TERRITORY

Brace yourself because limitless thinking is new territory for most of us. As I mentioned before, I did not start out looking for a specific answer or outcome. I just started looking at everything I believed with an objective mind; as if it was all new information. I put in a lot of spiritual work; studying endlessly to insure I could stand behind everything I share in this chapter as well as this book. When it comes to facts and information, I researched multiple sources. When I suggest spiritual exercises or practices to help you manage through the cognitive dissonance or mental/emotional disturbances that you may likely experience as we proceed, please trust that I had to teach myself how to manage my own distresses as I entertained new truths and evolved into an always ascending approach to life. I suggest you do the same.

If I say something you believe is untrue, I invite you to do the research and then, we can reason together to hash out any error in my reporting or my interpretation. Until then, let's proceed with the understanding that what I am about to disclose is true, to the best of my knowledge. In matters where a spiritual insight is shared, please note that I speak from a perspective of metaphysical spirituality, which encompasses the holistic wisdom of many ancient teachings. Some of which, have been plagiarized within texts used by the organized religions of the world. As you may have already guessed; I neither ascribe to, nor do I promote, any formal, organized religion or religious doctrine.

LIVING THE FANTASY

The **Disney Corporation** has gone to a mega expense to create and maintain the "***happiest place on earth***" and the happiest franchise in the film industry. The experience is carefully designed to mesmerize, excite, enchant, thrill and engage you in a fantasy world. What they have built, however, has nothing to do with the real world. Unfortunately, the real world, in which you live today, has also been carefully designed to mesmerize, excite, enchant, thrill, engage and, unfortunately, imprison you in a world of fantasy, make believe, and immersion in a well-designed hologram of matter, energy and thought!

Now, before you the doctor start working on you, the patient, it's important that you understand which "normal" ideals are hindering your ability to grow spiritually and emotionally. Since these influencers are operating in your subconscious mind and your unconscious Self, it is imperative that you recognize how you are being influenced behind the scenes and without your consent. Yes, it's time for a paradigm shift in your thinking if you plan to walk in the power of an Ascending Mind. But, to make this 180° turn in your thinking, you must give attention to the current paradigm you are working with.

Keep in mind that every person's paradigm is both uniquely personal and cumulative. Moreover, the paradigm you're stuck in, depending on your age, has probably had you glued down to a very finite rule of thumb for values such as right and wrong, good or bad, true or untrue. Such a state of being makes a paradigm shift almost impossible without conscious and intentional efforts to seek the truth, find it, accept it, experience the freedom of clarity and then, initiate a mental, emotional, and spiritual shift in your thinking and being.

> *"When a person thinks according to a specific paradigm, their thoughts and beliefs tend to be channeled into certain directions whilst other directions are excluded because they appear inconsistent with the given paradigm."*
>
> **Images of Time: George Jaroszkiewicz,** Associate Professor of Mathematical Sciences, University of Nottingham, UK; Oxford University Press

As you can see, I'm trying to prepare you upfront. Because some of this new information will be very difficult for you to accept. I'm certain some will fall away from their ascension journey and put this book down forever because of the facts that come into question. If you really want to let go of what ails you most, however, I encourage you to hang in there. As this book teaches you how to think for yourself, you will be empowered to see with new eyes and a more open mind. This too, is part of the "**Always Awakening**" way of life; to objectively scrutinize your personal paradigm, to remain open to new information, to examine that new information with objective eyes and logic, to recognize discrepancies of fact and fiction, and to accept the uncomfortable truth.

For your own good, you must first wake up from the nightmarish system of mind control you have been operating with since you manifested in this dimensional paradigm called The World. So, in order to wake up, you will have to face some hard facts about yourself and the world around you.

COGNITIVE DISSONANCE: THE UNCOMFORTABLE TRUTH

> *"It is the nature of the human species to reject what is true but unpleasant and to embrace what is obviously false but comforting."* **H.L. Mencken**

This chapter should have been called, "wake up and smell the poop" since once you realize everything you know is wrong, everything you know stinks. Once you realize this, the next step in your awakening is to accept that you have been served a crock of crap. This pill is very hard to swallow. Therefore, we will stop here to discuss the matter of cognitive dissonance. Cognitive Dissonance (CD) is a mental health condition wherein we know the truth but, because the truth is uncomfortable to know, we psychologically figure out a way to rationalize our irrational response to that truth.

Consequently, through irrational thinking, we convince ourselves that our inappropriate response is rational, regardless of whether it is logical or not. Later in the book we will examine the Christian apostle Paul's explanation of the apparent human disconnect between mental understanding, spiritual will, and actual behavior. Until then, here are a few simplified examples of how Cognitive Dissonance (CD) plays out in real life.

CD EXAMPLE #1:

THE UNCOMFORTABLE TRUTH:

"I am overweight."

But when I look in the mirror, I tell myself...

THE SELF-DECEPTION:

"Yes, I am overweight but that's only because I'm big boned and that runs in my family".

Of course, the obvious truth is that I know I am overweight. Furthermore, I know I need to lose weight. But the underlying inner truth is that I don't want to commit to the self-discipline required to lose weight. Though I know the benefits of reaching a healthy weight, i.e. better health, greater mobility and strength, longer life, etc., I have trained my mind to dismiss my inability to take responsibility for my own health by finding an illogical explanation for why I'm overweight in the first place. In cases of cognitive dissonance, sometimes the person figures out a way to justify the undesired truth by finding an excuse for why the undesired truth exists in the first place.

CD EXAMPLE #2:

THE UNCOMFORTABLE TRUTH:

"You can't trust the media."

But as I watch the nightly news, I say…

THE SELF-DECEPTION:

"Yes, but without the media I won't know what's going on in the world."

We watch the media, hear the stories, and know that each media franchise has a distinct, preferential political point of view. The night that Donald Trump won the 2016 election, for example, every media outlet biased in favor of the democratic party was in utter emotional turmoil. The commentators who had once, subliminally expressed this bias for Hilary Clinton basically came "out of the closet" and exposed their true personal preferences.

They became emotional, one even started crying, and they openly revealed their personal values and bias in what is supposed to be an allegedly unbiased forum. We know that journalists are supposed to report truth and facts, and yet, we participate in our own miseducation because cognitive dissonance will not allow us to say…

"the media is biased therefore I really need to do my own research and not rely upon biased sources for the news".

We do not say this because we really don't want to put in the work and do our own research. In fact, we would much rather have our information spoon fed to us. Even worse, these days we would rather just have information downloaded into our consciousness via repetitive subliminal signals transmitted by our government and other corporate entities. Unfortunately, far too many are fully plugged into this new techno-consciousness, immersed in an avatar-like experience with the physical world.

The truth is I am most certainly NOT loving it because I know the far-reaching mental havoc such messages wreak when they take root in our psyche and manifest in our choices and behavior.

Another, equally damaging, CD point of view on the media is...

CD EXAMPLE #3:

THE UNCOMFORTABLE TRUTH:

"I don't watch the news because it's always bad news"

But as I hide from the reality that the news is bad because the world condition is deteriorating, I embrace,

THE SELF-DECEPTION:

"Since all news is bad news, I will not watch the news at all."

So now you are truly ignorant of what's going on in the world because you refuse to see at all. Instead, you amuse yourself by posting pictures of your fingernail polish and your lunch just to kill the time you didn't spend getting the facts!

MYTH VS FACT: A FIREHOSE OF UNTRUTHS COME TO LIGHT

Now that you have a better understanding of how Cognitive Dissonance can influence your perception of reality, I thought it wise to discuss how myths also play a key role in how we perceive our world and our reality. Historically, myths emerged in many ancient cultures as interpretations and explanations of inexplicable phenomena, heroic deeds, seemingly supernatural events and the like. These fantastical tales were then passed down through cultural tradition and, like a rock rolling down a steep hill, collected more fantastical moss along the way.

The uncomfortable truth, however, is that a myth is much more than an exaggerated or fictional tale; for the Oxford Dictionary defines a myth as:

1. a widely held but **false** belief or idea
2. **a misrepresentation** of the truth
3. a **fictitious** or **imaginary** person or thing
4. an **exaggerated** or **idealized** conception of a person or thing

I don't know about you, but anything that is categorized as false, fictitious, imaginary, exaggerated, or a misrepresentation sounds very much like an out and out lie to me. And though that false belief may be widely held, it is, nevertheless, still a lie.

Now that we've got that clear, let's look at how we respond to the many myths of our society, which ring true for many people, (even though they are untrue), in our current social paradigm.

MYTH: MATTER IS SOLID

> *"Don't try to bend the spoon...instead realize, there is no spoon."*
> **Spoon Boy**-from the film **The Matrix;** Dir.
> Lana Wachowski, Andy Wachowski

I thought I would begin with the matter of matter and the physical world. Most believe that the world is made of solid matter. But as the famous quote from the film The Matrix implies, the "matter" that we are interacting with is technically not even real... at least not in the finite, physical sense that most of us confidently rely upon.

When you Google *"what is matter"* you may come across the definition given by **Answers.com** which states:

"Matter is the physical material of the universe. It is the "stuff" all around you."

And yet, if you research the true "matter" of matter, you will discover that most quantum physicists agree that what we perceive as our physical, material world, is neither physical nor material at all. In fact, according to Nobel prize winning physicist **Neils Bohr:**

> ***"Everything we call real is made of things that cannot be regarded as real."***

But what does Mr. Bohr mean when he says: *"things cannot be regarded as real"*? Surely, we experience the physical world as both real and tangible. For everywhere we look, matter appears to exist. Our world is, therefore, both visible and tangible, right? Or is it? Let's consider what other physicists are now realizing.

"Quantum physicists discovered that physical atoms are made up of vortices of energy that are constantly spinning and vibrating, each one radiating its own unique energy signature. Therefore, if we really want to observe ourselves and find out what we are, we are really beings of energy and vibration, radiating our own unique energy signature -this is fact and is what quantum physics has shown us time and time again. We are much more than what we perceive ourselves to be, and it's time we begin to see ourselves in that light.

If you observed the composition of an atom with a microscope you would see a small, invisible tornado-like vortex, with a number of infinitely small energy vortices called quarks and photons. These are what make up the structure of the atom. As you focused in closer and closer on the structure of the atom, you would see nothing, you would observe a physical void. The atom has no physical structure, we have no physical structure, physical things really don't have any physical structure! Atoms are made out of invisible energy, not tangible matter."

ARJUN WALIA, SEPTEMBER 27, 2014

From: **Nothing Is Solid & Everything Is Energy – Scientists Explain the World of Quantum Physics** *www.collective-evolution.com*

Now if that doesn't challenge the status quo of your understanding, nothing will. How utterly challenging to be expected to suddenly believe that at the core of every perceived solid surface, lies a vortex of energy void of any mass or volume. Furthermore, how does one reconcile with the fact that even the "matter" that makes you, you, is a void of intangible energy! Selah.

Here are more facts you think you know, but really don't...

MYTH: THE FOOD SUPPLY IS SAFE ENOUGH TO EAT

Wake up and smell the poop! It's literally all around. We know that most of the food is unhealthy, yet most of us continue to eat it. We go to fast food restaurants and convince ourselves that "angus" beef isn't just a regular old, GMO-fed, hormone enhanced, cow patty. Surprisingly we pay top dollar for such a meal. And just when we think it's safe to eat healthy, another outbreak of salmonella hits the market! If you really want to inform yourself about the food supply, I suggest you check out the documentary film **FOOD, INC.**, Directed by Robert Kenner. If you do your research, you will see for yourself how animals, such as chickens, are being raised in facilities so crowded that they can't even walk around. Yes, they are literally sitting in fecal squalor from birth to butcher. Some are even born without beaks!

Nevertheless, we continue to provide enough demand for the food industry to justify the need for such practices to continue. Now if you want to know how that alleged "food" is affecting you, be sure to see the documentary, **What the Health,** directed by filmmakers Kip Anderson and Keegan Kuhn. Though we understand that with truth comes the empowering freedom of choice, we still choose to retreat to the comfort of our Cognitive Dissonance, which keeps us paralyzed with inaction and indecision about making healthier food choices and demanding food growers change their practices for a healthy food supply. Nevertheless, we continue to reassure ourselves saying:

"I know the chickens and cows are mass produced, full of hormones and putting me at risk for illness... but I'll eat it anyway!"

Honestly, I have been guilty of this behavior in the past. I usually suffer the consequences in the form of a terrible stomachache after eating unhealthy food. The tummy ache certainly helps me to keep my toxic meal cravings under control. Most people, however, have not taken the time to get the facts on how their food is made, raised, or processed and thus, are ingesting very toxic substances that cause significant dis-ease and illness through the degradation of the immune system, the heart, the vascular system, the stomach, and other vital organs.

MYTH: THE AMERICAN EDUCATION SYSTEM IS SUPERIOR TO THAT OF OTHER COUNTRIES & OUR STUDENTS ARE GLOBALLY COMPETITIVE

The fact is, the American school system is falling apart across the country and our children are getting dumber every year. According to the **Third International Mathematics and Science Study (TIMSS)** involving a half-million students in 41 countries, test results indicated that:

> "*U.S. fourth-graders are performing poorly, middle school students worse, and high school students are unable to compete*" [internationally]. Moreover, "*By the same criteria which was used to say we were "average" in elementary school,* [data indicates] "*we appear to be "near the bottom" at the high school level.*" Nevertheless, "*People have a tendency to think this picture is bleak, but it doesn't apply to their own school. Chances are, even if your school compares well in SAT scores, it will still be a lightweight on an international scale.*"

Ouch! Is the correct response. And yet, most Americans boast of the quality of our education system overall and politicians running for office continue to portray us as fierce competitors on the global arena. Public school educators are ineffective because of over-regulation of the school system, limited resources and overcrowded classrooms.

Parents know that the teachers are overwhelmed, and yet, it is still a challenge to get parents involved and engaged in their children's education.

While working as Director of Development for a private elementary school in Los Angeles, for example, I created a parenting program designed to empower parents to tutor their children at home. Notices were sent home, reminders from teachers went out, etc. But although most of these parents possessed the skills to help their children grow and learn, we were only able to get 4 parents (*out of a student body of 250 children enrolled*) to show up and participate. The most common excuse given for failure to participate in the program was… ***"I don't know enough to help my kids with math or science or reading"***.

The irony was that most of these parents had jobs where these same skills (reading, spelling, basic math, etc.) were being used daily. Here again, is a clear indication of how CD paralyzes a person from engaging in actions that liberate them and others in this case. What makes this example even more confusing is that the children needing tutoring were grades K-6! I guess the parents were afraid they were not smarter than a fifth grader after all!

MYTH: HISTORY BOOKS ACCURATELY PORTRAY U.S. AND WORLD HISTORY

Let's keep it real. Those of us from my generation know that information which was once commonly taught in school is no longer included in today's schoolbooks. As a result, children are less learned in almost all areas of education not just math and science. The observation is certainly true when it comes to the subject of U.S. and World History. This topic could probably be the subject of an entire book but for now let's just say… the youth of today don't have a clue about what they don't know about world history. In all truth, I am sure there are many countries worldwide, besides the U.S., filled with people who don't know the truth about our country's historical beginnings.

A perfect example of history lessons gone completely bonkers is the current issue of whether the U.S. is a democracy or a republic. The irony is that we all endearingly recite *"I pledge allegiance to the flag...and to the Republic for which it stands"* (***from*** **The U.S. Pledge of Allegiance**); so, it would seem obvious at first review. The more important question, however, is... Why does this matter?

I think the distinction matters for several reasons. First, a republic stipulates that the leader of the government has been duly elected by the people. There should be no dictators, monarchs, executive orders, or electoral college votes in a true republic. Inherent to that stipulation, the duly elected leader or leaders of the republic are not granted the authority to act outside the general will of the people. The leader, therefore, would not be empowered to override the will of the people under any circumstance. In our republic, however, the president may use the power of executive orders to override existing laws if such an order is deemed necessary to protect the security of the land.

Like a democracy, a republic also allows "the people" to elect representatives who will vote on their behalf. In this governmental structure, the representative has an implied responsibility to submit a vote that directly expresses the will of the people he or she represents. This is an important distinction because in our current democratic Republic, the Electoral College elects the presidential candidates based upon the political party to which they are pledged; regardless of the expressed will of the people they are pledged to represent. These allegiances are made months before the presidential election and have a direct impact on the outcome of presidential elections.

Secondly, in a democracy, only the needs of the majority are represented by the law, even if the election that establishes that law is passed by a slim majority. In a true republic, the needs of all people are considered when forming public policy. What a jolt that truth is to our perception of the political system by which we are governed. In fact, many Americans confuse the republic approach to public policy (not the "Republican" party) as Socialism. I don't know about you, but I have yet to see the "needs of all" being a priority in American public policy.

To make matters worse, most people don't even know that the constitution we currently follow is a part of the formation documents used to establish the corporate entity known fondly as the United States of America. You see, my friend, **"America"** is the name of the land upon which we live. Upon the land is a union of states, formerly colonies, that agreed to unite under one governmental republic. Why does that matter? Because it means our union of states is, and has been, under the control of a separate corporate entity, commissioned to oversee this union from the "sovereign" land of the District of Columbia. As such, these united states are controlled by the corporation instead of by the people of these great and united states of America.

That is why, almost since its inception, the country has been held hostage by indebtedness to foreign interests such as The Federal Reserve Bank; which is neither controlled, nor owned, by the government of the united states of America. In fact, the Federal Reserve Bank, as well as most major banks of the world, is controlled by the Rothchild empire! That is also why the current, so called, "democratic" system is so corrupt. Because everyone in politics can easily be bought for the right price. And of course, the powers that be can, and do, pay that price; much to our expense and detriment. But I digress!

MYTH: THE ORIGINS OF MODERN MAN

One of the most profound phenomena of our history education system is the myth that Black History is limited to a list of firsts made by African Americans since the inception of America as a country. The reality, however, is that Black History, if properly portrayed, is, in truth, World History. Historians, archeologists and anthropologists all agree that Africa is the true origin of what we call modern man and that Africa is the birthplace of the first "civilized" people. We must further consider in our origin-of-man history discussion that archeologists, anthropologists and geneticists also know for certain that all modern-day Caucasians have DNA from both the Neanderthal and the African Homo Sapiens who predated the Neanderthals appearance in history by nearly two hundred thousand years.

Yet African people worldwide and throughout antiquity, are and have been, the most oppressed people on the planet; a people categorized as less than human who to this day continue to be oppressed at the hands of their younger, mixed-race descendants. The consequence of such a gross misrepresentation of the facts is a population of ignorant and racially polarized factions; all in denial about their own genetic origins. Nevertheless, the subject of Black History in schoolbooks begins and ends with Martin Luther King Jr. and a few other heroes thrown in for good measure.

I wonder if world history would have unfolded the same if those conquering nations of Europe had only stopped to acknowledge they were destroying their ancestors across the African continent. Furthermore, since most white people dismiss the fact that we are all genetically related, social systems such as racial segregation, apartheid, and "racism white supremacy", a term introduced by renowned psychologist **Dr. Frances Cress Welsing**, have basically set the tone for historical world events for the past 2300 years or so.

Now this is when "*wake up and smell the poop*" takes on an entirely new meaning! Is it poop for the White race to hear the bad news that they are, genetically speaking, basically African? For all Homosapien-sapiens (modern man) have their genetic origins in Africa. So if you've been misinformed or in denial about that all your life the answer is obviously, yes. Moreover, I imagine for those who don't acknowledge their DNA mix, this news is downright disturbing. Surely, cognitive dissonance runs amuck with this subject. The reality, however, is that this truth has the power to unify all humanity as a genetic family tree with many branches. Imagine what a peaceful world we would have if everyone simply acknowledged our familial relationship and eternal bond as one human race of people! For now, you can just be like me and greet all strangers as "cousin" (not cuz) everywhere you go. Be sure to smile and make eye contact. Then watch the reaction!

MYTH: THE AMERICAN DREAM IS ATTAINABLE

Probably one of the most significant hurdles in your struggle to break free from cognitive dissonance is the illusion of the American Dream. I will go out on a real limb here and say that the pursuit of this dream has probably killed more Americans than any other influence in American culture. In chapter one I spoke of many of the syndromes caused by our collective condition of Systemic Syndrome. I would say this psychosis, which comes from pursuing a dream that is virtually unattainable for most, is a clear indication of a collective illusion that seems to have no end.

As I write this book, the average cost of a home in Los Angeles county is at a whopping range of $500,000 to $1,000,000. Yet, household by household, couple by couple, Americans strive to attain this type of unreachable goal. And in a society where winning means everything, no one stops to acknowledge that for every winner, there is surely a loser who is probably experiencing the American nightmare, much at the hands of the collective wealthy. Homelessness, extreme poverty, unemployment, poor education, lack of access to opportunities and resources, etc. all contribute to a society and a world where economic disparities abound as most are stressed and unhappy.

Nevertheless, even the poor scurry about in pursuit of a dream that is, and always has been, reserved for a few at the top of a food chain of voracious competitors eager to devour the weak or less fortunate. And even though we know everyone cannot attain this American dream, we all plow ahead like racecars on a freeway that leads us to our own spiritual and sometimes, physical demise. I'd be remised here if I didn't mention my dear, deceased husband Carl. I believe years of stress, brought on by racial, economic and social struggles, was ultimately the cause of his premature death. For we know, the heart and the body overall can only endure so much in a state of stress. Health, more than anything else, is the clearest indicator of spiritual peace and harmony.

If we use the health of most Americans as an indicator of our overall cultural, social and spiritual health, we are clearly killing ourselves quietly and slowly in pursuit of a pointless outcome where success does not bring joy. A hard truth to face, to say the least. For as a country, most are sick in some fashion; clearly evidenced by the ever-pervasive use of drugs prescribed to treat a plethora of symptoms and ailments resulting from our collective condition of malcontent.

Here begins the part of your ascension where you must accept that you have been lied to and manipulated. Yes, now you must reconcile with many truths that have been suppressed in your consciousness or hidden from you altogether. This is the process of reformation and ascension; question everything, seek the truth, find it, unlearn the lies you have learned, and then learn and embrace the truth. Now you are prepared to make decisions based on fact instead of fiction. How many beliefs are you currently operating with that are harming you because they are, in fact, untrue? Only you know the answer...or do you? Keep learning and see where the rabbit hole takes you. This is just the beginning.

At this point, I want you to grasp hold to the fact that YOU must do your own research to verify whatever I've said so far that you find unbelievable or untrue. Like I told you at the beginning, everything I'm telling you in this chapter is true. I highly recommend that you start your own pathway to seek the truth for yourself. For only when you do your own research and seek the truth, will you find it. And when you put that kind of work in, seeking and finding, you learn to think for yourself. Once you learn to think for yourself, freedom is just around the corner because you no longer depend on biased sources to know the truth of things.

Now, I will tell you a few more things that may bother you upon hearing. Ultimately what I'm going to say will set you free if you let it. The first thing: According to many former government employees and officials, the U.S. government has been in the business of collective mind control for over 75 years. We've already covered the media's role in mind control. We also know that psychologists and educators verify the impact of repetition on the psyche of the human mind. Psychology tells us that if we hear a bit of information that is false, we will eventually believe that the information is true if we hear it enough times. That's the madness of people who are habitual liars. They tell the lie so many times that they eventually forget it's a lie, because over time they have convinced themselves that the lie is true. Similarly, when we are exposed to mass saturation of information that is false, we tend to accept it as truth over time. The proverbial *weapons of mass destruction* in Iraq, for example, has been proven repeatedly to be false. And yet, our U.S. military troops are stationed there to this day. But we heard that accusation so much that our presence in that country, though unwarranted, remains acceptable to most Americans.

I don't want to get into all the political activities of our government in this book. Truthfully, I do but this book would be 800 pages long! I do, however, want to emphasize how many times we have been told an untruth, accepted it as truth, and then suffered the consequences of making a decision that harms others based on a lie. This is, unfortunately, the modus operandi of the American people's impact upon the globe. Now CD says, *"well it's not us, it's the government, and they're only killing people to protect our freedoms"*. Okay you can stay there if you want. But the truth is, we all got the memo years ago that NO weapons of mass destruction were ever found in Iraq. Explain that one away if you can.

YOU ARE AT WAR

There is a war for your mind. That's the point of this chapter. That war is being waged on several fronts including the media, the political system, the church, the healthcare system, technology and social systems and networks. One of the most effective tools for waging war on your mind is being accomplished by attacking the body directly through poor nutrition and poorer healthcare. In addition, technology brings with it, electrical frequencies that transmit energy signals directly opposite of our natural polarity; altering our mental and emotional states of being, attacking our bodies at the cellular level, and generating an abundance of free radicals that cause cancer and other self-destructive dis-ease.

Right now, for example, your cell phone is operating on an energy that is the direct opposite of your body's natural polarity. In the same way, ELF (extra low frequency) towers across the country are also being used to alter our circadian rhythm, which is organically synchronized with the rhythm of Planet Earth. As a part of nature, we were once in natural harmony with these frequencies. Now, these

ELF towers emit energy signals that trigger moods of complacency, apathy, fear, stress, anger, numbness, and indifference. Just look around you and observe the behaviors of most people. We all know something is off, but we can't quite identify the source of the problem. I believe the Divine Creator within us knows exactly what is needed for this transitional time in humanity's spiritual emancipation and maturation. The question now is...Do you FEEL me?

INSANITY IS THE NEW NORMAL

Ultimately, this will be the chapter that determines whether you keep reading this book or not. If you only read the first two chapters of this book you have gotten enough information to enlighten you considerably; that is if you do your own research to verify the information contained herein. But this is where the book gets hectic because this is where we must face the truth; that insanity is the new normal. Because normal means you don't ask questions and you accept whatever you are told or given. Normal means that even if you know that people are being killed at the Dakota Access pipeline, yes protestors have been murdered, you will allow it because it's normal to turn away from the uncomfortable truth of what you see.

It's normal to not know your neighbors. It's normal to spend hours per day commuting. It's normal to let the school raise your children. It's normal for women well beyond childbearing age to have children, even though these children have a much higher risk of birth defects, disabilities, and other health abnormalities. Immunization is normal even though we know immunizations are causing some of the more prevalent illnesses found in young children born in America. Even though some of these illnesses can be linked to immunizations, children are, nevertheless, required to receive them before enrolling in most school districts across the country.

These days, we are inundated with social debate on a wide range of issues. Under the current regime of President Donald Trump, the entire U.S. is in an uproar about immigration reform. Though many countries have much stricter immigration laws than the U.S., it has become normal for Americans to argue and fight about this issue in the media and in the streets. To some Americans, normal is *let all immigrants enter the country for we are a country of immigrants.* For others, normal is, we don't need more immigrants because they place an economic burden on society. Still for other Americans, immigration reform is mostly about prejudice against a race of people whose ancestors were driven from the newly formed America as these disgruntled citizens chant *"build that wall"*.

Most of these biased viewpoints are not based in facts or data, but rather, they are based in a lack of understanding of how this country was formed in the first place. Therefore, for some, normal is that America was "discovered" by Columbus and 200 years later populated by well-meaning dissidents in search of religious freedom. The historical truth is that the "Americas" were populated over 20,000 years ago by Paleo Afro-Asiatic migrants, and their descendants... ages before the country of Spain was a thought. In fact, an overwhelming body of evidence actually proves that it was Africans who frequently sailed across the Atlantic and visited the Americas on trading expeditions thousands of years before the birth of Columbus and the emergence of Christianity.

THE TRUTH ABOUT "AMERICA" BEFORE AMERICA.

In his book, **Africa and the Discovery of America**, Leo Winer, an American historian and linguist at Harvard University, explained that according to Columbus' journal, the "Native Americans" that he "discovered" told him that long ago, black skinned people had journeyed to pre-America in boats and traded with the native people. Further evidence suggests that African explorers, from as far away as Kemet (Egypt), arrived in pre-America during the reign of the Ramses III, Pharaoh of the 19th Dynasty, sometime around 1292 BCE. Archeologists have even found numerous Egyptian artifacts in various locations across America including the Grand Canyon. And of course, everyone knows about the monuments left by the Negroid civilization of the Olmecs in the land we now call Mexico, Thus, most of the descendants of the ancient, indigenous people of the Americas argue that they are not immigrants at all. So, normal for them is that the Europeans are the ones who don't belong in America! Selah

The alarming truth about America is that the early Spanish expeditions to the New World, which landed in what we now call the Caribbean, resulted in the violent genocidal murder of an estimated 8,000,000 indigenous people as the Spaniards discovered "America". Their brutal colonization of the New World marked the beginning of one of the largest genocides of the modern era. It's a most egregious crime to face; particularly when you also factor in the millions of Native Americans who were later slaughtered by the United States Calvary and colonizing settlers who drove them from their homeland in a barrage of wars and genocidal massacres.

Thus, the more accurate truth is, that America is a country built upon the murder and exploitation of the indigenous people who settled here tens of thousands of years ago, as well as, the importation of African slaves who worked to build the economy of the colonies. If the European settlers had been immigrants, they would have taken on the customs of the people that allowed them to settle here right? Instead, the European settlers conquered the indigenous dwellers and forced them to adapt to their "new world" way of life. Today,

America remains a "new world" to every immigrant who comes here. And today, these beliefs are a part of our collective reality.

WHEN NORMAL GOES BAD

Of course, there are numerous examples of how our collective normal reality is woven within the fabric of our society. Most Americans know, for example, that a person cannot live in any major city in America on a wage of $10 per hour and still we passively accept a federally mandated minimum wage that keeps a large portion of employed workers living at or below the poverty level. Normal has certainly gone bad when over 50 million underemployed persons earn close to or below the minimum wage. Even so, the gainfully employed are annoyed by the prevalence of homeless persons living on the street. Ignorantly, these types of people simply do not consider that with one quick turn of circumstances, they could find themselves in the same condition.

Moreover, they also fail to see the direct correlation between normal wages and what has now become normal poverty. Thus, our normal efforts to address the "homeless problem" do not focus so much on the actual problems of the homeless as they do the problems that the homeless create for those more fortunate. Yet, regardless of the obvious connection, we continue to ignore the law of cause and effect and we collectively accept a minimum wage intentionally designed to keep a certain percentage of the population in poverty in perpetuity.

The truth is that if every major corporation were forced to provide a living wage instead of a minimum wage, CEOs making as much as 48x the average wage of the employee would become obsolete. But the mega corporations know that if they were required to pay a fair and living wage, they would lose control over the global economy. Thus, the unstable condition of the current global markets is evidence that big business is, in fact, quite bad for the world overall. Regardless of the overwhelming evidence, we continue to accept these mega corporations as not only "normal" but necessary. Just think, if everyone received a living wage. Maybe then the new normal might be a reduced need for the government enterprise of social welfare.

An obvious example of corporate growth gone haywire, is Monsanto's patented control of the genetically modified seed industry. This control of the seeds positions Monsanto to weave its footprint through the entire fabric of the food chain...from the feed used for the animals that will be consumed, to the use of high fructose corn syrup in almost every prepackaged food on grocers' shelves. No corporation should have the economic power to force feed entire countries with foods that can potentially alter the genetic chemistry of the global population, thereby, altering global health in irreversibly profound ways. This condition, too, is part of our collective normality, whether we like it or not. Nevertheless, such unchecked power over the food chain is considered...you've got it...normal.

Here is yet another abnormality passing for normal. Do you remember when I mentioned the significance of the difference between the united states of America and the corporate entity, the United States of America? Yes, it is normal, for the people of the great republic of America, to accept the fact that our money and our government is under the control of a separate corporation. The implication of this revelation, if it is one for you, is obvious as conflicts of interest, usury, and taxation without representation abounds.

Let's be frank. Americans turning over economic oversight of our money and economy to the corporate control of the Federal Reserve Bank and then, expecting them to look out for the interests of THE PEOPLE OF THE REPUBLIC, would be like turning the well-being of your family over to a predatory investment banker and expecting him to put the needs of your family before the needs of his business. Could you, would you, really expect or trust a predatory lender to look out for you when he stands to benefit from your economic exploitation? Hell No.! The conflict of interests makes it impossible for the lender to act for the highest good of your family.

Likewise, this is the case of the relationship between the FRB and America. However, when you accept that the United States of America, Inc., in the District of Columbia, masquerading as the Republic of America, is also the corporate business partner of the Federal Reserve Bank, it all makes sense. Once you accept that the USA is a corporation engaged in the oversight of America and the business of generating profit for our elite investors (Big Business), then you will understand why a Social Security fund that is mysteriously depleted, an IRS that has no laws to support it, a Federal Reserve Bank that is not controlled by the federal government, a privatized prison slave system (established under the 13th Amendment) and numerous other government enterprises like war and colonization, were systematically built on the backs of the well-meaning but ignorantly devoted, citizens of the Republic! WE THE PEOPLE have most certainly been bamboozled! Sadly, that condition, too, is normal.

ALL GROWTH IS GOOD GROWTH

Another normal perception held among most is that all growth is good. In truth, however, some growth is quite "un-good" if you consider the current condition of the planet due to man's unkind propensity for consumerism and consumption; two mental health conditions that most people are trapped in and addicted to in western culture. I highly recommend every American view a video which I found on You Tube entitled: **"The Most Important Video You'll**

Ever See" featuring a lecture by **Al Bartlett, Professor Emeritus at the University of Colorado, in Bolder.**

The subject of the video deals with the negative effect that exponential growth is having on the global condition. Using arithmetic, Professor Bartlett explains how *"the greatest shortcoming of the human race is our inability to understand The Exponential Function".* The term Exponential Function is used in mathematics to describe the size of anything that is growing steadily at a certain rate, expressed as a percentage, such as a population growth rate of 5%.

At first, Professor Bartlett demonstrates the mathematical structure of exponential growth. Next, he shows how a seemingly low growth rate of 7%, for example, can profoundly impact a city or country's environment and society. He then discusses how perceived tragedies like natural disasters, illness, and even war help to balance out the far-reaching effects of our obsession with exponential growth.

Professor Bartlett's objective is to demonstrate the pros and cons of exponential growth and to show, in quantifiable outcomes, how consistent exponential growth negatively impacts our world socially, morally, ecologically, geographically, and economically. More specifically, he emphasizes how exponential population growth impacts the planet in significantly dangerous ways. Your next **Ascending Mind Challenge** is to view this video if you are seriously seeking the truth about humanity's impact on the global condition.

I also recommend you watch the short film: **The Story of Stuff**, written by **Annie Leonard**, Directed by **Louis Fox** and produced by the **Story of Stuff Project**. The video clearly explains how everyone's mass pursuit of technology and other commodities, has affected indigenous peoples around the world, as well as, having catastrophic impact on certain resource rich areas of the world like Africa and South America. Both videos will help you decide for yourself whether exponential growth is good or bad for the world.

I also challenge you to write a journal entry to capture your reaction and response to the information you will learn from this video. Your response refers to what you will <u>do</u> differently, or even more vehemently, as a result of witnessing and inner-standing this film. Then, invite a few friends over to see the video and perhaps hold an old-fashioned 70's rap (discussion) party to review the personal and collective inner-standings derived from the film. What might you do as a group to act together in more peaceful ways toward all of humanity? What changes can you make as an individual to minimize your global footprint? What will you DO to make sure the cycle of global imperialism and oppression of indigenous peoples around the world comes to a long-awaited end? Or, will you accept this lingering virus of mass murders, global wars, destruction of nature, murder and displacement of indigenous peoples, pollution of water and air, etc. as a "normal" necessity of your personal convenience? If you choose wisely, divinely and humanely, you will choose to change for the sake of the collective good while creating an energy signature of peace, compassion and respect for our entire ethereal family. Asé

"NORMAL" CONSEQUENCES

If you're really trying to wake up, you will have to accept the fact that almost everything you think of as normal is... indeed... utter insanity. For, what is the implication of a world where parents don't raise their own children, old people are raising babies, children are less healthy, young people don't want to grow up, food is no longer nutritious fuel for the body, corporations control governments, etc.? Most who get as far as understanding these impacts on society and the world would say, "*yes, but there is nothing that can be done*" to change these conditions and move humanity in a more positive direction.

I believe if we wake up and face what is factually happening, we can change the way we think, and, manifest a healthier, happier wholistic outcome for all. Let's take the growing epidemic of diabetes which currently affects nearly 40% of Americans. It's big business for the medical and pharmaceutical industries; seeing as a 90-day supply of diabetic glucose strips gets a whopping $800 on the Medicare market. That is only one example of the corporate fraud that has become the new normal of the American healthcare system. No wonder the USA wanted so badly to create a law that requires all citizens to literally buy into this ponzi-scheme implemented by the government and the pharmaceutical industry. And that, my friends, is now also considered "normal".

The sad thing is that the overall food supply, as well as the entire fast food industry, is a key contributor to the phenomenon of the diabetes epidemic. The medical arena has known for years that diabetes is not hereditary. Yes, they know the truth… that a healthy, controlled diet, along with regular exercise, is the cure for diabetes. And yet millions of Americans are contracting kidney disease from the profound damage that unmanaged diabetes can have on the kidneys.

CASE IN POINT:

My mother was diagnosed with diabetes approximately 25 years ago. At first, she took pills to "manage" her condition. Like most diabetics of her generation, she was later switched to daily insulin injections as her doctors opted to treat her escalating glucose levels rather than treating her need for a nutritional behavior modification intervention. For in most cases, Type 2 diabetes is the outward evidence of a patient's lifestyle of unhealthy eating habits, improper nutrition, and lack of exercise. Thus, her doctor's failure to emphasize nutritional counseling over increased medication led to a 25-year battle with diabetes. As the dosage was increased, my mother's kidneys also began to deteriorate. Finally, the words a large percentage of diabetics eventually hear, that kidney disease was now irreversible, was added to the table for our family to digest.

At that time, my mom was taking as much as 46 units of insulin daily. When she was told it was time to put a fistula in her arm, in anticipation that she would soon need dialysis, Mom finally realized that her out of control diabetic lifestyle had to change. With lots of research and behavioral modification coaching, my mother began learning how to make the changes necessary to reduce her daily insulin. Since being diabetic had become "normal", the road to an insulin free life was chock full of triumphs and setbacks. Eventually, however, she was able to get her diabetes under control and is now insulin-free! After almost five years, my mother is still insulin-free to date. I attribute her success to an awakening in her mind that first, she should change and second, that she could change. Of course, our family is elated that she decided to save herself before normal killed her!

Though the mental and physical rehabilitation process was emotionally grueling, it was necessary and well worth it. The end-result is that we still have our mother, grandmother, great-grandmother and great-great-grandmother around to celebrate her new, healthier lifestyle and her newfound freedom from the pharmaceutical and governmental ponzi scheme. As I write these words, we are celebrating her 80th birthday! Not bad for someone who suffered with a disease for decades. Now, being insulin-free and more active is her new "normal"!

That is my prayer for this book. That you, the reader, will find somewhere in these pages, information that will empower you to make the changes you need to make to live a happier, healthier, more empowered life. Yes, you do have the power to set yourself free from mental bondage! This book is the roadmap. But only you can take the steps necessary to begin thinking for yourself and setting yourself free!

CONCLUSION: WAKE UP AND SMELL THE POOP

The world is going to hell in a handbasket. I wish it were not true but clearly wishing things would change is not enough to make them so. You must change the way you see the world, change the way you think, and, pursue a lifestyle of ascension in order to become your highest Self. We are living in the kind of world where you should expect a prophet to be on every corner preaching a need for everyone to wake up and get their acts together. Or as I like to say... a time when we must wake up and smell the poop.

Honestly the current world condition kind of makes you wonder: What is the good of church if not to awaken the spirit of mankind and draw us closer to the truth about our world? One would think that churches would strive to cultivate this kind of spiritual and social awareness and that the church itself would usher in a much-needed age of enlightenment. It is my experience, however, that the goal of most churches is, like every other enterprise, the pursuit of membership and money. Unfortunately, a spiritual revolution is not the agenda of organized religion. Instead, the pursuit of mega-church status has become the status quo.

So, if the journey to ascension will not be commandeered by the church, from whence, then, will come this spiritual revolution? From where will we draw the courage to stand firm in the belief that we must become the designers of our own destiny, the captains of our individual and collective ships? Will we ever come to know our own self-induced awakening? Or will we continue to allow institutional strongholds to steer us closer and closer to our collectively induced insanity? The truth is we are living in a world of people who want to have their cake and eat it too; even though doing both is impossible! Nevertheless, we continue to pursue all that we have been enticed to covet and all our minds have been trained to believe we need. Yet our ravenous appetite for the things of the world creates a vulture-like mentality that devours others and ourselves in the process. As such, life as we are living it, can only end in outcomes that become more and more chaotic, stressful, unhealthy and yes, illogical.

In addition, the prevalence of our collective cognitive dissonance, our ability to block out the uncomfortable truth, keeps us looping on a physical, emotional, and spiritual hamster wheel that is going nowhere fast. The question this book asks again and again is do you, as an individual, have the desire and courage to change, thus impacting change on the collective consciousness of our world? Keep in mind... one drop of dye in a glass of water changes the color only slightly. But with each added drop, the color becomes more apparent. This is the impact that a paradigm shift in collective consciousness can have on our world. Are you ready and willing to be one drop? Hopefully this book will foster such a desire and will to act in your mind, your heart, your spirit and ultimately your life.

CHAPTER FOUR

What is Reality?

"How can you continue to see the world as real, if the Self that is determining it to be real is intangible" **Ramtha** (J.Z. Knight)-from the film: **What the Bleep Do We Know** Dir. William Arntz

INTRODUCTION:

I think we should take the time now to discuss reality. What is it, where does it come from and how does it affect the way we interact with ourselves, each other and the world around us? After all this talk about *"everything you know is wrong"*, a plethora of facts must now be considered as we proceed on the journey of spiritual awakening, personal discovery, and self-empowerment. Unfortunately, the last two chapters have probably felt like a firehose of information blasting its way through your brain and spiritual consciousness. Certainly, much of the information given most likely disagrees with your current reality. And that's okay because reality is a relative and subjective experience. It is probably the one thing that is most assuredly NOT real.

Reality exists in the Mind. Since everyone's mind is uniquely different, everyone's reality is also different.

> *"For my thoughts are not your thoughts, neither are your ways my ways saith the Lord"* **Isaiah 55:8**

As indicated above, our ancestors once believed that the thoughts of our Divine Creator, whose "mind", we assume is expansive and limitless, are unlike our own. If we are so wonderfully made in the image and likeness of "God", however, shouldn't our experience of reality also be expansive and limitless? Sadly, for most people this is not the case. Because most of us operate with a finite construct of collective thoughts and beliefs which have been passed down and imposed upon us by others. Through these limiting thoughts and beliefs, we express and experience our collective reality.

For human beings, the expression of one's personal reality is called the Self or the Soul. In contrast, the expression of the Creator's universal reality is called the Universe. Though many might disagree on what this divine, universal life-energy should be called, most can agree that whatever you call it, the Universe, and all its wonderment, is much too expansive for us to comprehend, even in part. I suppose that is why we struggle to perceive and understand the oneness of humanity. Consequently, in our limited reality, we tend to focus on the insignificant details that make us different, such as, the color of another's skin, religious beliefs, sexuality, politics, social behavior, etc. In so doing, most experience a personal reality focused on difference instead of oneness. As a result, our collective "Self" is filled with disagreement, misunderstandings and chaos.

THE CHAOS OF OUR COLLECTIVE REALITY

What is the need for all this separatism? What is behind this quest to sequester a niche in the world that makes us feel unique and special? Can't you, just as an individual, be unique and special? Why is it that we can't all meet on the common ground of the singularity of humanity? We are all human and that is the common denominator. The fact that we have not learned how to just be man and be kind is clearly the source of much chaos in the modern world. If we could master being man and being kind or being mankind, all these other differences might become irrelevant.

Orange is the new black, 40 is the new 20, and insanity is the new normal. Is there anybody who is willing to honestly look at reality? Is there anyone that's willing to do that anymore because it's really time for everyone to stop pretending.

I believe one of the main reasons that the federal, state and local government so aggressively sought to destroy the Occupy movement was because it was completely based in a common truth. Everyone who was active in that movement had in common the belief that 1% (of 1%) of the population should not control 95% of the economic wealth of the world. The color of your skin, your race nor your station in life mattered in this movement. The power of it was based in the collective belief that corporate America was/is controlling our government and dictating what kind of life the common man or woman will live.

In response, "the powers" made sure that the movement was not only suppressed but annihilated. Please keep in mind that just as a social movement can be used to steer the public in a positive direction, so too can global control of information, propaganda, biased media reporting and popular opinion be used to steer us in a perceived direction that does not serve the collective interests of humanity. In such circumstance, the ultimate reality can manifest as conflict and chaos.

YOUR PERSONAL REALITY

Your personal reality is your own personal mental hologram. It is constructed by you and is a byproduct of your perception of the world; a perception which shapes and is shaped by, your individual and collective experience of the world and the people in it. Therefore, your personal holographic reality is only limited by your own perceived limitations. In contrast, it is expanded by your personal perception of the possibilities. What we often forget is that, being made in the image of the Universal Creator, we are endowed with the same limitless creativity as our Creator.

As the creators of our own personal holographic experience, we run the risk of creating a finite and inflexible life experience when we fail to approach life as an artist would; as both the objective observer and the passionate participant of the world we are creating. But if we see the world with a limited view, we will, in turn, design a personal reality that is limited in scope as well as lacking in possibilities.

Whether we realize it or not, our awareness of, and receptivity to, possibilities is the stuff which ignites our creativity. And it is creativity that empowers us to design our holographic lives with purposeful intention. Yet, many souls struggle with the realm of possibilities because they cannot turn their attention away from the appearance of limitation and lack. And, as we have learned, an existence crippled with mental limitation results in a reality that is overrun with disappointments, hopelessness, and despair. Since your personal hologram is the projection of your perceptions and experiences of the world, it is imperative that you cultivate the ability to see and experience the world both objectively and consciously.

YOUR PERSONAL HOLOGRAM

Think of your life as an interactive, holographic video game. You are the creative and interactive game designer. Yes, you are creator of the story that will be told and experienced. Because you are human, your holographic video game will be programmed using the database of your experiences, knowledge, perceptions, and opinions of the world around you. But, unlike an electronic video game, the parameters of your hologram are continually being upgraded as your collection of beliefs, values, triumphs, and alleged failures accumulates.

Through infancy and early childhood, or level one, you are simply learning the rules of the game…language, mobility, speech, emotion, etc. Let's face it. When you are a child, the world is telling you who and what you are. As you develop, you learn to comprehend some of what has been deposited within your mind and heart and emotions. Over time, these experiential deposits become your unique holographic reality; which you mostly act out unconsciously. That reality, whether based in truth or lies, trauma or ecstasy, is unique to you and you alone.

Evidence of our unique realities is most apparent when we analyze how several people can have the same experience, yet, process that same information with vastly different points of view, descriptions of facts, and, of course, reactions to those events that are uniquely different from the experience others may have had in the same situation. Everyone who gets victimized or traumatized, for example, does not have the same perception nor the same response to similar or even the same traumatic experience. How is that even possible? Because our perception and/or inner-standing of every experience is mostly determined by all the previous programming we've had in life from inception to that present moment! It is not until you begin to review your life, your emotions and your thinking as the conscious observer that you can begin to create and choose the type of features, elements, or opportunities your holographic life game might include.

The reality is, that everybody's reality is different. We may share some things in common, such as the names of colors in the color spectrum or the descriptions of shapes like circles or squares, but at the end of the day, everything is relative. In any society, there must be some commonality in the understanding of the collective, societal hologram for it to function. We share areas of common agreement, as concentric circles overlapping, wherein acts such as murder or theft, for example, are generally considered wrong by all. Accordingly, these common realities held by society birth and shape our understanding of the collective reality.

Our common reality, for example, tells us there most certainly is a spoon! Accordingly, those who believe otherwise remain on the fringe of society. It is no wonder that our common reality, therefore, remains somewhat consistent when it comes to certain truths passed down from generation to generation. Simultaneously, we also develop a uniquely personal reality which is shaped by the common reality, as well as, the individual's unique life experiences from conception forward. Before you experience personal ascension, therefore, you must accept that "reality" "truth", "right", "wrong", "good", "bad", and "normal", are all subjectively relative terms that require new eyes of scrutiny moving forward. For, no two people share the exact same interpretation of what is real or true or right or wrong.

The reality of a schizophrenic, for example, is no less real to him than the reality of a so-called sane, or mentally healthy person. Similarly, it is impossible for a White supremacist to empathize with the racism and oppression endured by the Black race at the hands of the White race. These comparative differences abound ad infinitum; but at the end of the day... whoever you are, you cannot run from yourself for your reality is yours, and yours alone. And yet, though your reality is separate from that of your neighbor, it is simultaneously, blended into the totality of the collective reality; a reality that was formed from the amalgamation of all the experiences of all humanity; past and present.

When you view your life as the conscious observer, however, you suddenly realize that it is you who sets the parameters of your inner reality; who you are, who you will become, and so on. You define the bad guys and the good guys, and label them accordingly. Similarly, when you live with an ascending self-awareness, you do not proceed through life on autopilot, like a stone rolling downhill and gathering moss. No. As the conscious creator of your present and your future, you learn to step outside of auto-pilot functionality and step inside of conscious awareness; learning to choose who you are and who you are becoming. You define how you will creatively respond to the challenges you must overcome, and you decide who you will be and more importantly, who you will become.

AN INTRODUCTION TO BEING AND BECOMING

Can you imagine a life where you decide what truly makes you happy without the obstacle of limitation? With a creative designer mindset, *"I would be a doctor, but I can't afford college"* becomes, *"I am becoming a doctor because day by day I am taking steps toward the goal which I have set for myself!"* Thinking as the creative designer of your life, therefore, keeps you in a constant state of expectancy as you are both being and becoming the person you desire to be. It's sort of like being pregnant. Even though the baby may not be at full term, you proceed with the confident understanding that there is a baby inside you and that baby will soon appear within your reality. It is this kind of thinking that resulted in the completion of this book. For nearly three years I kept saying, I am writing a book. And here you are… reading it!

Once you train your mind to step back and observe your thoughts, your emotions, your beliefs, etc., consciously choosing who you will be and what you will do, becomes a healthy, inspiring, evolutionary and yes, quite normal experience. Then, as you proceed through your holographic story, you gather your strength, destroy your enemies and grasp the golden ring that grants you access to more and more personal achievement, inner-standing, confidence and peace as you move up to level 3, level 4, and to infinity and beyond.

In theory this sounds easy enough. You are, after all, programming the features of your holographic reality, so how dangerous can it be? The truth is, since the global agenda has so effectively mastered global mind control, it is nearly impossible to have a unique and personal interpretation of the world and ourselves. As a result, there are many who will never experience the liberating satisfaction of being the creator of their own lives. Once again, in order to design a life of conscious creativity, you must learn the art of objective evaluation of your day to day choices, behaviors and interpretations of your current reality. Then, you must learn to adapt your thinking, your beliefs, and your responses to apparent limitations with confident creativity. That is what I mean by being and becoming. Three years ago, for example, I was being a person who wanted to write a book. After I started writing the book, I was being a person who was writing a book and simultaneously becoming an author. Now that the book is finished and published, I am being an author and becoming a world-renowned influencer on spiritual ascension and personal empowerment! As you can see, this thinking process requires practice, discipline, and exertion of your personal power over your own will. As this skill is cultivated, you will start to experience being and becoming more and more useful in your ascending life.

As I evolved through my personal ascension experience, I discovered many spiritual and practical principles which helped me "save" myself by becoming the designer of my own life. If you are serious about saving yourself before normal kills you, I strongly suggest you take the online course, Essential Principles of the Ascending Mind, which I created as a companion to this book. In it you will learn to stop, review, learn, let go, grow, adapt, and change your life trajectory. Until then, I encourage you to start the practice of viewing your life, your choices and your beliefs more objectively. I am confident you will soon come to inner-stand that more objectivity empowers you to envision your life goals with more creativity, imagination and limitless possibilities!

OUR COLLECTIVE SPIRITUALITY: THE DIVINE MIND

There is clearly an intelligent, self-aware, and powerful energy acting upon and within the design of the universe; take the sun, the moon and the stars, for example. There is an order to the universe and with it, the chaos of creativity which injects the unpredictable, the uncontrollable, and the unexpected. Similarly, we witness the impossible become possible in the form of "miracles", "divine interventions" and sometimes, even natural disasters. This divine design is also present in nature, as seemingly "spirit-less" creatures demonstrate the ability to respond, create, adapt, and evolve with brilliant ingenuity and creativity. These transformative properties of all "living" things are described as evolution and "natural selection" by Charles Darwin and others. But what if these perpetual evolutions of nature are simply the result of collective, selective, choice and creativity among species? Moreover, what if what we call "nature" is, like us, made in the creative and intelligent "image" of what we call God? I will call this ever-evolving creativity the Divine Mind.

As part of nature, human beings are also collectively aware of the creative, intelligence of the unseen Divine Mind, consciously or otherwise. For the evidence of it is always present in the material things it has inspired us to create since the dawn of humanity. But as our conscious awareness of this divine spiritual presence has been framed through the lens of religion, politics, social trends and big business, it has become normal to focus on the things we create, rather than the divine energy that inspired their creation in the first place. In most, the awareness of our innate spiritual power, wisdom, and creativity has been strongly suppressed. For some, it has been lost altogether.

Thus, our collective spiritual reality is a convergence of our individual and collective awareness and inner-standing of the natural world, the cosmos, the things we have created, and yes, our collective awareness and inner-standing of our individual and collective Divine Mind.

CHANGING OUR COLLECTIVE REALITY

One's impact on the world is directly proportionate to one's inner desire to have an impact upon the world, mixed with one's committed determination and skillful ability to perpetually learn, create, change, adapt, and grow. The pathway to our collective evolution is, similarly, contingent upon the degree to which we cultivate a society of evolving individuals. To evolve (ascend), one must remain in a constant state of change for the entire universe is never static, but expanding in each moment, to infinity! So too, must we. If we want to change the world, therefore, we must change first! For the process of evolution does not work backwards. The appearance of the forest, for example, changes as the trees change. Similarly, it is our individual inner-standings which are the catalyst for our collective, global evolution.

I hope that once we individually and collectively start to see the world system for the global mind control project that it truly is, we can begin to respond to our global challenges with cooperative, creative imagination. I happen to believe that the imagination is the most apparent evidence of the Universal Creator in all of us, as us! Because imagination allows us to see with new eyes, to explore possibilities, and then, choose to MAKE SOMETHING OUT OF NOTHING! Even if it's just a thought! I strongly admonish you to consciously choose who you are and who you are becoming, moment by moment. Never let anyone else define your holographic design parameters!

> *"Our personal holographic design begins with our desire and will to see ourselves through the eyes of The Conscious Observer; perpetually approaching the unknown with hopeful imagination, determination and creativity"* **Michelle Crenshaw**

Thus, the power of our imagination is made manifest by the degree to which our imagination expands. If your imagination is limited, you will have limited creativity and power; resulting in a finite personal hologram possessing little or no room to expand, grow, evolve, become or ascend.

OUR COLLECTIVE, NORMAL, REALITY

One thing I think we can all agree upon is that all reality is subjective. For even the energy in plants will react to outer stimuli when introduced into that plant's outer environment. It has been scientifically proven, for example, that plants will respond to musical frequencies by mimicking, memorizing and even transmitting these melodic frequencies to other plants! For the plant, the melodic frequencies were not a part of its previous reality. But, as soon as this new vibrational experience is introduced, the plant quickly responds by learning, adapting, evolving and teaching other plants! The chain reaction of this process resulted in a symphonic forest of musically aware trees that even created new melodies as these frequencies were passed on to other trees. What a miraculous experiment! And even though we may not all agree that the plant is "consciously" aware that this is happening, the example reasonably supports the premise that our Inner Self is, like the plant, being influenced by outer energies that significantly shape the Self. In our world, these energies operate in the form of family values, societal norms, rules, policies, laws, trends, news, propaganda, advertisement, etc.

Experts in Behavioral Science have already proven that human beings are a product of genetics, personal experience, and environment. All work to form the Inner Self. As a result, every person interprets life in a way that is unique to his or her individual and collective experiences. I am always amazed when I have an experience with another person and our interpretation of the events of that moment is profoundly different. How is this even possible? The implied interpretation here is that even if there were only two people on earth, they would most likely have differing views on the "reality" they are living together. Now just imagine the infinitely exponential differences that are possible in a world of nearly 8 billion people! With the entire collective simultaneously processing a daily dose of personal and collective experiences and interpretations, the possible outcomes of inner-standing and outer behavior of each individual Self is infinite!

Over time, however, the influence of the outer environment upon the individual has become the most influential force of our collective consciousness. For when we evolved from micro to macro societies, certain standards for normality; values, beliefs, dominions, kingdoms, laws, religions, governments, politics, trends, brands, and propaganda were established for the collective whole. Thus, it was the formation of collective "normality", that became the foundation for our Collective Reality. Our present reality, therefore, is most certainly the outer manifestation of our collective Inner Selves! For better or for worse, our current world is the evidence of what has been achieved (or lost) by allowing a global mind control project to run amuck for thousands of years! Hear Ye, Hear Ye! The Industrial Mind Control Complex is doing a fine job! The evidence is all around us; expressed in our collective and individual thoughts, beliefs, and, most significantly, behaviors; no matter how extreme or irrational.

COLLECTIVE COGNITIVE DISSONANCE

In the current age, normal has been equated with words like good or favorable; even if normal is known to be harmful to the individual and/or collective whole. Foods containing genetically modified organisms or as they are now known, GMO foods, are a perfect example of "normal" being bad for everyone. Yet, it is quite normal to find GMO foods sold in mainstream grocery chains in most cities. How often have you seen a protest or boycott of a local grocer who sells GMO foods? If your neighborhood grocer is like mine, the organic section is still the smallest portion of the produce department. Let's face it. If GMO foods were truly unacceptable to Americans, they would have been banned by now, right? Once again, the phenomenon of collective cognitive dissonance guarantees that we will continue to eat GMO products for the foreseeable future. Now if that's not an example of the duality of our reality, you can eat my hat!

Hence, the duality of our reality is rooted in our apparent inability to see our lives and our world with an objective view. With objectivity we can choose what we will think, believe, and do. But a subjective life perspective, in contrast, forces us to maintain a reactive mental and emotional stance as we are saturated with a barrage of conflicting signals from within and without daily. Here, collective cognitive dissonance plays a key role in keeping us prisoner to conflicting beliefs, impressions of the world, and intentions toward others.

The condition is perpetuated, of course, by a technological age wherein information, true or untrue, can be and is, disseminated daily via a barrage of propaganda and "fake news" across all technological mediums. Since this information network operates 24-7, it has become almost impossible to perceive the world objectively. When, therefore, we attempt to discern what is true or false, we find ourselves in a state of utter mental chaos because we don't know what to believe, nor, how to react. What makes this collective cognitive dissonance even more frightening is that it is administered to billions of people across the globe at the click of a button. Our collective reality, therefore, establishes a global social paradigm of perpetual inner and outer conflict.

OUTER CONFLICT VS INNER CONFLICT

As if we didn't have enough to worry about, we must now contend with the notion that this duality of reality is our inner-Self striving with the outer-Self to, consciously or unconsciously, manifest or express itself in the physical and spiritual realm of the human experience. If I am gay, for example, in a culture or community where homosexuality is viewed as wrong, I will probably experience the inner conflicts of fear or distress which could adversely affect my personal esteem and peace of mind. I would have even more anxiety if I lived in a society where homosexuality is against the law or considered worthy of death! Sadly, this is the reality of many in the LGBTQ community who live in places where out of date laws, superstitions, or religious beliefs prevail over personal freedoms. If I am overweight in a world where people think it is good and normal to achieve socially defined physical perfection by any means necessary, I am more likely to experience self-loathing or depression if my physical appearance does not meet the social standard. Just ask Richard Simmons! Of course, we have all seen the self-mutilation some are willing to endure to attain society's view of what is beautiful or attractive. Any plastic surgeon in America can attest to how far some people are willing to surgically alter themselves in order to achieve the world's standards of beauty. I could give examples ad infinitum but I'm sure you get the gist. In fact, I'd wager that as you're reading this, you can probably think of a few personal issues that have your inner-self at war with your outer-persona.

My personal example of my Inner Self struggling with my Outer Self became apparent when Carl and I "let go" of societal normality and decided to live in a motor home. At first, though my Inner Self was elated that we had achieved the ultimate "letting go" transformation, I found my Outer Self, very reluctant to admit to strangers that I lived in a motor home. It took many months before my inner conflict, worrying that I would be perceived as a bum or an "undesirable" of society, subsided. I had, after all, spent most of my life believing in the American dream of a house, 2.5 kids, a white picket fence and a new car in the garage. I even noticed that divulging this personal information greatly depended upon who I was talking to. In fact, even how I said it was predicated on how I anticipated being perceived or judged. What nonsense, right? Well, not really if you factor in how long I had believed in the American nightmare!

The point here is that breaking free from the choke hold of social order and living a life that is normal on your own terms will result in some inner struggle as you ascend. After all, the process of letting go of beliefs and values that may have been instilled within you from birth is not a simple set of steps that can be easily achieved without faith in your Divine Higher Self, personal discipline, as well as, on-going behavioral and spiritual modifications.

For in order to transform into your highest Self, you must have clarity on the new truth you desire to manifest and experience. In addition, you must have the inner strength and belief that what you wish to manifest is possible and necessary. As I have emphasized before, you must be fully persuaded that your subjective reality requires an objective review. Only then can your inner-Self clearly recognize the outer influences that are controlling your inner perceptions. For you cannot gain control of your thoughts, perceptions and beliefs until you consciously recognize that most of what you believe has been purposefully designed to control you. If you still haven't accepted that truth, the emancipation of your inner-Self, and the ascension to your highest-Self will not, and, cannot occur.

CHAPTER FIVE

The Matter of Time

> *"What then is time? If no one asks me, I know what it is. If I wish to explain it to him who asks, I do not know."* **Saint Augustine of Hippo** from Confessions of St. Augustine, Book 11

Time has always been a peculiar phenomenon in our universe. Cosmologists, astronomers, astrologists and shaman from all cultures of antiquity have tracked and measured time, while philosophers, psychologists and others have urged us to make time, save time and try not to waste time. Nevertheless, time is, unlike most elements of our world, still an intangible. Like the wind, it can neither be seen nor controlled, but rather, only experienced. Still, people will agree that time exists. For it is through the medium of time that we experience the events of the past. Though the events end, our brains readily retain and even sometimes relive them through the retention of memories stored in the brain. The more profound the experience, the more vivid the memory. This is true of benchmark moments in our lives such as the birth of a child, the death of a parent, or an achievement like graduating from college, or a wedding day.

Likewise, the lesser moments of our lives, casual conversations with friends, a trip to the local market a few days ago, or even where you last put your keys or eyeglasses, create short term memories which quickly fade away into the obscurities of the mind and are eventually forgotten altogether. Still, the awareness of time (or the lack thereof), remains at the center of most of our lives. In so doing, time instills an urgency in most people to reach some desired outcome before time runs out. This way of thinking has brought us to a widely accepted belief that time is therefore, a finite medium, in a finite world, through which we experience all life. Time is how we measure the events and activities of our lives. Accordingly, we mark the time with dates and holidays and work schedules and personal accomplishments. Time is our keeper; helping us to gage where we were, where we are, and where we ought to be by tomorrow.

When we examine time in relation to our spiritual journey, however, it becomes necessary to revisit our perception of what time is and how time may be used as a medium for our spiritual ascension and evolution. In the realm of the mind, time functions in somewhat of a loop that replays itself based on our mental programming; dictating and manifesting many underlying aspects of our beliefs and our behaviors. We say things like, *"I've always been this way or that way"* or *"I don't have time to pursue this dream or that dream"* or *"I would be able to achieve this goal or that goal…if I had the time."* As a result, we unconsciously project our collective perceptions of time as a finite realm which holds us prisoner to our past, present and future selves.

As a former Christian pastor and current spiritual advisor, I cannot tell you how many times a person has said during a discernment session that they do not feel they have the time to work on their spiritual growth. Consequently, I've found that these people come back again and again in the same state they were in the last time we met. That is what I mean by the spiritual loop that replays itself. Unlike Bill Murray's character in the movie Groundhog Day, whose life loops many times before he realizes he can change the circumstances of the day, most people simply keep reliving their same spiritual loop of beliefs, choices and outcomes until they leave this earthly plain. The result is a spiritual stagnation which traps them in the time loop of the past, and, finds them making the same autopilot choices again and again in the present. Subsequently, I must emphasize the need to consciously function in the present if you wish to change your future.

Such a pattern not only leads to spiritual stagnation, but it also creates a stressful tension in the person, exacerbating an already frustrated hamster wheel existence. When you tell a person that first you must stop, they always say… *"I don't have time to stop, I don't have time to wait, or I don't have time to focus"* etc., etc. Thus, the need to understand what time is and how time works in the spiritual realm is a necessary subject for analysis if you wish to save yourself and pursue a path of spiritual ascension.

TIME AND SCIENCE

In classical physics (that is physics before the discovery of quantum physics) time was a very manageable phenomenon. Time was finite, predictable and orderly. And people's response to this perception of time was to live in the finite possibilities that time would allow. But the discovery of quantum physics has sparked a curiosity and fascination with the possibility that time can be manipulated, and, that this manipulation brings with it, an infinite number of possible choices and outcomes that were never considered when time was perceived as being predictable. I realize that acceptance of what I will be proposing later in this chapter will create a paradigm shift in most peoples' thinking. Nevertheless, such a shift is imperative if you truly wish to let go of what was and proceed with the understanding that the only time that is of actual value, is right now.

For it is in the present, right now, that you can choose to see with new eyes, to think with fewer limitations, to act in new ways, to affect the world around you more profoundly and to experience new and different outcomes based on the presumption that time is, among many things, a medium through which we conceive, incubate and manifest the possibilities of the now and the yet to come.

In the first chapter, I asked you to stop. I am certain many who are reading this book did not stop and I imagine that for those who tried, stopping was a challenge. Of course, it was a challenge. It was meant to be a challenge. And it is a practice I recommend if you wish to master the art of mind clearing in order to settle your thoughts and spirit in preparation for reprogramming your internal time clock. For now, let's take another look at time from a new perspective.

> *"Yesterday is history, tomorrow is a mystery, today is a gift of God, which is why we call it the present."* **Bill Keane**

I am sure by now most of you have seen or heard this quote. It's catchy, quick and to the point. Yet how many of us have really lived the truth of these words with any consistency? Yesterday is history, for example, seems simple enough. But many people find it difficult to live without yesterday creeping up into the reality of today. Your spouse did something to hurt you last year... and Dr. Phil keeps telling you, you've got to let it go but you can't. Your boss pissed you off yesterday and you and your co-workers are in the break room the following day planning a strategy to set him/her straight by tomorrow. Your child misbehaved in school last week and he's grounded till next Saturday, but you find yourself badgering him/her about what he/she did so that they will not forget... thus bringing the scorn and shame of that past sin into the present repeatedly. And on and on... I cannot tell you how many times I did that to my poor children; reiterating the past to prevent repeat mistakes in the future. I was always, as the age-old idiom says... "beating a dead horse". And the phenomenon continues every time I tell myself what can or cannot be because of what was or was not before.

YESTERDAY IS HISTORY

In Earth Time, the past does not exist. This is the first truth you must accept if you want to save yourself by letting go of your old life and creating your new one.

The past, however, does continue to exist in mental and emotional time. For the past remains in us in the form of memories which remain with us as far as our minds can reach back and retain them. Once I got clarity on that concept, I soon realized that it was essential to my inner-standing of the process of letting go. For how could I let go of thoughts, emotions, and beliefs that were imbedded in me from birth?

That is when I first considered the notion that perhaps the past can only live within me if, I allow it. Now that's where the fun began. For in that moment, I realized I had my work cut out for me! How could I know what parts of my memorial history were toxic or helpful? How could I get to the core of myself to see what was hidden within me? Furthermore, how would I know what thoughts and beliefs no longer served my highest good? From that moment on, I began the ongoing practice of analyzing and purging my apparent thoughts, as well as, the memories in my mental and emotional library.

Once this mind clearing project got underway, I realized I would have to identify which memories I was consciously clinging to, as well as the entire arsenal of experiences and memories which had left their mark in my subconscious mind, heart, soul and body. My body fat, for example, was an outward sign of my body remembering all the unhealthy eating habits I had engaged in over the years. That was easy. My insecurities, in contrast, sprouted from the memory of all the mistakes I had made without reconciling the truth that "shit happens" to everyone and that, sometimes, *"the best laid schemes"* (Robert Burns) often do "go awry". My residual memory vault was also home to thoughts that foster low self-esteem or the inability to forgive myself for not making better choices…and on and on.

Regardless of how these residual thoughts and beliefs got planted, watered and rooted within my mind-soil, the result was a mental and emotional garden chock full of self-destructive weeds lying in wait to choke out the good seeds that were also planted there. These dormant seeds then dictated how I thought, felt, behaved and interacted with the world and the people around me. I admonish you to participate in all the exercises in this book, as well as, those found on the Ascending Mind website. The mental exercises and principles I've provided there will surely help you begin to clear the weeds of your spiritual garden and empower you to plant new thoughts, ideas and beliefs that serve you and the highest good of the people in your life.

TIME TRAVEL

We do not go back to the past, though quantum physics says that we probably can. And even if we could go back to the past, could we change even one moment to achieve a different outcome? Perhaps, but such an act would require such a high degree of spiritual focus, faith, science and power that most people would be remised to achieve it. Especially if one doesn't even have the discipline to pause for ten minutes of silence as the STOP exercise suggests. Unless you possess some exceptionally supernatural spiritual powers, returning to the past is simply not an option. You cannot change it and you cannot return there. You cannot undo what has been done or said. You cannot right wrongs, bring back the dead, nor change any aspect of the past. With that said, the past is, indeed, history. It only remains in the form of memories, which only exist as far as our minds can reach back and retain them. When that memory of the past is gone, the last remnants of the past dissolve into the abyss of a time forgotten. And if we could return to the past, would it not then become... the present once we arrived there?

But how can I say that the past is not real? Simply put, if I, for example, ate a Snickers candy bar yesterday, I can remember it and even visualize it. My memory might even trigger my glands to secrete saliva based on the strength of the memory of it. But I cannot relive that same candy bar eating experience today. I cannot taste it again. I cannot eat it or enjoy it. I can only remember it and perhaps buy another and have a new snicker eating experience that will also, become the past as soon as it's eaten. Both experiences will forever remain inaccessible to me to experience again. Each additional snicker eating experience will be new and at any time in the present, I can choose to eat something different.

If it's not here, today, in my possession, therefore, it is not real, no matter how many times I fantasize about it. And if I fantasize about it, only the fantasy, in the realm of now, is real and yes, temporary. For as quickly as an experience occurs, the concept of time forces that experience to slip into the unreality of the past. Finally, when people remain stuck in the past, believing it is real, they are usually a candidate for some psychological or psychiatric evaluation! Fortunately, the memories of the past can provide us with many valuable lessons and with a point of reference for making better decisions and exploring new possibilities in the present.

Time has revealed that much of what we accept as factual history has now, after thousands of years, been firmly disproved. Some of those debunked "truths" of the past now include accepted facts like; the earth is round and not flat, the earth revolves around the sun and is not the center of the universe, there are an infinite number of galaxies besides the Milky Way, and the earth is a result of millions of years of evolution and not a finite mass created in 7 days by an unseen God, and so on and so on.

In a similar way, our personal history is often dictated by prejudices, preferences, and limitations which give us a selective or distorted memory of the facts. The result is that we perpetually exist in a subjective view of the past, as well as, the present reality. But how powerful is a memory that you once believed was true and later realize is quite untrue? Furthermore, if we fail to reconcile these conflicting facts, how will these memories or resulting beliefs which are based in untruth, impact our present, and future, choices and perspectives?

I will never forget, for example, the day the news announced that Rock Hudson was in fact, gay, and not the virile, manly, woman-loving hunk whom women had swooned over for several decades. What happens to the memories of all those women who fantasized about someday meeting a man just like Mr. Hudson? Were those memories shattered for some? Did some women decide to remain stuck in holding onto the belief that Mr. Hudson was not gay in order to preserve their memories of the past, intact? Did this new information change the desires of the women who once believed they wanted to someday meet a man just like Rock Hudson to have as a husband? I ask... are all those thoughts, wishes and beliefs grounded in a lie any less valuable to the present once they are exposed in the light of now? The point I am making here is if we can't even be sure about the so-called "facts" of our history, how can we allow these "facts" of the past to influence our perception of now, and, the future?

Thus, as we remember the past, we realize we always run the risk of remembering it amiss. This truth alone makes the past an unstable starting place for gaging one's true reality in the now and establishes even more support for the notion that the past (our history) is not as real as we may realize or believe. Even now, with the evolution of quantum physics, mankind has much to reconcile about the notion of space and time and our relationship to the perpetual expansion of what we call "the Universe". Selah (*pause and think about it*)

WHAT WE THINK WE KNOW ABOUT TIME

Let us first discuss the phenomenon of time itself. Though I am not a physicist, I feel confident sharing my understanding of time based upon the research I've conducted...over time. For I hypothesize that the science of time is intricately connected to human spirituality. In addition, I believe that this connection significantly influences our understanding of the world and ourselves, as well as physical and spiritual phenomena.

According to renowned physicist Stephen Hawking, "time began at the Big Bang". His reasoning for this theory lies in the current scientific evidence that the universe, inclusive of all that we know of it, is expanding. Moreover, in his book, **A Brief History of Time**, Mr. Hawking states that this expansion has been in motion for "about 15 billion years" and that the path of this motion can be observed and measured. Though some scientists first refuted his claim, Mr. Hawking's theory is more, or less, the prevailing view of the overall scientific community for now.

Surprisingly, even the religious and philosophical have begun to embrace the Big Bang Theory since it seems to support the possibility that at some point, a supernatural being could have created the universe out of one singular galactic event. Furthermore, through the technological advances of civilization, scientists are now much more equipped to observe the cosmic bodies and to measure their movement through space. These observations and measurements have led to the current, prevailing theories of time and how time functions in our day-to-day existence here on Earth. Hawking and other physicists generally agree that the universe is expanding and not collapsing. Through advanced technology, they now measure the speed and distance of this expansion in terms of time, which is defined by the Merriam-Webster Dictionary as: "*the measurable period during which an action, process, or condition exists or continues: duration.*" So, with this understanding, we will proceed with the notion that time began with the Big Bang.

THE BEGINNING OF TIME

So, in the beginning was the Big Bang and the Big Bang created time as we understand it. Since Mr. Hawking's' Big Bang Theory proports that in the beginning, "*all matter in the universe would have been on top of itself*" and that the "*density would have been infinite*", scientists have no way of knowing what was before this moment of universal expansion which we are currently experiencing. Similarly, they have no way of knowing if "time" as we experience it, even existed before the bang for the Bang created the energy particles, that clustered into galaxies and these galaxies, by the force of the bang, are now moving out and away from the source and from each other. Miraculously, these galaxies move in synchronicity away from each other, like ripples in a pool of water. And the changes in these ripples are measured as they move from one point on their trajectory to the next. The measurement of this distance and velocity translates in our reality into the phenomenon of time. As far as we know, the observation of the cosmos has been documented by humans since the existence of humans. The Sun, our daily indicator that a new day has dawned, is also the indicator of earthly time, measured in days, hours, minutes, seconds, nanoseconds, etc. Thus time, on earth remains constant and predictable, as long as the sun remains in our galaxy.

TOMORROW IS A MYSTERY

In general, I think most would agree that the future is indeed a mystery. Afterall, most people still marvel at the mystics, sages, seers and clairvoyants who predict future events that do, indeed, come true. That awe-struck impression of the future exists because in classical physics, we are taught to recognize time in linear terms; defined by the sequential order of past, present and future events. Regardless of the mystery of it, however, I would argue that in truth, the future also exists in the present as hopefulness, promise, preparation and anticipation or, as fear, trepidation, anxiety, stress and frustration. The latter arising when one perceives that one is not ready for what the future may have in store. Fortunately, as we mature, we come to realize that what we didn't finish today, can be completed tomorrow. And, what we do today, can create a new opportunity or experience for tomorrow. Even though we understand this concept in theory, we continue to forewarn ourselves and each other that tomorrow, with all its potential, is still, not promised.

If I hope for something, that hopefulness heightens my awareness of possibility. As I discover the possibilities, I fortify my awareness and recognize that what I hope for is indeed, possible. Once I believe that possibilities exist, confidence in my ability to take actions toward the desired outcome is ignited. As I grow in confidence and inner-standing, so does my faith. As a result, I am empowered to continue acting in synchronized agreement with my beliefs more effectively. It is then, that my creative actions manifest in my present reality. As I learned in my Christian days, faith is the "substance of things" (**Hebrews 11:1**), or rather, the ingredients and processes necessary for the "thing" to exist; just as flour, sugar, eggs, butter, mixing, baking, etc. are the necessary ingredients and processes needed to make a cake. But it is the "making" of the cake, the action, that causes the final product of cake to exist. Thus, hope is the catalyst which activates our faith, which in turn, prompts the action that makes "things' come into "being".

Subsequently, we discern and, therefore, can conclude that hopeful intentions, apparently project a certain kind of Creation Energy into the spiritual ether. Though unseen, this Creation Energy projects the frequency (or tone) of expectancy from the present that then comes into being, sometime in the future as a result of the synchronicity (or agreement) between our beliefs and actions. Though we seldom recognize our coincidences as deliberate outcomes emanating from us, we do recognize when this moment of synchronicity manifests. We may not realize that this manifesting process is facilitated by the synchronized cooperation of heart, mind, will and action emanating from the creative idea that triggered it. As we act with expectation that we are making a cake, for example, we subsequently manifest a cake which is consistent with the original recipe, or tone of expectation, which thought to make cake in the first place! I generally operate with the inner-standing that the future is, therefore, a creative manifestation of the collectively synchronized frequencies of the Heart, Mind, Will, Soul and Spirit of the Self. For all that is in the future was born of Creation Energy, moving through our decisions, choices and actions; manifesting predictable outcomes from one point in time to the next.

When it comes to personal ascension, I propose that the future is more a manifested outcome of the spiritual, mental and emotional intentions of the present, than it is a mystery to be feared with anxiety or trepidation. Hopeful people, for example, plant seeds of possibility, watered by hopeful intentions, nourished by emotional desire, and powered by specific action.

(THOUGHT/MIND	*"I THINK I may go to college."*
(INTENTION/HEART)	*"I WANT to go to college"*
(DESIRE/WILL)	*"I WILL go to college"*
(ACTION/REALITY)	*"I AM attending college"*

This repeating loop of {thought + intention + desire + action = REALITY}, is the operation of our Present/Future experience. *"I think"* becomes *"I want"*; *"I want"* becomes *"I will"*; and *"I will"* eventually becomes *"I AM"*. Consequently, thoughts, desires, and actions, powered by the Creation Energy of Spirit, become established within us as what most would describe as our individual faith.

With each reinforcing act of faith, confidence in our belief grows within the conscious and subconscious Mind and Heart. There, it is established as clarity and truth. It is the force of faith, that is the catalyst for changing the present into the future, manifesting whatever you truly believe, inner-stand, feel and intend in the Mind, Heart, Soul, and Will into the physical reality! The law of cause and effect applies even when these inner thoughts, beliefs, etc. are perceived as negative. Therefore, who you are in your truest Outer Self, is the product of your cumulative inner experience of your personal history. Thus, faith is the operation of the energy-action of cause and the energy-re-action of effect in our present and future reality. As such, the spiritual law of faith is eternally tied to the scientific law of cause and effect.

> *"As above, so below, as within, so without, as the universe, so the soul..."* **Hermes Trismegistus** from **The Emerald Tablets of Thoth**

The element of faith is also key to this past-present-future time travel trip because, to experience growth or change within the Self, we must first address the Mind, the Heart, the Will and the Soul. That's why spiritual ascension is a way of life, rather than just a single process of steps to engage in for one everlasting result. For to change anything, we must first believe that what we desire to manifest in our reality is possible. As our belief in the possibilities grows stronger, we begin entertaining creative ideas that can make the possible happen. As creativity becomes a regular operation of the mind, possibilities transform into beliefs, beliefs into expectations, expectations into actions and actions into desired outcomes. It is the strength of our beliefs, and acting upon them, that makes possibilities materialize into our physical experience. So, then, faith is the evidence of things seen, not with the eye, but with the Mind, Heart and Soul! Powerful stuff, right?!

To experience the power of what I call, intentional faith, you must begin to seek truth, clarity, and divine purpose. In so doing, you are establishing a foundation upon which you can design a creative manifestation-plan of action. This plan will support you in intentionally influencing your outer reality.

> ***"THIS IS FAITH:***
> *power, creativity, truth, clarity, divinity, purpose, passion, planning, expectation and action; all working in concert to become apparent in our daily lives"*
>
> **Michelle Crenshaw**

As I stated earlier, the law of cause and effect is always in operation here. That means, if you don't inner-stand your Inner Self, you will not inner-stand your Outer Self. You will not know or understand why you feel and act as you do. And you will not understand why you fail to act with purposeful intention. Once again, cognitive dissonance and low self-esteem arise and become problematic. That is why I recommend that you practice a life of ongoing, self-awareness, self-analysis and self-diagnosis. For if you do not practice going within to assess the contents of your cupboards and refrigerator, you'll never be able to cook dinner. What tools are you working with? What are the origins of your beliefs? What do you want and who do you choose to be? What are you willing to do to see your best Self come into reality? If you fail to consciously define these answers, faith simply responds to the Inner Self that already exists; for better or for worse. Therefore, until the inner you, evolves into the ascending you, you will continue repeating cycles which do not represent the positive, creative, fruitful potential of your Spirit, Mind, Heart, & Soul. Selah

On the flip side, fear, anxiety, doubt and disbelief (lack of faith) also create outcomes in the present/future. Fretful people, for example, tend to plant fearful seeds of impossibility within the Mind. Without a hopeful vision for the future, there is no room for positive possibilities or outcomes. Instead, the worrier usually thinks, consciously or subconsciously, in terms of past failures and disappointments, causing that pattern to continue. The past, then, acts as a predictive catalyst for repetitious patterns of destructive thoughts and behaviors that result in undesirable, yet predictable, outcomes. The Mind, in this instance, loops thoughts of defeat, failure, or fear. The Will oppresses desires and establishes doubt within the Heart, and subsequently, the Soul is paralyzed to act toward positive outcomes for the future. Unfortunately, many people live a life filled with doubt and worry, looping outcomes of disappointment that are sustained by destructive or limiting beliefs and lack of creative faith.

The point here is that if I hope for something and back that hope up with action, my hopefulness automatically heightens my belief in possibilities as soon as my actions cause that "thing" to come into existence. That is the miraculous beauty of childbirth. Two people joining their belief in possibilities, backing it up with action, and realizing they have created something/one by sheer will and action. The more I have this Creation Energy experience, the more I believe in my ability to create. And the more I create, the more the desire to create grows. Therefore, my desire and ability to act is consistently strengthened. With more confidence comes more understanding and more faith. That is because hopeful intentions project a certain kind of energy into the spiritual ether. Though unseen, this energy propels our intentions from the present into future by means of the energetic hopefulness which projected it.

THE GIFT OF THE PRESENT

Can you imagine what your life would be like if you constantly found yourself completely immersed in the moment of all your experiences. Someone says: *"Hi, how are you?"* and you reply in full detail disserting "how" you really "are" in real time. Would anyone have the time or patience to stop, listen or care about "how" you are doing if everyone took the present time to express that answer fully? I shudder to think! In such a world, the "present" would surely become the past by the time we evaluated each moment in this manner.

Quite frankly, in our current world, we don't have time to dissect our experiences moment by moment. If we tried, we would have one heck of a time getting anything done or making any progress in our lives. As a result, most have conveniently learned to truncate their awareness and experience of the present moment down to simple words like, fine, well, awful, great, tired, etc. But in the spiritual realm, the ability to compartmentalize and discern the energy of the present becomes a key element on the journey to manifesting infinite possibilities.

THE POTENTIAL OF THE PRESENT

On the pathway of spiritual ascension, the present gives us the opportunity to stop, savor the moment and connect with our creative energy. Have you ever seen a scary movie or had a dream where someone is walking down the hallway of a mysterious house and as they walk, the hallway just seems to stretch longer and longer? Oddly, this moment in the movie generally fills us with tension and dread, because we are waiting with baited-breath, convinced that something bad is going to happen. Now in contrast, let's pretend the movie is reality.

What if, instead of moving down that hallway with fearfulness and apprehension, you proceeded with the anticipation that something wonderful is about to happen? Furthermore, what if, halfway down that hallway you decide to stop and admire the paintings on the wall, the beautiful grain of the woodwork on the doors, the intricate patterns on the draperies, etc.? What if you decided to paint the walls another color, to install new lighting, to stop midway and have a sack lunch in one of the plush chairs, or to knock at one of the doors, expecting someone handsome or beautiful to answer, and so on? What if the hall appears dark and ominous but you decide to flip on a light switch and illuminate the darkness? And what if that illumination dispelled all the darkness and fear, replacing it with awe and admiration for all the beauty that you discover as you journey down that hallway in peace?

That, my friends, is the beauty and gift of the present, in the spiritual realm. For in the Spirit lies all possibility. And possibilities, once presented, inherently bring with them the reality of choice. So here, in the present, you can pause and decide to choose a different path, direction, perspective or response to the moment. But before you can savor the moment you have to be able to stop.

PLEASE PAUSE FOR A 10 MINUTE MOMENT

LIFE LESSONS ON ASCENSION
BE STILL AND KNOW THE POWER OF STILLNESS

I am including the following journal entries to help you begin thinking through the process of letting go of prior belief systems that could limit your ability to have success with this exercise. The quotes noted were taken from **The Secret Universal Mind Meditation by Kelly Howell** (on YouTube). I strongly recommend that you listen to this meditation daily for at least 30 days. It is a valuable ascension tool that can open your mind to the notion of limitless possibilities and the power of faith; a skill that must be cultivated if spiritual ascension is the goal. For now, I'm asking you to listen to this meditation at least twice before reading the following reflections.

Journal Reflection: August 6, 2014 (excerpt)

It's still Wednesday, August 6th-evening…at McDonald's listening to a new meditation. I am changing. Seeing the world from a different view. It turned out to be a good day. We made some money, lightened the load of what we carry around. A productive day. And then, we went to dinner at Sizzlers.

> *"I am one with the Universal Mind. I know this mind is perfect and I may rely upon it for guidance in all my affairs; which responds to me when I ask. All the answers are speeding their way to me Right Now. Each day brings evidence of the power and wonder of the universe and myself… of the greatness and perfection of God that is in me and is me…In the strength of my belief my faith will make it so…The great reality is good and is always attempting to manifest itself."* **Kelly Howell**

The Universal Mind is constantly manifesting that which I believe. So, each day I must believe (know) I have enough resources for all that I need.

DESIRE =CONCEPTION. *My world is ordered by my own thoughts and convictions.*

Journal Reflection: August 8, 2014 (excerpt)

I snapped at Carl. I shouldn't have. I was just hot and tired and reactive. That's a dangerous and un-useful behavior and mentality. It shows a lack of order and control in the mind. It means-your emotions are ruling the moment. I let go of my emotions having final reality. My thoughts must always be reviewed before they are accepted and displayed in emotion...

We are more honest now I think, honest without malice. It is the emotions that seek malice because emotions reflect intent. And if intent is not chosen, it becomes quite simply...reactive to all the contributing factors in our physical and mental retention... memories and experiences both well and unwell. So, when you are reacting to the moment with the sum-total of the history of your life experiences, history prevails and most likely, we do, therefore, err.

Journal Reflection: August 11, 2014 (excerpt)

Great day today. We slept well and woke pleasant. Today we went to Westchester Park. Carl slept in the sun. I was energized. Today I kept telling myself... it's okay to do nothing but that which brings me joy... resting, relaxing, and being still. That was the message today "Be Still". So finally, I surrendered to that.

> *"I hold my thoughts ...in contemplation of the good"* **Kelly Howell**

I have complete faith in the power of stillness. I accept only the good. I conceive today the answer to the repair of the truck. I desire a solution to this situation and will receive it. I refuse to accept the mechanical problems of the truck having final reality. It is impossible to fail with this faith present. My world is ordered by this belief. So today we asked the question "what will we do with this new freedom?" Our Purpose. It is important we identify this. For our prayers, our ascension and our fulfillment are tied to this… Purpose. The preliminary answer… minister to the homeless.

We have learned together that our prayers and desires must not be out of need but out of our purpose. We need the truck to reach and help people. Its function is to facilitate our purpose.

> *"I have complete confidence that every circumstance that comes my way is part of a perfect plan to convert the image of my faith into physical reality… As I believe in my heart, so it will be done. This is the law of life and of living. I do not seek, I know. I do not strive, I am guided."* **Kelly Howell**

NOTE: This understanding, for me, is profound.

THE ILLUSION OF TIME AND SINGULARITY

It is in the present moment that you train your mind to stand still. For in stillness, the very source of many fears may be allayed. In the stillness we can choose nothing or everything, joy or sorrow, hope or despair. In stillness we can also imagine and will to create something beautiful! The key, however, is that you must savor the present and recognize that each new moment brings with it, the chance to create the next present moment again with every step forward.

But, it is important to pause here and acknowledge that certain methods have been put in place to keep us ignorant of our collective power as One Divine Mind. Be clear. Those who control the thinking of the masses understand that the physical world, though an expression of the energy of the Divine Source, is also subject to and a prisoner of time. For the Earth vibrates at a slower energetic frequency than the Universe. This vibration allows us to perceive and experience time within an earthly, physical and multi-sensory context. I believe this context was purposefully designed to allow the creator to experience creation. As a recording artist, I equate it with listening to recordings of myself and experiencing the same love, joy, and emotion that others may encounter when they hear me sing; or, the experience of preparing a meal, and then enjoying the fruits of your culinary labors.

In creative experiences, I am the conscious observer of my life and that objective view enables me to love and appreciate the Self that I AM more abundantly. In those moments I recognize that I AM walking in my truest purpose. Such a feeling and awareness renders an energy of peace, contentment, self-esteem and gratefulness that stirs me to rejoicing. Maybe that's why the ancients believed that "God" created the world, looked at the creation and recognized that it was, indeed, all good.

I believe that humankind is made in the likeness and image of the divine creative energy, and as such, exists with the same spectrum of divine attributes as the divinely creative force from which we emanate and with which we co-exist eternally. Thus, as both creator and creation simultaneously, we each possess the shared nature and limitless abilities of the Divine One! Have you ever considered that all the glory of the Creator is within you, and is you?

Without sounding cliché, I am reminded of the parable of the creation of man in the garden of Eden, which most attribute to the bible. Here, the author tells us that "God" said... *"let us make man in our image"* (**Genesis 1:26**), which implies that humankind was intentionally endowed with the fullness of the Creator when we received the divine *"breath of life and man became a living soul"* (**Genesis 2:7**); for no other living creation was described in this way. Though we cannot say for sure if these descriptions were facts, we can at least glean from these words that from the beginning, humans believed they were created in the image and similitude of a Divine Creator.

I happen to believe that this understanding and intention is expressed by the words... "**I AM THAT I AM**" (**Exodus 3:14**) which I translate to mean: *"I am all things co-existing as the Creator and Creation"*. Just as all colors of the spectrum exist within the energy vibration of the color black, all life exists within the energy vibration of the Divine Creator and is expressed on earth as all creation, of which we are a part and with which, we too, are one.

The rulers of this realm understand that in this dimension, what we observe as the physical world is just the frequency or rhythm of the divine energy being observed. Just as music waves appear on recording software, these musical frequencies appear as one line of energy that moves (vibrates) in continuum until the origin of the music stops. Variations in the music create frequency wave patterns of highs and lows emanating from the source. Yet the frequency being observed is really one sound, with the variances of pitch and intensity appearing as waves which can be observed, measured and manipulated. The concept is easy to perceive if one considers the visual experience of stop action or slow-motion effects used in motion pictures. Though the event was recorded at one speed, the film editor can slow down that speed to give the illusion that the event occurred more slowly than it did. The perceived space between the vibrational waves of motion, light or sound, are simply a continuation of one unified movement, that when slowed down, can be measured in terms of space. This measurement of the distance between vibrational energy events is what we refer to as "time". I highly recommend that you read **A Brief History of Time** *by Stephen W. Hawking* for a broader understanding of how time exists and can be manipulated.

What better way to control humankind than by attempting to interrupt the frequency of our divine, collective mind, through the manipulation of time with all its implied limitations. By training our physical brains to forget the divine Universal Mind and instead, think within the limitations of linear time, it becomes easier with each new generation to control our thinking and, thereby, control us. Thus, humankind finds itself trapped within a time loop that begins and ends within a matrix of deceptive limitations.

Why is this kind of thinking deadly to humankind? Because the life within all living things is a timeless continuum of divinely unlimited abundance and eternal regeneration without end. That, I propose, is the meaning behind the passage found in the book of **Revelation** stating, *"I am Alpha and Omega, the beginning and the ending"* (**Revelation 1:8**) *"the first and the last"* (**Revelation 1:11**). For in that "revelation" lies the truth of all living things. Because the truth is, we are all one with all creation and one with the vast and limitless whole of the eternal life-force. Thus, time has no relevance in divine creation… because our existence is by its very nature, eternal. Still, most have succumbed to the mental programming described herein, and so, they live a limited reality sandwiched within the prison of time.

As expressions of the Divine Creator we are here to manifest abundant life and to perpetuate the miracle of eternal creation abundantly. This is what the man we call Jesus understood; reminding us of ancient wisdom that can be traced back through the antiquity of many cultures to the very dawn of humankind. So, as the deceivers have persisted and succeeded in using time to teach us the apparent limitations of past, present, and future thinking, we have simply forgotten who we are. As a result, we now exist in a constant mental & spiritual state of running out of time, making time, losing time, worrying about the future, trying to forget the past and struggling to live in the present moment. Sadly, we live this way without even realizing that time is completely irrelevant to our divine awareness.

Ironically, it is these "lords" of the earth who are the true and eternal prisoners of the time, which they sought, and seek to manipulate. It is they who will always repeat the time-life cycle here on the Earth. While, on the other hand, we are the ones who will live on as the eternal evidence of The One; far beyond the limitations of this current physical realm. That is, unless we succumb to the illusion of time and singularity. For it is only in the awareness and acceptance of our collective expression of The One that we are empowered with conscious determination to reeducate our spirit, mind, soul and body. And, as we pursue this divine pathway of enlightened thinking and doing, we can move through time and space on the pathway which leads us back to our divine source. Just as a single drop of water returns to its source through the process of evaporation and precipitation, we too, as divine drops of the Divine One, return to same through a brief process of life and ascension. This yearning for perpetual connection and reunion with our source is, therefore, innate within each of us.

For we know, deep within, that we are merely on a brief journey which leads us back to completion when we reunite with our beginnings, our Source. Accordingly, our soul yearns for this refreshing, just as each drop of rain rejoices in the reunited glory of the mighty, life-sustaining waters of the ocean!

CHAPTER SIX

No One is Coming to Save You: Part One

INTRODUCTION:

Somewhere along this evolutionary journey on Earth, humans decided that their salvation would come from outside of themselves. It is understandable since in ancient times, man's life and livelihood was contingent upon a vast world of the unknown, the inexplicable and the awesome. Their view of the world, therefore, fostered respect, admiration, reverence and fear of nature and the cosmos. These apparent "mysteries" birthed heroes, deities, mythologies, allegories, saviors and gods. Consequently, many basic spiritual mythologies and religions were birthed from these beliefs; as well as, many divinely profound life-lessons. These lessons and mythologies were eventually adopted by the so-called world religions which appeared centuries later. Today, most of our religious beliefs and teachings remain anchored in this ancient spiritual dichotomy of mythology vs spirituality and allegory vs human history.

For this reason, I am certain that the next few chapters will prove to be the most disturbing part of the book if you are practicing any version of formal, organized religion; particularly, Christianity. In fact, the notion that no one is coming to save you contradicts nearly every social teaching of our age. For it is the belief of most people that somewhere, somehow, some entity outside of themselves will intervene and rescue them from themselves, the consequences of their actions, and the discomforts of the human experience. So, if you're counting on being rescued from whatever ails you, get over yourself and suck it up buttercup, because no one is coming to save you!

THE NATURE OF ORGANIZED RELIGION

The primary advantage of "organized" religious doctrine is that ultimately, you can create whatever kind of religion you want. Once the doctrine is formalized, it can then be systematically taught by its leaders and conveyed by loyal converts to each new wave of eager initiates. This systematic process of orientation and initiation still applies to the world religions of the modern age. Since each of these religious powers has remained over many centuries, any opposing doctrines are generally classified as cults. But, before they became world religions, all three began as cults, just like the host of other "cults" which came into existence long before them.

Sadly, the one thing that the three world religions have in common is a history of violence. Formed at the behest of nation states and kings, their creators simply "organized" their way to power. The irony is that by violently annihilating the cults from which they came, the true intention and function of the many rites, rituals, and traditions they adopted was lost or grossly distorted in translation; resulting in traditions void of the true meanings and understandings that inspired them in the first place. As we begin to examine the origins of Christianity, therefore, we must acknowledge that most of its tenets are deeply rooted in the ancient "cults" and religious traditions that preceded it. The result is that many of our current religious beliefs and practices are now, mere "knock offs" of the originals and thus, lacking in the rich cultures and allegories from whence they were derived. So, before we delve into the significant ancient influencers that made organized religions what they are today, let us begin with a few basic & useful concepts as we proceed on this journey of discovery. Accordingly, I admonish you to do your own research on any statements herein which conflict with your current belief paradigm. In so doing, you may find more information than what I have provided here. If you do, that would be awesome!

THE PROBLEM WITH CHRISTIANITY

The following section provides a summary of the historical and cultural origins of the fundamental dogma and doctrine of Christianity. It is not, however, a history of Christianity in entirety. There are plenty of books you can read on that subject. Instead, I thought it more useful to highlight the origins of the beliefs, philosophies, sacred cultural practices, mythologies, and rituals that influenced and/or became the foundation of Christian church tenets. These ancient religions, practices, and beliefs predate the invasion of Egypt by Alexander of Rome, in 325 BCE, by thousands of years. Hopefully, this information will provide a roadmap that illuminates the truth about where these "Christian" beliefs came from and how they found their way into the formation of the Roman Catholic Church in the first place.

More importantly, I hope to shed a light on how the church's adopted dogma became the tool by which the Roman Empire gained control over the already civilized world it invaded. As we proceed, you should be able to follow the dots that led to Christianity. Facing these facts is imperative to this ascension from "normal" process. For it is better to know the beginning of a thing, if you wish to understand its end. Most importantly, you should be able to see how time can erase so much of our historical memory when the powers that rule the world are writing their own historic narrative. But before you begin reading this section, I need you to STOP and take a 10-Minute Moment. Why? Because this is the point where you either "wake up and smell the poop" or you cover your mind's eye with the poop and remain an ignorant product of your systemic programming. Ouch! I know, that was a bit harsh.

Why Christianity? Why do I have to "go there"? Because the global agenda that sparked the birth of this religious mind control project over 2000 years ago, is the same global agenda that remains alive and well today! The same global agenda that keeps nations at war. The same agenda that seeks to keep the people of the world imprisoned in the mind. Yes, I am speaking here about the unholy alliance of the:

- Holy Roman Empire, administered by the Holy See and The Roman Catholic Church
- The State of Israel led by Prime Minister Benjamin Netanyahu
- The World Jewish Congress under the oversight of David de Rothchild (the Ashkenazi)
- The Rothchild Empire -which owns/controls over 50% of (almost) every central bank in the world excluding North Korea by the way
- Her Royal Majesty's Government of the United Kingdom
- The United States of America, Inc.
- The United Nations

Just to name a few!

The agenda of this unholy alliance is complete and comprehensive global control of the economies, societies, governments, religions, and military powers of the world, as well as, the thoughts and behaviors of all humankind. That goal is facilitated and achieved through manipulation of political leaders, governmental policies, social programs, religions, banking, stock exchanges, as well as, control of commodities, laws and legalities. In particular, the religious agenda is strongly promoted and supported through the teachings of Christian churches and Jewish synagogues, where the false messianic tenets are promulgated, knowingly or not. Furthermore, the alliance between elite secret societies and the industrial military complex relies heavily upon global media, entertainment, political propaganda, and control of core industries (pharmaceuticals, health care and food related commodities, etc.), to keep a tight grip on what and how information is disseminated to the global community.

For starters, the Holy Roman Empire set a precedent for world religion when it initiated the crusade to put the entire world under Christian, and later, Judeo-Christian control. Whether modern-day non-Catholic Christians accept their culpability in that agenda or not, it is still true. The non-Catholic Christians may try to disassociate the origins of their Christianity from the Catholic church, but the uncomfortable truth here is, there would be no protestants if some Catholics had not protested the Catholic church in the first place. Likewise, there would be no non-denominational Christian churches if the founders of same had not protested the many denominational protestant churches which preceded them. To disassociate the connection between the two, would be like modern day White Americans, (who benefit across the board from White Privilege in America), denying that this "privilege" was acquired as the byproduct of a country built upon the most egregious enslavement of Black people across the world over many centuries!

These religious institutions have one thing in common. That is, that they are being used as a tool to control the thinking of masses of people worldwide. Is it the only tool for mass control? Most certainly not. I have already mentioned many tools of control that the system maintains. Throughout this book, I have addressed as many of these tools as I can. But because religion is an organized, group belief experience, it is the most powerful tool of the System besides media, entertainment, and political propaganda. I did not include the origins of Islam because it evolved several centuries after the Roman Catholic Church was already conquering the world. I include Judaism because, as the falsified documentation of the historical legacy of the Black people of Africa, it remains one of the most egregious falsifications of stolen legacy of a race of people in the annuls of modern history.

I do not have time to visit that big, ugly elephant in the room in this book. The point here is that the two religions are forever in partnership in this global deception and control project.

According to the Oxford Dictionary the following definitions apply:

Doctrine: a belief or set of beliefs taught by a church, political party, or other group.

Dogma: a principle or set of principles laid down by an authority as incontrovertibly true.

Principle: A fundamental truth or proposition that serves as the foundation for a system of belief or behavior or for a chain of reasoning. Synonyms: *truth, proposition, concept, idea, theory, postulate, assumption, basis, fundamental, essence, essential, philosophy*

In consideration of the cognitive dissonance that could possibly result from reading this section, I highly recommend that you take a 10 Minute Moment to process the barrage of information that follows. If you are a church going person, a devout or actively participating

Christian, a pastor, a preacher, an evangelist, etc. I ask you to say the following prayer:

"Divine Spirit who is within me and is me... Help me see today with new eyes. Help me to listen. Help me to be open. Help me to connect with the part of me that knows that everything in my life is working, in cooperation, for my ultimate benefit and growth. Help me to trust that ancient understanding. I call upon my inner courage and my desire to know the truth. As I read these passages, I open my mind to gain knowledge and know wisdom; seeking to know the truth rather than live a lie. For it is my deepest desire to be free. I release myself from fear. And, I will live in the blessed grace of divine spiritual wisdom and faith. And so, it is"

PLEASE PAUSE FOR YOUR 10 MINUTE MOMENT

DOCTRINE: THE ULTIMATE MIND CONTROL WEAPON

By creating the doctrine of salvation by grace through faith in the self-sacrifice of a savior-god, the Roman Empire served as both author and finisher of what Christians would believe for centuries. For, as I mentioned earlier, the people longed for saviors! So, with each new mission, crusade, conquest or war came more converts. The more converts the empire produced, the more this religious virus spread. For the converted became the ambassadors of the doctrine. For most the message was, indeed, good news. Those who would not convert to Christianity, however, were expendable in the name of Christ. But those who accepted this "salvation" were saved and forgiven of their sins for life! All one needs for this grace-filled "salvation" is belief.

By establishing the foundation of the Church upon the premise of faith, the substance of things hoped for and the evidence of things not seen, Christianity became the ultimate Mind Control Marketing Plan! For the Church simply found a need and filled it! Since the dawn of Christianity, therefore, people need only believe that they are "saved" to be saved. Furthermore, every sinful act can also be forgiven by, you guessed it…faith. For in Christianity, one is always forgiven if one believes that one has received forgiveness by God's grace. Sort of like switching over to a new brand of ice cream and believing you'll never suffer the fat-assed consequences of your dietary "sins". Heaven! Who wouldn't take that deal? Unfortunately, that is how the Unholy Roman Empire, and the Church it created, conquered and killed the minds of the "civilized" world…with doctrine and very aggressive marketing! And, to think, these converted "believers" helped fund their own mind prison project through offerings, tithes, and penance! Selah

As I mentioned at the beginning of this chapter, humankind has always yearned for a savior, a hero, a leader who would rescue the world from the unavoidable circumstances of the human condition. From many traditions and cultures, many heroes, deities, and saviors were formed. The dilemma here is that the creation of "Jesus the savior" did not just evolve organically through folklore and allegory. Instead, the messianic message of the man they call Jesus was deliberately organized to facilitate and reinforce the military/political agenda of Rome; which was to conquer the people of the world. Rome accomplished this goal by initiating the global mind-control project we call Christianity.

Since Christianity remains the largest religious group in the world, over 30% of the world identify as Christian, I would say the mission of The Roman Church has been a success for sure! Furthermore, when you also consider the enormous wealth of the

Vatican, with billions of shares in the most powerful international firms in the world, the largest land holdings in the world, and ownership of the largest reserve of physical gold bullion and gold treasure in the world, the Roman Catholic Church certainly hails as the *"biggest financial power, wealth accumulator and property owner in existence"* according to philosopher Avro Manhattan, author of "The Vatican Billions". Now when you factor in the church's alliance with the Ashkenazi Jews, who make up less than 1% of the population of America yet, control nearly 70% of the wealth in America (as of 1999) via domination of the broadcast news, film, television, and music industries, as well as the financial markets, you get a very clear picture of how successful this collaborative mind control project has turned out. Which just goes to show that the Mind Control Industry turns out to be the most lucrative industry of the modern age!

But this chapter is not about bashing Christians. For most practicing Christians do not benefit from the financial wealth of this religion. Instead, this chapter is about addressing the big yellow gorilla in the room that, through cognitive dissonance, we all dismiss or justify through lack of research, lack of knowledge and lack of courage to face the uncomfortable truth.. But when we study the history of the formation of Christianity and the bible, we can examine how formation of the "good book" has been at the center of the global mind control agenda to which we are currently subject. Now if you truly want to save yourself and know just a little more truth about how we got here, please read on.

HUMAN HISTORY VS BIBLICAL HISTORY:

Before we proceed, let us agree to agree from the start. When ancient text is used to define the parameters of any belief system, one should always research the origin of that text and the context in which it originated. Then you can discern the intention of the author(s) who created it. The "Holy" Bible is no exception to this rule. For it has been promulgated as historical documentation of the messianic legacy of the "Jews" and the "Christians" for almost 2000 years. But in truth, this "holy" book is an amalgamation of fact, fiction, allegory, wisdom and tradition evolving from many cultures over many centuries. By merging ancient wisdom and truth with modern lies, The Holy Roman Empire, the clergy, and the aristocracy of the Christian faith have used this so-called "holy" book to form the religious and social infrastructure that has imprisoned the minds of millions of followers. These followers, and the rest of us, are now trapped in a perpetual paradigm of world domination through mind control, behavior modification, deception, and war.

THE STOLEN LEGACY OF THE CHILDREN OF ISRAEL

In order to distinguish the lies from the truth found within the good book, we must first research the alleged facts contained therein. Then we can discern how and why, the overall Judeo-Christian narrative was formed in the first place. The legacy starts with Abraham and Sarah, generational descendants of Shem, son of Noah. Abraham was born in N.E. Africa, (modern-day Iraq) which was still part of Nubia prior to invasion by the Arabians centuries later. Abraham was married to Sarah, who was either his sister, half-sister, or niece. Legend has it that they left their homeland and settled in Canaan (modern day Israel). Abraham and Sarah from

Nubia, birthed Isaac. Prior to that, Abraham and Sarah's Egyptian slave Hagar, birthed Ishmael. Yet, we are expected to believe that the modern-day children of Israel, (Ashkenazi descendants of the Asiatic Mongols of the Steppes of Central Asia) are the descendants of these ancient Nubians. Surprisingly these Ashkenazi converts of a non-Semitic race have successfully convinced the world that they are, indeed, the "chosen people" of God. I contest first and foremost, therefore, that OT history in its current packaging, is as fictitious as a film screenplay, with the subtitle *"based on a true story"*. Through restructured ancient text, substantial military power, and economic alliances, the true legacy of the East African descendants of Abraham, Isaac, and Jacob (Israel), was taken hostage by a race of people known then as the Khazars.

A BRIEF HISTORY OF THE KHAZARS

The Khazars are the ancestors of the Ashkenazi "Jews" who sought to insulate themselves from the Roman and Muslim religious wars leading up to the Crusades. Acknowledging this stolen legacy instantly invalidates the authenticity of the testament as a representation of true history; especially when one realizes that the Old Testament, as we now know it today, was assembled well over a thousand years after the events therein allegedly occurred.

For the record, the Euro-Asian Ashkenazis, who claim to be the "children of Israel, are descendants of a formidable clan of Turkish-Mongols known as the Khazars. The Khazars were allegedly driven out of central Asia centuries before they settled in the Steppes of the Caucasus mountains in southwest Asia (a region that is now a part of Russia). Over several centuries, the Khazarian Empire spread as far west as Eastern Europe and as far south as what we now call the Middle East, inclusive of the trading seaport of Crimea. The location of the empire proved to be an ideal position for both commerce and war, as trading on the Silk Road between East and West emerged.

The Khazars became a formidable nation. For they occupied the Caucasus region for approximately 700 years (circa 300-1000 CE). Approximately 300 years after the formalization of Christianity, turbulent conflicts emerged between the Christians and the Turks, for the Turks had taken Jerusalem and forbidden Christian pilgrimage to the Holy Land. In response the Khazars, clever in war, commerce, and political strategy, seized the opportunity to carve out a niche for themselves by funding both the Christian and Islamic armies as tensions between the two factions escalated. The nation even served as a proxy between the Byzantine Empire (an extension of the Roman Empire in the eastern provinces).

To insulate themselves from the emerging holy conflicts, the Khazarian king, Bulan, met with leaders of the three Abrahamic religions of the day (Christianity, Islam and the newly formed Judaism). Bulan opted to convert himself and his people to Judaism. I say newly formed because the version of Judah-ism practiced today by the Ashkenazi Jews did not exist until the codification of the Hebraic (Afro-Asiatic) scriptures circa 600 CE. The codification agenda merged ancient Afro-Asiatic traditions with the messianic narrative of Christianity and exists today as the Old Testament. Thus, this codification process forever solidified the stolen legacy of the Hebrew speaking, people of Afro-Asiatic ancestry by modifying their true history to serve the interests of the conquering nations of the time. If you think about it objectively, you might ask…Why did these traditions need to be formalized into a religion and synergized with the Christian narrative? What was the motivation behind that strategy? I would say that this strategy forever placed the people of Khazaria and their Ashkenazi descendants under the powerful and protective covering of the Holy Roman Empire. Or, so they believed.

Eventually, however, the Byzantine Empire broke the alliance with the Khazarian Empire (circa 900 CE) and convinced the Alans (Aryans) of modern-day Iran, to attack Khazaria and weaken its stronghold on the commercial trading routes they controlled in the Caucasus and the trading port of Crimea. In the end, the ruler of Kiev (to the East) conquered the Khazarian capital city of Atil and destroyed the Khazar State. With their stronghold breached, the now converted Khazars fled to Eastern Europe, taking the formalized religion of Judaism with them. It is this nation of non-Semitic converts who now masquerade as the descendants of the Hebrew speaking, people of East Africa. To this day they continue to promulgate the propaganda of their messianic link to Christianity.

MORE ON THE SO-CALLED JEWS

If you search out the etymology of the word Jew, you will see it originates from the word Y'hudah or Judah; connecting its roots back to East Africa. In fact, the letter J did not even exist in the original Hebrew language! Furthermore, the Hebrew speaking Africans did not call themselves Jews, neither did they practice Judaism as it exists today. That name was given to them by the Romans who conquered them; just as the name Egypt was given to the kingdom of Kemet once the Romans arrived. If you research the history of the Ashkenazis for yourself, you may come to realize that the people of the Old Testament are not the same people who lived in Kemet when the Romans arrived. If you attempt to link the Ashkenazi's to the historical origins of Christianity, you will discover that the Ashkenazi Jews of today were most assuredly not the indigenous inhabitants of Egypt nor Israel at the time of the man called Jesus. If you consider the history of the Khazars, you will recognize the disconnect between the so-called children of Israel (modern day Ashkenazis) and the actual children of Israel cited in OT history. For how could these non-African, descendants of the Mongols of Asia have occupied Israel, at a time when their actual ancestors were living far to the east and warring with the kingdoms of Asia?

Honestly, I do not have time to delve further into this historic discrepancy, but the bottom line remains the same, which is... We have been force fed a false narrative which fails to offer factual evidence linking Old Testament "history" to the modern-day Jews of eastern Europe; those who currently control the nation state of Israel. In truth, there is very little that the Ashkenazis and the true children of Israel have in common. For even the original Hebrew language was altered by the Ashkenazi converts who later authored the present form of Judaism that is practiced today. For now, just know that when it comes to connecting the modern-day Jew to Old Testament history, let's just say; the names, places and circumstances have been changed to obliterate the innocent!

The karmic, consequence of masquerading fabricated history as biblical history, however, is that historical records, in the form of ancient texts and artifacts, have a way of eventually materializing in the modern world. I guess the divine Spirit responds to those who seek by ensuring the truth is brought to the light. One such example, of ancient historical records re-emerging to expose the inauthenticity of biblical text, comes to the surface in the analysis of the historical origins of the OT Book of Proverbs; one of the most celebrated books of the Judeo-Christian Bible. The events therein were later credited to an alleged "Jewish" king commonly known as Solomon, son of David.

AUTHENTICITY OF THE OLD TESTAMENT

Unfortunately for the sake of truth and history, the Old Testament Book of Proverbs has masqueraded as the writings of an alleged Jewish king known as Solomon for nearly 1500 years. In fact, the legacy of the Africans' role in ancient world and biblical history was almost completely obliterated after the Ashkenazi converts to Hebraic tradition took this plagiarism one step further by also claiming themselves to be the "children of Israel", simultaneously bastardizing the posterity of ancient Kemet and rewriting world history with a lie that is widely accepted among most of the "civilized" world.

OLD TESTAMENT TEXT-REVISITED

According to renowned paleographer, Jaroslav Cerny, the words of wisdom found in the Book of Proverbs were *"clearly predated by and derived from the writings of an Egyptian scribe and sage named Amenemopet"* or (Amen-em-apt). Amen-em-apt's literary work titled ***Instructions of Amen-em-apt, son of Kanakht,*** dates to the Ramesside Period of Egypt, sometime during the 20th Dynasty (1189-1077 BCE). It is believed that he served as a scribe for the Pharaoh Ramesses III. The Ramesside Period marked the beginning of a time of multiple civil wars, tremendous corruption in the leadership, and great chaos in the overall society. It was a time like our own, where ancient words of wisdom about righteous living were, and are, surely needed.

The 20th Dynastic period also marked a time before non-Africans usurped the kingship of Egypt's royal dynasties. Though the original pharaoh/kings of Egypt were African, history books and popular films, ironically, still portray Egyptian Pharaohs as non-Blacks in most media. I would be remiss if I failed to bring attention to the deliberate deletion of the contributions of the African race in both world and biblical history. For the people of Kemet, (modern day Egypt) were the originators of written language, metaphysical healing, alchemy, cosmology, physics, mathematics, and chemistry for starters. All disciplines that the Greeks quickly plagiarized as their own.

Nevertheless, as we dig deeper for the origin of biblical truths, we learn that the writings of Amen-em-apt are believed to be derived from an earlier Egyptian literary work composed by the Vizier Ptahhotep entitled ***The Maxims of Ptahhotep,*** which dates back to the 5th Dynasty (2494-2345 BCE), some 1400 years earlier. The vizier, by the way, was the highest official chosen to serve the pharaoh. It is now also quite accepted in the archeological community that Ptahhotep's maxims are a later version of an even older work of wisdom literature attributed to the Vizier Kagemni; who served during the reign of Pharaoh Sneferu during the 4th Dynasty (2613-2589 BCE). Now that is what I call "ancient" wisdom! And who knows? Perhaps Kagemni's work can be traced to another sage dating even further back in antiquity. I suppose that's why the Book of Ecclesiastes states clearly:

> *"What has been will be again, what has been done will be done again; there is nothing new under the sun"* **(Ecclesiastes 1:9)**

INTRODUCTION TO THE HISTORY OF ANCIENT EGYPT:

In the days of the Old Kingdom, prior to invasion by the Persians and the Greeks, the land of Egypt was known as Kmt (aka Kemit, Kermet); an ancient word that means "Black Land". The inhabitants of that land even referred to themselves as *remetch en Kermet* which is translated as the "people of the Black Land". The word Egypt, (from the Greek word Aigyptos or Aegyptus) appeared in more modern times when it was used by the Greeks who began trading with the Africans of the Nile Valley circa 800-600 BCE.

Over the centuries, western Egyptologists interpreted the word black as a reference to the fertile soil of the Nile Valley after the flooding-season. I, like many others who study ancient Kemet, propose that perhaps the "black" land refers to the Black people of that land. For I do not think it a coincidence that the people of Kemet clearly represented themselves as Black in the ancient art and hieroglyphs. In this case, the writing clearly appears on the walls of Egypt! Perhaps the word had an implied double meaning. You can think for yourself and decide for yourself on that one. By the way, did you happen to note the lack of vowels in the root words translated here? This is also a unique trait of the "Hebrew" language. Sound familiar? That is because the origins of the original Hebrew speaking people are deeply rooted in ancient African beginnings.

The bottom line is, if you are one who views the Bible as an accurate depiction of world history, which it is not, this discussion becomes much more problematic, since you probably already believe the popular narrative that has been preached over the past couple of centuries. This book, however, was written to help you see what you have not been shown, told nor taught. And see you must! For how can you know where you are going if you have an inaccurate view of where you began? The far-reaching implication of the misrepresentation of the African in world and biblical history should be acknowledged if one wishes to inner-stand how this misrepresentation has played out in both biblical and world history.

IN CONCLUSION

At first thought it may seem insignificant that these words of wisdom were written by African scribes who lived centuries before the man called Solomon allegedly existed. What difference does it make, right? But if you accept that this wisdom did not originate with the "Jewish" people to whom it has been credited, how can you trust other assumptions made about the historical validity of the bible without conducting the necessary research to verify the facts? But before you can jump on the research train, you must first acknowledge that your personal interpretation of biblical literature has been based upon unreliable facts and even outright lies, whether you like it or not. Yes, you must face this truth because most modern Jews and Christians still accept biblical history as a reasonably true depiction of world history!

But when you consider the catastrophic effects that these beliefs and values have had upon the world for the last 2000 years or so, however, the need for us to save ourselves from this "normal" way of thinking cannot be emphasized enough. For the "righteous" have been fighting the other "righteous" for so long. And here we are, thousands of wars later, still fighting! To think that so many have died fighting over the validity of one righteous view over another righteous view is simply ridiculous. In fact, knowing that these unholy wars and other crimes of man's inhumanity to man were not even waged for the sake of righteousness, but rather, for greed and power is the most disgusting truth of this book! When we factor in the number of people who have died because so many rely upon fallible sources for shaping their overall view of the world, the situation becomes problematic on a global scale to say the least!

For isn't righteousness just...righteousness? And just think... the belief that the Old Testament books are accurate depictions of "Jewish" history, offered a strong argument for the creation of a "Jewish" state in Israel after WWII. My issue is not that the state of Israel was formed, but rather, that those who benefited most from its formation and strategic location were not African people. If, instead, the original Black people of Kemet (and not the Ashkenazi converts who have exploited this stolen legacy for centuries) are the true "chosen" people of God, then the world has been living a lie of epic proportions for much too long! With so much at stake, we all have a collective responsibility to revisit and scrutinize all the ancient works in their entirety before using them as the basis for our religious tenets and beliefs. At this point of my life, I Question Everything!

> *"QUESTION EVERYTHING! and when you have questioned it all, 100 times... Begin Again!* **Michelle Crenshaw**

Now, when I say **we**, I really mean, **YOU**. Considering the number of world conflicts stemming from perceived religious differences, we (you) have a responsibility to investigate, scrutinize and question everything you believe if it's based on religious literature. I cannot emphasize this enough because the consequences of not doing so are simply too severe. If you know your current events, then you have a glimpse of the chaos that fear can inflict upon the world. Perhaps this too is a topic for another book. For now, however, I simply hope you can and will acknowledge that biblical "truth", as it has been given to us, is not always in agreement with historical facts. Perhaps this acknowledgement alone will spark your curiosity enough to seek out the origins of other biblical "facts" that you have assumed coincide with, or accurately depict, world history.

I believe the stolen legacy of the Black people of Northeast Africa, formed by the alliance of Roman and Khazar empires, is the most diabolical conspiracy of all time. And, I truly hope this book brings this most egregious crime to the light so that you, and many others, may see and inner-stand the truth so you can be truly free. Asé

CHAPTER SEVEN

Ancient Religion before the Modern Age

The synergistic merging of Greek, Persian and Egyptian mythology evolved organically over many centuries before the modern Christian Era. The Greeks traveled east and south bringing their gods with them. The Persians, highly influenced by the Indo-Iranian god Mitra, practiced Mithraism, which merged with the tribal practices of the people of Babylon and East Asia (modern day Iran, Iraq, & Turkey). The tribal peoples of Egypt and the near East practiced the spirituality of Kemit, Kush & Canaan (modern day Israel).

Let me emphasize here that this fusion of competing beliefs, practiced by a diversity of people from a vast array of traditions and cultural influences, occurred over nearly 1000 years of military campaigns and conquests across the entire region we now call the Middle East. Along with these wars, came the battle for the minds of the people as competing kingdoms, tribes, cults and civilizations strived to bring their mythologies to the forefront of public acceptance. Just imagine what it would be like if America was under the control of constantly changing conquering nations. It would be like the imperialized nations of Africa and South America are even today... shifting and adapting to one foreign regime after another; each with an agenda to dominate the people conquered.

Clearly, we can see why a unifying state mandated religion became the objective of the competing empires of Egypt, Persia, Greece, and eventually, Rome. The ebbs and flows of power sparked the emergence of several state mandated religions and eventually led to the formation of Christianity.

PERSIAN/INDO-IRANIAN INFLUENCE ON MODERN HISTORY & RELIGION

THE WORSHIP OF MITRA (1500 BCE-500 CE)

The first written record of the Indo-Iranian-Persian deity Mitra (later known as Mithra) appears in texts dating back to the 15th century BCE. Worship of Mitra is first documented in the ancient texts of the Vedas; a collection of religious writings, rituals and hymns that later became the Hindu religion. The four Vedas (Veda is Sanskrit for knowledge), include the Rig Veda, a collection of poetic hymns, the Yajur Veda, containing the rituals of Vedic liturgy, the Sama Veda, music used in rituals and finally, the Atharva Veda, a manual including the sacrificial rites for the chief priests and Brahmin.

Some believe that the Aryans of central Asia brought Vedic spirituality with them when they entered northwest India around 1500 BCE. The jury is still out on the validity of that claim, though linguists agree that the origins of the Sanskrit language lie somewhere in central and southern Asia. Like most ancient spirituality, the Vedas were most likely first passed down by oral tradition. Archaeologists and linguists presume that some version of Vedic spirituality could have existed as far back as 3000 BCE. As a result of this hypothesis, the worship of Mitra is believed to be one of the oldest religions of antiquity.

Mitra, in his earliest form, was a male deity of justice, fairness and covenant. He was the god of the earth, who created all life and vegetation. His name can be found on tablets, temples and even treaties between nation states. He was known as the god of light, the god of the sun, the giver of life, the way, the truth, the life, the word, the son of god and even the good shepherd. Sound familiar? In India, Mitra was merged with the Varuna, god of the heavens, the night and the waters. Thus, the invocation of Mitra-Varuna, embodied the fullness of creation as earth, water, moon, sun, stars, day, night, life and death.

The worship of Mitra spread among the indigenous peoples of the Indo-Iranian world via the military conquests of the Assyrians, Persians, Hittites, Canaanites, Babylonians, and other conquering tribes. With these conquests, Vedic spirituality spread and synergistically merged with the existing beliefs and rituals of the indigenous tribal people of the region; specifically, the Chaldeans and the Babylonians. Over many centuries, tribal spiritualities evolved into many synergized beliefs and customs. Some scholars believe the Mitra-Varuna evolved into the Ahura Mazda, that later became the central deity of Mazdaism; which rose to the forefront of Persian culture as the empire spread across east Asia during the last millennium BCE

MAZDAISM (1000-500 BCE)

It is also important to note here that the worship of Mitra, aka Mithra, and finally Mithras, continued, or a better word might be resurfaced, well into the Christian Era. Mithraism was later adopted by the Greeks and Romans after the invasion of Egypt and the near East under the conquests of Alexander and later Constantine. These spiritual mysteries were later brought back to Rome by soldiers returning from campaigns in the east (circa 70 BCE). Mithraism in this new form became known as the Mysteries of Mithras; being highly influenced by the astro-theology of Chaldean and Babylonian astrology and infused with the mysticism of the Magi.

Over the next 400 years, Mithras in the Greco-Roman world became known as the Divine and/or Unconquered Sun as well as the mediator between heaven and earth. By the 2nd Century CE this new "mystery" religion, now fully synergized with the Egyptian-inspired philosophies (brought back by the likes of Socrates, Pythagoras, and Thales), became the prevailing practice of the Roman priesthood. As such, Mithra was honored as the patron saint of loyalty to the emperor. The Mithraic "mysteries", no longer accessible by the common man, flourished in cults shrouded in secrecy among the elite influencers of Rome. Most Roman priests associated the origins of the Mithras Mysteries with Zoroasterism.

ZOROASTERISM (AKA) MAZDAISM: (1500 BCE-500 BCE)

The life of Zoroaster, the founder of this ancient spiritual tradition, can be traced back to somewhere between 1000 and 600 BCE. Evidence suggests, however, that the worship of the Ahura Mazda, the supreme deity of Mazda spirituality, was practiced for centuries before Zoroaster transformed Mazdaism into a formalized spiritual philosophy. That being true, Zoroaster was not so much the creator of a new religion, but rather, a learned philosopher and spiritual teacher who recorded his interpretation of the elements of the Mazda faith tradition into a collection of doctrines, beliefs and rituals that could be practiced and taught to others.

In reviewing the teachings of Zoroaster, one can see that much consideration was given to helping the practitioner achieve a higher level of spiritual awareness and morality. It is likely that Zoroaster, an educated holy man, held court with Persian royalty to teach and advise in matters of the state. Like many other philosophers and holy men before him, Zoroaster was revered among the royalty and the priesthood. In its written form, the religion easily spread among the priestly elite who were the keepers of all knowledge and education. It is not surprising, therefore, that Zoroasterism eventually became the official religion of the Persian Empire, lasting from the 6th century BCE through the 7th century CE.

This 1300-year period of institutionalized spirituality marks the beginning of what I would now call organized religion though there was no separation of church and state in the ancient world. This was true from Egypt to Asia, for the king always retained priestly advisors, holy men, and keepers of the wisdom of the kingdom who were masters of: mathematics, science, astronomy, medicine, astrology and spirituality. In these ancient times, the wisdom of the priesthood was a mystery to the common man and the king was usually the one endowed with spiritual authority. The element of mystery gave the priests tremendous responsibility and, in some cultures, absolute power; thus, keeping the priesthood in a safe and protected position of spiritual, political and social authority.

Like religions of today, the more mystical the leadership is perceived to be, the more divine they become in the eyes of the common man. In this manner, the divinity of Zoroaster and his spirituality spread across the civilized world over the 1300-year reign of the Persian Empire. To date he is still recognized as the most significant spiritual leader and teacher of the Persian era of world history. Many still practice some form of Zoroasterism or Mazdaism to this day.

The primary spiritual elements of Zoroasterism include: (**a**) the Ahura Mazda, the Supremely Wise Lord Creator and (**b**) the Amesha Spenta, the immortal holy principles or six divine sparks of Ahura Mazda. Zoroaster's teaching focused on individual responsibility and accountability and, did not recognize a "devil" as a deity. Zoroaster proclaimed that there is only one God, who is the singularly creative and sustaining force of the Universe; making Zoroasterism among the first monotheistic faith traditions of archeological record. It's important to note here that this claim is shared by several other ancient religions; but I will not get into those claims here. For the truth is that most ancient mythologies had a supreme god who reigned over all the other gods. Even in modern Christianity, Jesus is given the title King of kings which was a name also attributed to the god Aten of Egypt, the god Mitra of Indo-Iran, and yes, the Ahura Mazda of Zoroasterism. These points will become more relevant later as we summarize how these ancient faith doctrines made their way into modern Christianity.

Zoroaster taught that human beings are endowed with the ability to make their own choices. His philosophy also taught that due to the law of cause and effect, human beings are, therefore, responsible for the consequences of their choices. Finally, he taught that the works of the Ahura Mazda are evident to humanity through the Amesha Spentas, or the six primary principles for living which are: Purpose, Truth/ Righteousness, Dominion, Devotion, Wholeness, and Immortality. These goals were possible with the help of the Spenta Mainyu or Good Spirit, which was comprised of the bounteous immortals.

Although the concept of a devil did not appear in earlier Persian faith traditions, the doctrine of Zoroaster included mention of the Angra Mainyu or, angry spirit, who was described as the contesting force of the Ahura Mazda. This teaching, consistent with the belief in cause and effect, also included the belief that Angra Mainyu and its forces were born of Akem Manah, or evil thinking. Thus, adhering to the Amesha Spentas was the divine pathway to enlightenment and a good life.

EGYPT'S INFLUENCE ON MODERN HISTORY & RELIGION

It is important to consider that science, alchemy, mathematics, astronomy, astrology, magic and spirituality were seamlessly integrated into the ancient culture of Africa. With kingship, the priesthood, and the social culture so deeply rooted in cosmic, metaphysical, mystic-spirituality, it is easy to comprehend how many mythologies evolved from an evolving understanding of the universe.

The influence of scientific discovery upon modern culture and spirituality is apparent even today. Just consider how the big bang theory or the science of quantum physics has altered modern concepts of creation, consciousness and spirituality, for example. It is, therefore, easy to see how the cosmos became the inspiration for the spiritual life of all ancient peoples across the globe.

As Egypt, or Kemet as it was originally known, grew over the centuries, its culture and mythology went with it, spreading to Canaan, Sumer, and as far as the Dogon tribes that migrated west out of Kemet toward Mali. Keep in mind, the Pharaoh was not only a king but also, the spiritually appointed leader of the nation and spiritual steward of the people. Subsequently, the Pharaoh's advisors, comprised of priests, astronomers, scribes, metaphysicians, scholars, and mathematicians, advised both the political and spiritual leadership of the nation. This merging of social culture and spirituality was, likewise, synergized into the everyday lives of the people so there was no need to impose a formal religion. Evidence of the allegorical spirituality of Egypt, revealed through the elaborate tales of ancient gods and heroes, remains on the walls of Egypt to this very day.

Ancient Kemet survived for thousands of centuries as the dominant civilized culture of the world. With time, however, adventurous explorers, warriors, and seekers of riches, resources and knowledge came to know of The Black Land and all the wisdom, mysticism and treasures it had to offer. With each new century came seekers, hungry for wisdom, knowledge, and riches. As the notoriety of Egypt spread west, foreign kings with military agendas sought to conquer Kemet and the resource rich lands under Egyptian control, which stretched eastward toward the emerging Achaemenian Empire circa (559-330 BCE).

GREECE DISCOVERS EGYPTIAN WISDOM

Over these centuries, many non-Africans came to the place they called Egypt in order to learn the ancient mysteries of Kemet. These mysteries included education in mathematics, science, herbal healing, internal medicine, astronomy, and metaphysical spirituality. In fact, some figures considered to be the greatest minds of European history received their education and training from the secret mystical schools of Egypt. Some of these so-called "fathers" of wisdom include:

THALES OF MILETUS (624-546 BCE)

Thales has been called the Father of Pre-Socratic Greek Philosophy. He was a philosopher, mathematician and astronomer from Miletus in Asia Minor (present day Turkey), which was a stronghold of the Egyptian Mystery schools. Aristotle named him the first philosopher of the Greeks. Historically, he is described as the first person from Western civilization known for scientific philosophy. His most notable work was influenced by ancient Egyptian mathematics and religion as well as Babylonian astronomy. His work influenced the philosophies of Pythagoras, Anaximander and Anaximenes.

PYTHAGORAS OF SAMOS, GREECE (570-500 BCE)

Pythagoras was an Ionian student of Thales who also studied mathematics, science, metaphysics and ancient mysticism at the Egyptian Mystery schools. He was the founder of Pythagoreanism; a secretive religious mathematical cult that promulgated his theories in metaphysics and mathematics.

According to Aristotle (384-322 BCE), Pythagoreans were "*the first to take up mathematics*". After the murder of Pythagoras (500 BCE), Pythagoreanism split into two distinct schools of thought, namely, the Mathematici (Greek for "teachers") and the Acusmatici (Greek for "listeners"). The former was concerned mainly with the science of mathematics, wherein the latter discipline dealt mostly in the realm of metaphysical healing using music and medicine to cure certain conditions and diseases. This practice was directly derived from the metaphysical teachings of the mystic priesthood of Egypt.

Like the Egyptians, the Pythagoreans believed that *"everything that can be known has a number; for it is impossible to grasp anything with the mind or to recognize it without this"* **Philolaus (470-385 BCE).** Pythagoras was said to be divinely inspired by the rule of virtue, a spiritual awareness by which a metaphysician could reverse various desires and appetites.

SOCRATES (470-399 BCE) AND ARISTOTLE (384-322 BCE)

According to **Wikipedia.com,** Socrates of Athens, Greece was *"credited as one of the founders of Western philosophy"*. His philosophies, however, are known only through the writings of his students; namely Plato, Xenophon and Aristophanes. Furthermore, no known writings by Socrates have survived from antiquity. As a result, comparisons between these secondary sources reveal contradictions that cannot be reconciled to Socrates as the source. This dilemma of unauthenticated information about the man has been coined the Socratic Problem. Nevertheless, Aristotle attributes Socrates with originating the doctrine that "virtue is knowledge".

In the area of metaphysics, Aristotle states that Socrates was the *"first to search for universal definitions"* for moral virtues. Despite the lack of historical evidence for this claim, Socrates retains the celebrity of being the Father of Western Philosophy. It is believed that Socrates was condemned to death and required to poison himself with hemlock after the Athenians found him guilty of refusing to honor the gods which were recognized by the state and for corrupting the minds of the youth whom he taught and mentored.

Although modern historians credit these notable persons as the originators of the disciplines of mathematics, philosophy, mysticism, science, physics and metaphysics, these Ionians, Greeks and Romans were all aware that the Egyptians were the true authors of the wisdom they brought back with them to Greece. In fact, after Aristotle's death, his Athenian pupils compiled a history of philosophy recognized at the time as the Sophia (or Wisdom) of the Egyptians. Because this "history" was produced by Aristotle's pupils, modern historians erroneously negated the origins of the wisdom therein, calling it Greek philosophy instead. This point is even more significant when we recognize that from the time of Thales through Aristotle, Ionians were considered Egyptian citizens (640-559 BCE) and later, Persian subjects.

GREECE'S INFLUENCE ON MODERN HISTORY & RELIGION: THE FALL OF EGYPTIAN SPIRITUALITY

The Egyptians were themselves, conquerors whose culture had followed them into Canaan and east Asia before the arrival of the Persians, the Greeks and eventually the Romans. The Persians invaded Egypt during the Achaemenid Empire (559-330 BCE). The Persian Empire had become the most militarized empire of the time; making it easy to usurp the throne from Egypt following Persia's victory at the Battle of Pelusium in 525 BCE. That final blow to Egypt came through an alliance between the Persian king Cambyses II and the Greek tyrant Polycrates of Samos, who offered a fleet of

40 warships to ensure the success of the invasion. The Egyptians, unprepared for the assault, were overtaken by the Greeks and the Persians, and soon Cambyses II became the first non-Egyptian to hold the throne of Egypt.

Cambyses II brought Persian culture and mysticism with him to Egypt. By now, the Greeks were already trading with the Persians and the Egyptians. While the Persians focused on the governing of Egypt, merchants from the East and West focused on commerce and enterprise, and the Greeks learned all they could from the Egyptian mystery schools.

When the Greeks who studied in the Black Land returned home, they refashioned the mythology of the Egyptian god Osiris into the mythology of Zeus, who they then claimed was father of all the gods. The Persians in the region practiced Mithraism, already the official religion of Persia. While the diaspora of tribal peoples practiced Mazdaism, one of the oldest spiritual traditions of antiquity, in various ways determined by individual tribes and clans. It was just a matter of time before all these varying beliefs became integrated and rooted into the overall culture, practices, mysteries, mythologies and politics of greater Egypt and the rest of the world under the next 200 years of Persian rule in the region.

Remembering that by this time the Persians already had a state religion (Mazdaism), in the following chapter we will look at how the fusion of these cultural dynamics brought forth the emerging pre-events of what we now call modern history and modern religion.

CHAPTER EIGHT

The Dawn of the Christian Age

INTRODUCTION:

In my research over the years, I have found many historical discrepancies in the doctrines and teachings of the Christian faith. Suffice it to say, the information to this regard is/was difficult to find and certainly harder to verify. Sadly, the true history of ancient Kemet was nearly obliterated from history altogether once Alexander "conquered" Egypt in 332 BCE. His victory marked the beginning of the Hellenistic era of world history and what we now call The Modern Age.

SERAPIS: THE CREATION OF A NEW GOD

After the death of the Emperor Alexander, his appointed emissary, the Greek general Ptolemy I, became the first Greek king of Egypt when he quickly usurped the Egyptian throne by force and declared himself Pharaoh. Ptolemy quickly claimed the entire nation as his own. By this time, the Sophia (or wisdom) of Egypt had already been rebranded as Grecian knowledge, philosophy and mysticism by the secret societies of the elite christos (the anointed). Thus, Ptolemy usurping the Egyptian throne dealt a final blow to the reign of the African kings of the Black Land. Fortunately, the truth eventually managed to push its way up through the cracks of history thousands of years later!

Ptolemy I, a non-African general turned self-appointed Pharaoh of Egypt, took the holy name Meryamun Setepenre, meaning "beloved of Amun." Amun was the ancient deity of Kemet depicted as the "creator" god. That's because along with the sun god, Ra, Amun was usually depicted as Amun-Ra, holding the title "King of Gods," as well as many others. Although Ptolemy I gave himself a divine title and the throne, he could not garner the support of the priesthood, who were officially tasked with anointing all the Pharaoh kings. Nor could he win over the hearts and minds of the people without that priestly blessing. Yet, neither the people of Egypt, nor the spiritual priesthood to the throne, would support Ptolemy; because he had taken the throne by force.

Ptolemy knew that he needed the approval of the spiritual arm of the Egyptian throne to successfully rule over the Egyptian people. A general of the Roman army, as well as a brilliant politician, he quickly used brutal tactics to infiltrate and "persuade" the priesthood of the temple at Memphis, in lower Egypt, to create a god in his image and likeness. For Ptolemy desired to be worshipped alongside the existing image of the god Osiris. To "save" themselves, they agreed to create the Greco-Egyptian god Serapis in his honor knowing that failing to do so would certainly end in their eminent demise.

And so, the new, white god, Serapis was introduced to legitimize the conqueror by merging the spirituality of Egypt and with the mythology of Greece. The name Serapis was chosen to join the attributes of Osiris, (the Egyptian god of the underworld, the afterlife and rebirth) with those of the god Apis (or Bull), the symbol of the fertility of the earth, life, and kingship. Since, by this time, the Egyptians and the Persians had co-mingled for over 1500 years, the imagery of the bull was already accepted and worshipped by the followers of both Osiris and Mithra, who were both described as the god of gods and "king of kings". As an amalgamation of these two deities, Serapis, was also endowed with the same attributes and divinity. Accordingly, his image was often paired with Auset, the wife of Osiris, who is now known as Isis in Greco-Roman mythology.

As Roman influence spread in the region, the mythology of Serapis spread with it; becoming more widely accepted by the people. Like Osiris, Mithra and all the other gods before him, Serapis was also endowed with many names. Among them, the name chrestos, meaning good in Greek, was used to describe Serapis just as it had been used to describe both Osiris (Auser) and Mithras (Mitra) centuries before. Now endowed with the same names and attributes as the Egyptian/Persian gods from whence he was created, his "divine image" was forged in stone, clay, wood and golden coins. The ultimate deification of Ptolemy I, however, was instituted by his grandson a few decades later; raising his divine status from Ptolemy I to Ptolemy I Soter (*translating as Ptolemy the Savior*).

This image of a non-African as a divine savior in Egypt forever cemented the European takeover of Kemet in the annuls of antiquity and modern history. The savior/king mythology replaced the allegorical wisdom and spirituality of the ancient deities of Kemet. Subsequently, the truth about the Afro-Asiatic people of the Black Land gradually faded from the records of modern history.

THE SIGNIFICANCE OF THE TEMPLE AT MEMPHIS

The priesthood of Memphis was held in the highest esteem within the government and the spiritual leadership of Egypt. Memphis was also the commercial and spiritual hub of the Egyptian nation state. The city of Memphis sat on the west bank of the Nile river. Keep in mind, the installation of Ptolemy I and the creation of Serapis occurred nearly three hundred years before the Christian Era of history. In addition, it was this priesthood of Memphis that would later become the first Egyptians to call themselves "christians"; nearly 200-300 years before the lifetime of the prophet called Jesus.

SERAPIS "THE CHRIST"

The anointing of a European as a Pharaoh by the priesthood of Memphis raised the position of Ptolemy to the same divine status of the god-kings who came before him. The acceptance of the image of Serapis as a god solidified Rome's authority over the Egyptian priesthood, as well as, the politics and spirituality of the nation. Thus, these once revered wisemen, healers, physicians, scribes, and leaders of the conscience of the nation became mere figureheads of Rome, which leveraged spiritual and military power over the people and the kingdom.

With the newly created savior/god Serapis merged with the divinity of the Pharaoh king, the battle for the minds of the Egyptians and the rest of the world was now in full swing. Over time, the divinity of a Serapis the Savior, depicted in the image of a Greek king, became legend, and eventually for some, a mythological reality. Consequently, the name *christos* was given to Serapis and the name *christianos* or christians was accordingly attributed to his followers. Christos is also the Greek translation of the Hebrew word *mashach* (pronounced *maw-shakh*) meaning, *oil, to smear with oil, anoint.* Over time, the god Serapis, like all the other gods before him, became a very real God to be revered, honored and adored among a variety of communities and religious sects. But even though the prominence of Serapis grew, his "foreign nature" gradually became a growing problem for the various debating religious sects among the African Egyptians. Nevertheless, the worship of Serapis, grew and spread mostly toward Greece and Rome.

ETYMOLOGICAL ORIGINS OF THE WORD CHRIST

According to **Strong's Exhaustive Concordance**, the adjective *christos* (pronounced *khrē-sto's*) is a Greek word meaning *anointed.* The words *christos* and *messias* were also used interchangeably by the

Greeks as the Hebrew translation of the word(s) *mashach/mashiach;* which also means *anointed.* the adjective *chrestos* (pronounced *khrā-sto's*) is of Greek origin meaning *fit, fit for use, useful, virtuous and good.* Please keep in mind, that Hebrew was the dominant language spoken and written in Egypt for centuries BCE; centuries before the arrival of the Greeks or the Romans.

The word chrestos, one of many titles appearing on Greek tombs pre, and post Christianity, was often used to reference gods, demi-gods, other deities, and heroes. The word christos was often used to describe spiritual status of the king, anointed by the priesthood upon ascent to the throne. The word was also given to the priests who facilitated this anointing. As would be expected, the term was also used to describe Ptolemy I, the new Pharaoh King, and later to Serapis, the god that represented him.

With the spread of Egyptian and Persian mythology, christos was also used amongst the brotherhood of the various mystery schools around the Mediterranean because, they too, had been anointed upon initiation. Subsequently, the Greek term *christianos* and later the Roman term *christianus,* were used to describe the followers of Serapis and the priesthood that promulgated his mythology.

ROME'S INFLUENCE ON MODERN HISTORY & RELIGION

Over the next few centuries, the Greeks, Romans, Egyptians and Persians interacted militarily and culturally. And just as the wisdom of Egypt re-emerged in Greece as Greek philosophy, the spirituality of the Persians emerged in Rome as the Mithraic Mysteries. But the mythology and wisdom of the East was closely guarded by the priesthood and the elite of Rome. The common man was not privy to these mysteries. Only those deemed worthy, by virtue of their initiation into the priesthood or by their social status, were anointed for initiation into the cults inspired by the ancient rituals, dogma and magic of the East. Accordingly, these Roman converts to eastern mythology were also called *christians* because they, too, were anointed upon their initiation, just as the priests of these ancient religions had been for centuries.

It is important to note here that the co-mingling of religious practices in upper Egypt, which included the indigenous Afro-Asiatic people of Northeast Africa, (what we now call the middle east), was a slow and somewhat volatile process. During this 600-year transformation of the government and spirituality of Egypt from Egyptian, to Persian, to Greek, to Roman military control, the region became muddied with many overlapping cultures, ethnicities, and religions. Like in all megacities of today, the muddy competition between conflicting cultures and mythologies would eventually prove to be a pivotal factor in understanding how the Christian religion was later formed. Suffice to say, the mission to garner support for Serapis as the anointed Savior required the conscious tenacity of the Greek, and later the Roman, aristocracy as they sought to synergize cultural and religious norms.

CHAPTER NINE

Historical Influencers of Christian Doctrines

INTRODUCTION

In the year 30 BCE the Roman Empire, led by Octavian (soon to become the Emperor Augustus Cesar) won the final battle for ancient Kemet, by annexing the Greco-Ptolemaic Kingdom into the Roman Empire. By now, the cult of Serapis was the prevailing mythology promoted by the Greeks and Romans in Africa. The Greek clergy had also infiltrated the previously Coptic (indigenous Egyptian)) priesthood. As the anointed of Egypt, they too, were learned in the Egyptian and Mithraic mysteries of the gods. Thus, the many attributes and names given to the ancient Egyptian gods, including mashiach and christos, had also been attributed to Serapis, further legitimizing his divinity among the masses.

But as the worship of Serapis spread, the debate over his origins and spiritual nature came into question among the diverse religious factions in Egypt and Rome. For starters, calling Serapis christos presented a philosophical and spiritual dilemma amongst the Coptic (African) priesthood of Memphis whose predecessors had succumbed to Ptolemy's tyranny decades earlier. For the Coptic priesthood knew that Serapis was not a god, but a created image of a man, made by the hands of man. After all, they are the ones who created him!

Moreover, according to Egyptian historian Walter Williams, inserting a non-African "son" into the Ancient African Egyptian Triad (**AAET**), consisting of Osiris, Auset, and their son, Horus, became more problematic for the Coptic bishops as Rome's domination of Africa and the near east grew over the next century. It was also during this period that the prophet known as the man they call Jesus appeared on the scene. His anointed (baptized) followers, Hebrew-speaking Africans of Jerusalem and the surrounding region, also eventually came to be known as christians.

Of course, the debate escalated once Rome gained full control of the government and the religions of the conquered world. Like the Greeks before them, the Romans continued to push for a non-African god to reign at the center of a state religion. But the Coptic priesthood still would not accept Serapis as christ; even though the common people had tolerated it. But when Rome sought to place Serapis within the **AAET**; the Coptic priesthood defiantly refused. For how could this created thing take the place of Osiris, the creator god, beside Auset (his sister/wife) and Horus, their divinely conceived son; all of whom had been clearly depicted as African for centuries? This familial relationship of the AAET is consistent with numerous artifacts and reliefs depicting Auset holding and often nursing her African man-child son, Horus. You can search **Google Images** for *"Black Madonna"* or *"Osiris, Horus, Auset"* and you will see how much evidence of the Ancient African Egyptian Triad exists in the coffers of archeology.

At this point I think it is important to provide a brief overview of other historical influences on trinitarian spirituality in the ancient world.

ANCIENT ORIGINS OF TRINITARIAN SPIRITUALITY

> *"The search for the origins of the Trinity begins with the earliest writings of man...and most of ancient theology is lost under the sands of time."* **Cher-El L. Hagensick**

The concepts of both a holy trinity and a savior had already been well documented in the spiritual doctrine of many ancient cultures; predating biblical times by tens of thousands of years. Although the word trinity may have its origins in early Christianity, the concept of a holy triad was clearly apparent in most mythologies that preceded it in Africa and the Afro-Asiatic lands to the East. The AAET, which I mentioned earlier, is only one of many spiritual mythologies grounded in a holy trinity at the forefront of its spirituality. Since I've mentioned several of these trinities earlier, I will recap them here for your review.

> *"The concept of a trinity or triadic nature of the divine has been a part of our psyche for thousands of years and has appeared in creation tales, myths, religious writings and holy texts the world over. Yet to this day, the Trinity is always thought of as having its origin in Roman Catholicism-most notably at the Council of Nicaea in AD 325, the ecumenical council of Christian bishops, where the consensus of beliefs was decided upon for all of Christendom, including the Trinity as the three-fold nature of the persona of God"*
>
> **3: The Perfect Number-Trinity Symbolism in World Religious Traditions by Marie D. Jones**
>
> *From:* *www.ancient-origins.net* Ancient Origins: Reconstructing the Story of Humanities Past

VEDIC TRINITIES

As I mentioned earlier in this chapter, Vedic spirituality dates back thousands of years before the arrival of Christianity on the world stage. The Vedic Trinity, comprised of Brahma, Vishnu and Shiva, represents that the concept of God or Supreme Reality is expressed in the triple function of God as Creator, Sustainer and Destroyer. In this spiritual tradition, the trinity or, Trimurti, in Sanskrit, also includes numerous other gods and goddesses who aid in facilitating the nature of each of the three gods in the Trimurti.

The Vedic Trinity is based on three basic spiritual functions of the Universe: Create, Sustain, and Destroy. As such, the Vedas, the earliest literary record of the Indo-Aryan civilization, are the most sacred texts of the Hindu religion. Some believe their roots date back as far as 7200 BC when the first hymns of the Rig Veda were composed. Like most ancient traditions, the Vedas are rooted in cosmic spirituality. The Gods of the Vedas, therefore, poetically express space, time, the heavens, the firmament, the sun, moon, earth, day, night, wind, rain, sunshine, etc.; all ministering to the divine care of man. and converging in one eternal voice of praise and adoration. In the **Puranas**, one of many Hindoo books of scripture, ritual and ancient gods, a passage reads:

> *"O ye three Lords! Know that I recognize only one God. Inform me, therefore, which of you is the true divinity, that I may address to him alone my adorations." To which the three gods Brahma, Vishnu, and Shiva reply: "Learn, O devotee, that there is no real distinction between us. What to you appears such is only the semblance. The single being appears under three forms by the acts of creation, preservation, and destruction, but he is one."* (Sinclair, pp.382-383) From the article: ***"How Ancient Trinitarian Gods Influenced Adoption of the Trinity"*** published by: **United Church of God, www.ucg.org**

SUMERIAN TRINITIES

The people of Sumeria and Babylon worshipped many deities described in the context of several divine triads. For example, the distinctions or attributes of the universe were divided into three regions which were the domains of God. Anu, the father and king of the gods, was the God of the sky. Enlil, the son, was the wind God and creator of the earth while Enki was God of the waters. He was also credited with the creation of mankind. The history of ancient Sumerian text date back to at least 3000 BCE.

BABYLONIAN TRINITIES

> *"All things are three, and thrice is all: and let us use this number in the worship of the gods; for, as the Pythagoreans say, everything and all things are bounded by threes, for the end, the middle and the beginning have this number in everything, and these compose the number of the Trinity."* **Aristotle (4th century BCE)**

The religious reputation of ancient Babylon has been the subject of many critiques on the spirituality of false religions and pagan gods. I believe this has to do with how negatively Babylon was depicted in Old Testament scriptures. The truth is, that like many ancient cultures, Babylon had multiple influences from the Afro-Asiatic region which, resulted in a culture chock full of concentric trinities as well as the deifications of Babylonian rulers such as Nimrod.

The Babylonian Magi dealt in the creative art of what some called magic and what others now call esoteric knowledge; astronomy, astrology, mathematics and alchemy. Since the number three is a very powerful number in numerology, it's easy to understand how trinitarian doctrine made its way into Babylonian spirituality and ritual. The influence of the Magi upon leadership played a key role in how various trinitarian beliefs developed in Babylonian culture. Since the Sumerians, who had lived in the region long before the rise of the Babylonian empire, believed in many trinitarian deities, we can assume that their beliefs were synergized in Babylonian spirituality. Since there is also record of people living in the region before the Sumerians, we can assume that many deities must have emerged as various peoples settled there.

There is additional archaeological evidence that the people of the region were among the first civilizations to believe in the *three persons in one god* doctrine. Artifacts depicting god with three heads and using an equilateral triangle to express the trinitarian unity of god, for example, have also been uncovered. Despite this three-headed god, Babylon, like other ancient cultures mentioned in this chapter, had multiple triune personifications of god which reflected their understandings of creation, nature and the elements.

EGYPTIAN TRINITIES

> *"No god came into being before him (Amun) and all gods are three: Amun, Re and Ptah, and there is no second to them. Hidden is his name as Amun, he is Re in face, and his body is Ptah.* From: **Hymns of AMUN, Chapter 300, vs. 1-15, Leiden Papyrus I,** (*circa 350-1213 BCE*)

I discussed the trinity of Osiris, Auset and Horus earlier. In the next section I will expound further on the interwoven doctrines of a Holy Trinity and Holy Conception. Pay close attention and I am certain you will see, as I did, how the currently dominant Christian narrative is most certainly not a unique story of salvation nor a triune God. But rather, a conveniently plagiarized tale of stolen legacy and the diabolical agenda of the quest for a one-world religion. But I digress.

CHRISTIAN TRINITARIAN TEACHINGS

Surely, many would be surprised to discover that the word trinity does not even appear in the bible. In fact, it was not used until the close of the 2nd century CE by an early Christian apologist and author named Quintus Septimius Florens Tertullianus. Tertullian, as he is now called, was known as the father of Latin Christianity.

According to the **New Bible Dictionary**, *"The formal doctrine of the Trinity was the result of several inadequate attempts to explain who and what the Christian God really is"*. This statement also explains why the debate over the relational nature of the trinity, was such a bone of contention among the early Church Fathers who met at the Council of Nicea (325 CE) *"to set out an orthodox biblical definition concerning the divine identity"* of God the Father and God the Son. Tertullian's terminology was later incorporated into the Nicene Creed at the 2nd Ecumenical Council in 381 CE. **New Bible Dictionary, Douglas & F.F. Bruce, Trinity, p 1298.**

In addition, Tertullian introduced trinitarian ideas of pagan origin such as dipping the initiate 3 times and making the sign of the cross on the forehead, into the initiation of new Christians during baptism. He believed incorporating these practices would make it easier to add the "pagans" into the Christian fold. He also admitted that he had adopted these practices from "pagan" teachings and that he could not support them from Scripture. His use of the word trinity or "trinitas" (Latin for, threeness) emphasized the character of God, not necessarily the existence of three entities.

In his writings, Tertullian's trinity doctrine taught that the Father, Son and Spirit were one substance, not one person and that this was Jesus' meaning when he stated, *"I and my Father are one"* (**John 10:30**). He also stated that the Son was not co-eternal like the Father but rather, had a beginning as the only begotten son of God. He even taught that the Holy Spirit was a literal "being". These differences in doctrine make his terminology of the trinity much different than the trinity doctrine the Christian faith now teaches.

Furthermore, since trinitarian doctrine does not appear in the bible, proving its meaning or intentions, beyond the mere speculation and explanations offered by the early church fathers, becomes a daunting challenge for most modern theologians.

Another reference, the **HarperCollins Encyclopedia of Catholicism** says, *"Today, however, scholars generally agree that there is no doctrine of the Trinity as such in either the OT or the NT... Likewise, the NT does not contain an explicit doctrine of the Trinity."* (**Richard McBrien, general editor, 1995, "God," pp.564, 565**)

Seeing as most Christian scholars can agree on the singular fact that the bible is not the source of trinitarian Christian theology, it becomes imperative to identify the origins of this theology from whatever sources the concept originated.

In the realm of Christianity, however, *"the doctrine of the Trinity developed gradually after the completion of the New Testament in the heat of controversy" and, "the church fathers who developed it believed they were simply exegeting (explaining) divine revelation and not at all speculating or inventing new ideas.* From the book **"The Trinity"** by **Roger Olson and Christopher Hall (2002, pp. 1,2)**

ANCIENT ORIGINS OF HOLY CONCEPTION AND VIRGIN BIRTH

> *"...the origin of the conception is entirely pagan..."*
> **Arthur Weigall-*Egyptologist***

Historically, there are many ancient religious traditions which include mysteries of how their deities came into being.

THE VIRGIN BIRTH AND THE LEGEND OF AUSET

In ancient Kemet, the adoration of the star Sirius was the inspiration for the spirituality of the gods. Like the star Sirius in the heavens, the god Osiris (or Ausar) stood at the center of earthly culture. At his side was his wife, the goddess Auset (or Aset or Isis as she was later idolized by the Greeks), to whom the stories of a virgin birth were first attributed. It is important to note here that these mythologies appeared thousands of years before the Christian Era. From the union of Osiris and Auset comes the allegory of the hero-son, Horus (or Heru), who avenged his father's death by killing his evil uncle Set.

The story of the birth of Horus appears on temples dating back to the 17th dynasty (1580-1530 BCE). However, sources writing for Wikipedia.com estimate it is likely that the full legend of the holy triad of Osiris, Auset, and Horus dates to at least the 24th century BCE. Though the tale of Osiris is categorized as a myth, many historians presume, that the story may have been partly inspired by a regional conflict in Egypt's early history or prehistory thousands of years earlier. Throughout antiquity, the story is expressed mostly in part rather than in its entirety; appearing in ancient texts, rituals, funerary rights, and allegorical stories. To date, it remains the oldest and most influential tale in ancient Egyptian culture appearing and reappearing throughout antiquity. The key spiritual elements of the story include birth, life, conflict between good & evil, death, afterlife, and rebirth. These elements appear in ritual practices integral to Ancient Egyptian life and cultural beliefs. It is very important to note here that these elements also mirror many of the key divine tenants of the holy trinity appearing in modern Christianity.

The legend says that Osiris married his elder sister Auset. Later, a great battle ensued when Set, the brother of Osiris, attempted to take over the kingdoms of heaven and earth. Osiris had already defeated Set in an earlier battle and had received power over the Sun, Sky, and Earth as his reward. In this second battle, however,

Osiris was not only defeated, but brutally killed and dismembered by Set and his minions. When news of his death reached Auset, she was overwhelmed with grief. Isis being a goddess with great powers of magic, then turns herself into a bird, searching the earth for the 13 pieces of Osiris' dismembered remains. She finally finds all the missing pieces, except his phallus (or penis).

In the Ceremony of the Opening of the Mouth, a common ritual intended to re-animate the deceased so that they can fully partake of life, after life, Auset violently flaps her wings creating a great whirlwind that causes Osiris' physical members to animate and reassemble as his essence (or spirit) rising from his body. Auset then takes the blood, flesh and spirit of Osiris into her womb (without the phallus) and miraculously conceives a son; thus, establishing the oldest account of an immaculate conception.

Thus, Horus is born, battles and defeats his evil uncle Set, and avenges his father's death. Through the birth and victory of Horus, the spirit of Osiris is raised from the dead. Osiris becomes the Judge and King of the afterlife and Horus is crowned the king of the living. Set, the jealous brother, is now the banished lord of the wilderness. It is notable that over the centuries, Osiris was depicted often as a mummified human body carrying a shepherd's staff and flail. The staff signified his role as the shepherd of mankind and the flail or sickle, symbolized his ability to separate the wheat from the chaff (or the good from the bad). Sound familiar? Auset became known as the protector and defender of Horus, the appointed Pharaoh King. Her image was often depicted with a man-child king on her lap. Sound familiar? When Horus destroys Set, he is granted the highest honor of all; that is...the king of all the kings and the god of all the gods. Sound familiar? To honor his father, who is now restored, Horus gives his eye, which was snatched out by Set, to his father Osiris. To this day the Eye of Horus remains a symbol of royal protection, power, restoration and good health.

CONCLUSION

Now it is not my intention to upset you if you are Christian, but on the other hand, it is my intention. I want you to get out of your autopilot religious complacency and start doing your own research. Start with this chapter. Because it is imperative that you learn the truth. And you cannot learn without engaging your mind to think independently and to seek and find the truth about everything you think you know. Truth that was accepted by you without questioning.

The point here is that there is a huge chasm between religious history and true world history. This is not unique to Christianity. You will discover it is also true of Judaism and Islam if you do your own intensive research. My journey of research began with Christianity because I was ordained in the Christian tradition and studied the bible for 30 years before discovering what is included in this chapter. Sadly, most practitioners of modern religions don't even know they are operating with partial information, lack of information, and even false information that has been mixed in with fundamental truths to facilitate a certain outcome. That outcome being the inevitable centralization and control of information in matters of history and faith. This fact should be enough to make any so-called responsible person investigate further when it comes to matters of beliefs and values.

Unfortunately, most people just assume that the Bible, the Tanakh and the Koran are completely true and mostly infallible. What a mess for those truly seeking spiritual enlightenment. And what a disservice to the past, present and future generations of truth seekers who are only receiving a mere glimpse of actual world history instead of all the facts. With that said, let us look at how these incomplete and/or inaccurate faith presumptions keep us bound in thinking that can harm and not heal. For we must know the truth to be able to use it for our spiritual liberation and ascension. And we must face these truths head on in order to stop the cycle of dependence that keeps us from growing and ascending to higher and deeper experiences and knowledge of the Universal Mind of "God" which is and is in, all living things.

CHAPTER TEN

No One is Coming to Save You: Part Two

THE HISTORICITY OF THE MAN CALLED JESUS

> *"The first Christian writings to talk about Jesus are the epistles of St Paul, and scholars agree that the earliest of these letters was written within 25 years of Jesus's death; while the detailed biographical accounts of Jesus in the New Testament gospels date from around 40 years after he died"*
>
> **The Guardian: *What is the Historical Evidence That Jesus Christ Lived and Died*; Dr Simon Gathercole, Friday 14, April 2017**

HISTORICAL REFERENCES TO JESUS

The issue here is that if the bible is an historical document, there should also be other historical documents which corroborate the events and persons described therein. And yet, even the evidence of the existence of a prophet or savior named Jesus is still very hard to come by. The most celebrated non-biblical reference to a man called Jesus, however, is attributed to the Romano-Jewish historian

Flavius Josephus. Josephus' acclaim began as leader of the Jewish forces of Galilee in the first Jewish-Roman war (66-70 CE). As the war escalated, he was forced to surrender.

But because Josephus had predicted that his enemy, the Roman general Vespasian, would one day be the Emperor of Rome, he found favor with Vespasian; who made Josephus his slave and Hebrew interpreter. Two years later, Vespasian became Emperor, gave Josephus his freedom and granted him Roman citizenship. Josephus' defection to the Roman government was complete when he took the emperor's family name (Flavius) and assumed the role of advisor and friend to Vespasian's son, Titus.

Nearly ten years later, Josephus wrote *The Jewish War,* an historical account of the Roman occupation of Galilee, and, *Antiquities of the Jews,* the alleged history of the world from a Jewish point of view. Both literary works were commissioned by the Roman Empire. Subsequently, Josephus was branded a traitor to the Jews. The accounts leave many to believe that Josephus' works simply propagandized the agenda of Rome. Nevertheless, Josephus did mention a man named Jesus who was crucified in *Antiquities of the Jews;* an account written more than 60 years after the time Jesus supposedly lived.

Non-historical accounts of the life of the man called Jesus are also found in the four Gospels of the New Testament, all of which were written in the last 30 years of the 1st century CE. It is important to note here that the gospel of Mark, who was not a disciple of Jesus, is believed to be based upon the oral accounts of Peter. In addition, historians believe the gospels of Matthew and Luke were based upon the gospel of Mark. Though the original gospel of John, who was a disciple of Jesus, was written only 20 to 30 years after Jesus' alleged crucifixion, the final edition found in the holy bible was written circa 90-100 CE.

In "**Antiquities of the Jews**", Josephus includes two references to Jesus. In Book 18, Chapter 3, he refers to Jesus as māšīah (anointed) and states he was "a wise teacher who was crucified by Pilate". Later, in Book 20, Chapter 9, Josephus refers to James *"the brother of Jesus, who was called christos"*. Many historians, however, believe that the reference to Jesus as "the messiah" was inserted into his work as Christianity became the conquering world religion. In addition, historians also note that Josephus' works reference at least twenty other people with the name Jesus, and that he most likely indicated that the Jesus who Pilate killed was the one *"who was called christ"* in order to specify which "Jesus" he was referencing. After reading this **Antiquities of the Jews** in its entirety, I am certain that the text provided the content for most of the Old Testament Books currently appearing in the Christian Bible. I also recommend that you read **War of the Jews**, to get a more in depth understanding of how the Hebrew speaking people of East Africa were persecuted, particularly for not excepting the Greek and Roman gods which were forced upon them. The works of Josephus Flavius are readily available online if you wish to read them and come to your own conclusions.

Remember, I'm not here to tell you there was no prophet named Jesus. As Josephus said, a man by that name was crucified and had a brother named James. But the question is not, did a man named Jesus live and die...the question is... did he intentionally die for the sins of all humanity? Unfortunately, this narrative can only be verified by the bible; a document created by the church of the Roman Empire. The same document that reinforces our own self-loathing as sinners who memorialize the death of a man who died because of our shortcomings. What a guilt complex!

I believe, instead, that there was a man, a prophet and revolutionary who probably lived and preached and criticized the Roman Empire. It is likely that such a man would have been killed on a cross as a result. But I also believe that those who sought to rule the world took the story of his life and his teachings to form a state-imposed religion that looks more like an amalgamated imposter of the ancient religions that came before it. I also contend that it was the man they call "Saint" Paul who, conspired with the bishops of the time, and assisted in creating the doctrine that would be used to bring all civilized and soon to be civilized peoples of the world together under one Roman world rule. Does anyone reading this see the parallel between one world rulership and the current New World Order agenda that was announced under the Bush and Bush/Chaney administrations. If you dare, you can also research The Project for a New American Century; which is the blueprint for how this one world government rule will be/ is being executed. Remember, if you truly want to manifest ascension, you must conduct your own research. Then you will know the truth, gain clarity, and be prepared to let go of information that no longer serves your highest good.

The government that benefits from Christianity these days, however, is the U.S.A. Inc. and its corporate partners, Queen Elizabeth and The Vatican (The Holy See of Rome). It is also no coincidence that these three world entities are the only self-declared "sovereign" entities in the world. And right now, on planet earth, in 2019, this is considered normal. Just think of all the people who died under the hand of the Roman Empire and the Vatican funded Crusades that helped them conquer the world. And the aristocracy of Europe, with England at the helm, successfully ravaging the rest of Africa, South America, North America et al and killing more indigenous people that can 'ere be counted. Now, in these modern times, the corporation of the United States of America has been tasked to navigate the final blow to all nations that oppose this unholy trinity of world rulership. And all this, my dear friends, is accepted as normal! What we have here is a clear case of normal killing us. Do you agree? Take a knee. So, what in heaven and hell does all this information have to do with saving my eternal soul Michelle? What's the message and what in heaven and hell am I supposed to do about it now, centuries after the fact? Good question. I was hoping you would say that…keep reading.

HORUS, PTOLEMY, AND JESUS: THE DOCTRINE OF THE "SAVIOR" GOD

Now anyone who has lived at least 30 years knows how quickly social norms can evolve, degrade or even disappear in a very short time. Well, the new dynasty of Ptolemy I endured for several generations. It was not long before the image of the Pharaoh-King had taken on the divine persona of soter, or savior. Along with this transition of race in the leadership came new traditions and mythologies, which gradually integrated into the culture in a variety of tribal interpretations. There was great diversity of beliefs, customs and spiritual practices…and great confusion because many of the stories of the "savior" conflicted. I liken the process to the communication exercise where one person whispers a story to their neighbor, then the neighbor whispers what he heard to person #3 and so on. By the 9th or 10th rendering of the story, the details are usually altered or lost. And so, these tales, that existed much like proverbs and parables of today, were turned into social, political and spiritual narratives shaped to help the new non-African leaders rule over and eventually overtake the Kemetian people.

But by the time the prophet called Jesus appeared on the scene, (300 years later) the so-called modern world was ripe for a different kind of savior. One who would rescue the people from centuries of oppressive tyranny at the hands of the Roman Empire. The news about the anointed prophet, teacher, and martyr, took root in the folklore of the modern culture of the day. Under the great tyranny of the Greeks and Romans, Christianity organically began to take shape and spread throughout the civilized world; which now included

Rome, Greece, The Mediterranean, Egypt and the rest of North East Africa, Persia and southwestern Asia.

By the 3rd century CE, there was much debate among the sects who called themselves christians. Significantly the argument over the divine nature of God within man rose to the forefront of discussion between the anointed factions. The Gnostics, for example, believed the Spirit was in all mankind and simply needed to be awakened through the pursuit of gnosis, or experiential, mystical knowledge of the divine. Once this gnosis was reached, the divine within man could return to the Great Divine. This process of pursuing and achieving knowledge of the divine selves was the catalyst for that person's individual salvation. Archeologists are now convinced that Gnosticism predated the Christian era by several centuries; having its spiritual roots, once again, in ancient Kemet.

Perhaps the ministry of the man called Jesus inspired the bishops of the emerging Roman church to include the concepts of forgiveness of sins into the official theology of Christianity. Or, maybe they knew that guilt is a tremendous motivator for those seeking salvation. Sin, after all, was a human condition that had confounded mankind for as long as could be remembered. With ancient spirituality corrupted and the Roman empire at war, I imagine it seemed impractical to assume conditions would improve anytime soon. The Greeks and the Romans, after all, entertained themselves with lascivious behaviors, philosophical debate, and political corruption. So, the banter about God, salvation, sin and the like continued. It only took a couple hundred years for the leadership of Rome to seize the opportunity and quickly amalgamate the various mythologies, into one cohesive salvation dogma that would be used to subdue the beliefs, traditions and spiritual practices of the now conquered people of Egypt, as well as the rest of the known world.

But it was at the Council of Nicea, (325 CE), where the plan to merge Christian folklore with Egyptian allegory was forged into official church tenants and Jesus, the savior of the world, was born. It is no coincidence that modern Christianity was formed within a decade of the invasion of Egypt by the newly converted Christian Constantine, the Emperor of Rome. Knowing what we know now about the objectives of Rome, which was to control the entire world, it should be plain to see how beliefs, that started as interpretations of allegories and spiritual mysteries, eventually became what we know today as the modern religion of Christianity.

In addition, the need to shift the center of the world from Africa to Rome brought with it, a need to convert even more peoples to one unifying theology. So, Rome became the new center of the civilized world and the "church" set up shop with its newfound savior, Jesus. With time, the founding fathers organized their salvation theology into the tenets of "*one holy, catholic, and apostolic church*" (From the: **Nicene Creed of the Holy Roman Catholic Church**); evangelizing and coercing many tribal peoples to convert to Christianity. Under this one, worldwide umbrella, all became "sinners" in need of salvation. Though many of the spiritual truths of life remain woven through Christianity (like the ***Instructions of Amen-em-apt, son of Kanakht***), as well as the liberating lessons attributed to the man called Jesus, the historical fact is, the "church" is simply an institution of religious doctrine contrived by men who sought to ascertain power and control over masses of people worldwide. The fact that this creed has gone virtually unchallenged for over 1700 years is certainly a testament to the power and tenacity of organized religion!

Now it is not my intention to upset you if you are Christian, but on the other hand, it is my intention to upset your mental processes. I want you to get out of your autopilot religious complacency and start doing your own research. Start with this chapter. Because it is imperative that you learn the truth. And you cannot learn without engaging your mind to think independently and to seek and find the truth about everything you think you know. Truth that was previously accepted by you without questioning.

The point here is that there is a huge chasm between religious history and true world history. This is not unique to Christianity. You will discover it is also true of Judaism and Islam if you do your own intensive research. My journey of research began with Christianity because I was ordained in the Christian tradition and studied the bible for 30 years before discovering what is included in this chapter. Sadly, most practitioners of modern religions don't even know they are operating with partial information, lack of information, and even false information that has been mixed in with fundamental truths to facilitate a certain outcome. That outcome being the inevitable centralization and control of information in matters of history and faith. This fact should be enough to make any so-called responsible person investigate further when it comes to matters of beliefs and values.

Unfortunately, most people just assume that the Bible, the Tanakh and the Koran are completely true and mostly infallible. What a mess for those truly seeking spiritual enlightenment. And what a disservice to the past, present and future generations of truth seekers who are only receiving a mere glimpse of actual world history instead of all the facts. With that said, let us look at how these incomplete and/ or inaccurate faith presumptions keep us bound in thinking that can harm and not heal. For we must know the truth to be able to use it for our spiritual liberation and ascension. And we must face these truths head-on in order to stop the cycle of dependence which keeps us from growing and ascending to higher and more meaningful experiences with the Universal Mind of "God" which is and is in, all living things.

Remember, I'm not here to tell you there was no prophet named Jesus. As Josephus said, a man by that name was crucified and had a brother named James. But the question is not, did a man named Jesus live and die...the question is... did he intentionally die for the sins of all humanity? Unfortunately, this narrative can only be verified by the bible; a document created by the church of the Roman Empire. The same document that reinforces our own self-loathing as sinners who memorialize the death of a man who died because of our shortcomings. What a guilt complex!

I believe, instead, that there was a man, a prophet and revolutionary who probably lived and preached and criticized the Roman Empire. It is likely that such a man would have been killed on a cross as a result. But I also believe that those who sought to rule the world took the story of his life and his teachings to form a state-imposed religion that looks more like an amalgamated imposter of the ancient religions that came before it. I also contend that it was the man they call "Saint" Paul who, conspired with the bishops of the time, and assisted in creating the doctrine that would be used to bring all civilized and soon to be civilized peoples of the world together under one Roman world rule. Does anyone reading this see the parallel between one world rulership and the current New World Order agenda that was announced under the Bush and Bush/Chaney administrations? If you dare, you can also research The Project for a New American Century; which is the blueprint for how this one world government rule will be/is being executed. That too, is a subject for another book!

The government that benefits from Christianity these days, however, is the U.S.A. Inc. and its corporate partners, Queen Elizabeth (The Royals) and The Vatican (The Holy See of Rome). It is also no coincidence that these three world entities are the only self-declared "sovereign" entities in the world. And right now, on planet Earth, in 2019, this is considered normal. Just think of all the people who died under the hand of the Roman Empire and the Vatican funded Crusades that helped them conquer the world. And the aristocracy of Europe, with England at the helm, successfully ravaging the rest of Africa, South America, North America et al and killing more indigenous people that can 'ere be counted. Now, in these modern times, the corporation of the United States of America has been tasked to navigate the final blow to all nations that oppose this unholy trinity of world rulership. And all this, my dear friends, is accepted as normal! What we have here is a clear case of normal killing us. Do you agree? Take a knee. So, what in heaven and hell does all this information have to do with saving my eternal soul Michelle? What's the message and what in heaven and hell am I supposed to do about it now, centuries after the fact? Good question. I was hoping you would say that...keep reading.

JESUS IS NOT COMING TO SAVE YOU

Let's start with the fact that all Christian religions have one essential belief in common: that God the Father sent his only begotten son Jesus to the earth to sacrifice his life so that sinful people would be forgiven. Once forgiven, the sinner is born again into a new life of perpetual forgiveness and grace. The offer of forgiveness stands if that converted sinner believes that God has in fact bestowed this eternal forgiveness upon him/her. Remarkably, that is the prevailing truth for nearly 31% of the world's population (as of 2010); regardless of the specifics of how each believer practices, or expresses, that Christian faith.

According to the apostle Paul, father of NT Christianity, every Christian knows "...how that Christ died for our sins according to the scriptures" (1 Co 15:3). And it is the Gospel of John (John 3:16), that captures the most fundamental belief by which Christians confess their salvation from sin by grace through faith in Jesus:

> *"For God so loved the world that he gave his only begotten son that whosoever believes in him should not perish but have everlasting life".* **John 3:16**

Now, let us assume for starters that this statement is completely true. A sinless man, who was also God, was born into a sinful world solely for the purpose of dying for the sins of everyone else. The only condition of this salvation contract is that the sinner believe

1) that Jesus is the only begotten son of "God" and
2) that Jesus died for his/her "sins."

But, if this statement is true, some very puzzling questions gnaw at my brain. Taking on the objective view of the Conscious Observer, the following questions come to mind:

Question #1

> **Do you mean to tell me that my sins will be forgiven by God, if I just believe that a God-conceived God/ man died so that my sins will be forgiven by God?**

ANSWER:

Yes, I am simplifying the differing Christian points of view down to one unifying creed. I did so because it's the one point I think most Christian denominations seem to agree on.

Question #2

Hey, wait a minute! Should I really want someone else to pay the consequence for MY bad behavior, actions, wrongdoings, debts, or "SIN"?

ANSWER:

From a moral and biblical point of view the answer is most certainly no. You should not want an innocent person to take the blame for your wrongdoing. In any case other than Jesus, this situation would be criminal, to say the least. But before we get into the exegesis of the scriptures used to support this fundamental truth, let's just look at the implications of the belief itself from a practical, social, and psychological point of view.

Question #3

What kind of person would I be to do wrong; then put the consequences of my wrongful behavior on an innocent person?

ANSWER:

The answer, put bluntly, is that such a person would be considered a sociopath according to today's mental health definitions. Sociopathy is an anti-social personality disorder wherein the individual has a pathology of long-term violation of the rights and well-being of others. With a violent affinity to adherence to social norms or obligations, the sociopath lacks the capacity to experience guilt, regret, or compassion for others, is unresponsive to punishment, and possesses a cruel disregard for the feelings or sufferings of others. This is the kind of person that would commit a crime and feel absolutely nothing about letting another take the blame for the heinous act they have committed.

Nevertheless, this is the lot of the man called Jesus in the annuls of Christendom. An innocent man, taking the blame for a wicked, undeserving world of sociopaths. I am truly ashamed of myself for not recognizing the psychosis of this kind of thinking years ago! That is, however, what happens when you take on or inherit a belief system that you did not question nor investigate against all the available evidence. I reiterate, "against <u>all</u> the available evidence"!

I think it's safe to say that most people would probably be unwilling to take responsibility for another's dastardly deeds, crimes, debts or "sins", especially if the punishment for that crime is death. I imagine that's why martyrdom is quite rare in this modern age. Still the element of martyrdom, with which so many are so fascinated, remains embedded into the Christianity narrative. Let us remember that the spread of Christian faith came on the coattails of miraculous legends of the martyrdom of saints who were persecuted for their beliefs. Even in this type of scenario, these saints were dying for their own beliefs, not for the actions or wrongdoings of others.

Yet, herein, we see the mindset of the founding fathers of the Christian church; to create a narrative of faith, established upon a foundation of sociopathic mental illness! Now I just made every devout, bible thumping, rosary praying, crucifix wearing, tongues-talking, shouting, praying, believer in the Christian world disturbed or angry. For the purposes of this book, I will give these men the benefit of the doubt and pray that they did not intentionally form a religion founded upon a theology of psychosis. Neither is it my intention to blaspheme the Creator-God, the Divine Spirit nor the people who now experience their spiritual faith through the medium of organized religion.

So why would anyone want to put the consequences of their wrongdoings on another person? I think the point here is that most people would not want to do that, especially if that other person was a tangible, human being. I suppose the man called Jesus being somewhat of a mystical, mythical, entity is just intangible enough for us to accept it as normal. One step further asks... if Jesus is God incarnate, why would one want to put the consequence of one's sins on an all-loving, all-forgiving, all-powerful God in the first place? For isn't "God" all things? And, if "God" is all things, then "God" is each of us individually and collectively? Simultaneously, "God" as the totality of all things, would also be both "sin" and "salvation". Would he/she not? Or, perhaps, are we assuming that our limitless and omniscient "God" is somehow limited in the capacity to render salvation through our uniquely personal experience of humanity and divinity? The irony of all this is that in OT scripture, "God" allegedly spoke through the prophet Isaiah saying...

> *"For I am the Lord Thy God, the Holy One of Israel, thy Savior; I gave Egypt for thy covering, Ethiopia and Seba for thee".* **Isaiah 43:3**
>
> *"I, even I, am the Lord and beside me there is no savior.*
> *I have declared, and I have shewed, when there was no*
> *strange god among you: therefore, ye are my witnesses*
> *saith the Lord, that I am God".* **Isaiah 43:11**

Now why would "God" need to negate his own promise by deciding that we suddenly needed another savior? And if "God" is all things, we are all one with "God", right? Thus, there should be no need for a distinction between us and Jesus, right? And, if "God" is "thy Savior", there is no need for another "Savior" to do what "God" did long before the doctrine of salvation through faith in Jesus was ever introduced by the Roman Church, right? Furthermore, if we are one with "God" are we not all the begotten of "God"? Do you see? I guess the Roman Church did not expect us to be able to discern this flaw in doctrine!

Question #4

What is going on in the mind of a person who would allow another person to take the blame for their wrongdoing?

Answer:

As I stated earlier, the diagnosis for anyone operating with this type of anti-social behavior in the world today, would certainly fall somewhere between a sociopath and a psychopath; depending on the definition you wish to attribute to both terms. For it is well known in the field of psychology that a lack of guilt or remorse for your wrongdoings is a very common trait shared by both mental disorders.

Yet, few perceive themselves as sociopaths when praying for God to forgive them for wrongdoing, because few probably consciously give scrutiny to how that forgiveness and salvation has been made available to them. That is, through believing that "God" loved us so much, that he came to earth in the form of a sacrificial human being to give us a clean slate to go forth and do wrong again. I'm pausing for a chuckle here as I reflect upon the sacrament of confession/penance and all the money the church collected over the centuries knowing that repeat offenders were inevitable! For we Christians are assured that "God" will always forgive. Even after 2000 years of martyrdom-based religion, most Christians still find themselves repeating the cycle of sin, repentance, and forgiveness from an unseen savior.

Regrettably, reconciling a transgression committed against another by some act of your own will is rarely emphasized as a doctrine of the church, though it may come up in the cycle of scriptures read at morning services. Have you ever heard of a church sponsored "forgive your neighbor" service? I mean a service where the offender and the offended gather to reconcile their differences? If such a service was held regularly, I'm sure there would be fewer murders and shootings in the world. For by now we would have learned better ways to reconcile interpersonal and global grievances. I believe the problem with this repentance/ salvation cycle is that confession and penance do not, necessarily, foster the development of the virtues of integrity, humility, remorse, truth, honesty, self-discipline and accountability; all character traits that are needed when reconciling transgressions with another person. Selah

ON ORIGINAL SIN AND FORGIVENESS

It is our sin, after all, which creates a need for salvation in the first place. And it is our collective and individual understanding of the nature of sin, or the lack thereof, that causes us to believe that only an outside force can conquer it. Unfortunately for humanity, we have simply been incapable of consistently living and walking in love, peace, harmony and righteousness with one another. These sins: pride, covetousness, lust, anger, wrath, greed, gluttony, envy and sloth, to name a few, rest upon the person's conscience as a constant reminder that we are somehow less than the perfect beings who were created in the image of God.

How confusing it must be to possess the spiritual wisdom to understand that you are made in the image of god and yet, lack the insight to understand that an omniscient and perfect God would not make a flawed being. For everything in nature is miraculously pro-creating and self-sustaining. Nevertheless, this conundrum has been the struggle of the ages. Herein also, enters another mental health issue we now recognize as low self-esteem. For God knowingly made us flawed so we would subsequently need saving? I think not!

LIFE LESSONS ON ASCENSION

HOW DID I GET HERE?

As a former Christian pastor, trained, ordained and licensed to preach the gospel of Jesus Christ, I was well versed in the artful skill of biblical exegesis, especially for someone who was not raised in the church. To the contrary, from ages 12 to 19, I was a professed atheist with a passion for persecuting those who condemned non-believers to hell with little hesitation. Surprisingly, my mother and father were quite shocked when I told them I didn't believe in God; though neither of them was what one would call religious. To save my soul, I was immediately christened in the Presbyterian faith. Sadly, I was no closer to salvation after the baptism, than I had been before; as I donned that pretty, white chiffon dress with the big, blue satin ribbon that hallowed day. As I mentioned earlier, it wasn't until I reached the age of 19, that my first boyfriend, almost eight years my senior, sat me down and told me that because he loved me, he didn't want to see me go to hell. He then shared **John 3.16** and explained that all I needed to do was believe that the man called Jesus died for my sins.

Well that proclamation of damnation sparked a crusade to prove him wrong. In fact, each of his *"you need to give your life to Jesus"* pep talks pushed me deeper into the scriptures in search of anything that would negate or contradict his theory that I was a sinner in need of salvation. Since I, like most people, suffered from low self-esteem back then, I guess I identified with the concept of sin and knew that I surely had committed some sin. After all, haven't we all? So, I started with the Genesis creation story and began my relationship with biblical scripture.

Remember the little girl who questioned everything? Well, she read and studied and took notes and pondered the psalms, the proverbs, and the salvation doctrine of the New Testament. But the part of the bible that got her full attention was the gospels. Most specifically, the words attributed to the man called Jesus. Can we keep it very real here? Because I admit that when I first encountered the words of this man, whoever he was or if he was, I connected with what he had to say. Coming from the rather militant perspective of the sixties and seventies, I found the words of the man they call Jesus to be bold, courageous and revolutionary. I think that is what I liked most about the man portrayed in the book...He was radical! But the truth is, the man described in the gospels never said he was the savior of the world. He was never quoted as saying he was the king of kings nor, the lord of lords. At the time I didn't catch this plot flaw between the book and the doctrine. I suppose, with time, the doctrine became normal to me. Especially after I started attending church and hearing these messages repeatedly.

As I meditated upon what I read, I think I let my guard down as new belief paradigms took root within me. I was inexperienced and naïve then, so I had no idea of the power that repetition was having on my Mind and Soul. In hindsight, I now understand that in the war for my mind, I was helping the system program me, as I steadfastly downloaded the tenets of Christianity into my belief system.

I am certain that neither my boyfriend, nor the loving community of Christians with whom I served the Church over the years, were aware that they had fallen prey to a one-world-order agenda. Nor did I know this as I preached the gospel and taught the bible to many. No. I didn't know the information I am sharing here, in the detail that I know it now, until I put in years of research, study, time, cross referencing, deductive reasoning, faith, and inner reprogramming to become who I am today. For the conquest to control the hearts, minds, and behaviors of the masses began long ago and is intricately woven into every strand of our collective social experience!

In fact, the agenda was implemented so precisely, that most would be remised to imagine such a sinister plot was even possible. How could anyone come to comprehend the vast scope of this global agenda? For it took the Holy Roman Empire thousands of years to spread the gospel across the world. From Africa, to Rome to Asia and the Americas, the promulgation of Christianity was the primary tool the Empire used to conquer all, in the name of The Church. Those who resisted the gospel were killed or enslaved. Those who believed became the indentured servants of the master. It is, therefore, easy to see how so many succumbed to the so-called faith during many centuries of "holy" wars.

Anyone who ever studied the Unholy Roman Empire knows that conquering the world was its primary objective. We studied it in high school, remember? Well, that agenda continued throughout the modern era up to this day. The hardest pill for Christians to accept is that this religion was specifically organized for the purpose of holding the people of the world mentally captive and molding them into tools for religious propaganda in perpetuity. Hence the call to "spread the gospel", even unto death, made all who believe and evangelize the false narrative culpable in the same offence! Can you imagine how I felt the day I made myself accept this responsibility! Me, a self-proclaimed militant Black woman, teaching the curriculum of the slave master!

CHRISTIANITY AND SLAVERY

For the Black people of Africa and their descendants throughout the African Diaspora, Christianity and religion has been the oppressive tool of choice for the slave masters who caught, bought, sold and controlled Africans in the name of god and money for many centuries. It is only logical that this happened to most of the descendants of that diaspora. For who, more than the brutally enslaved indigenous Black people of the Americas, along with the Africans who were stolen from the homeland and shipped far, far across the great sea, needed a message of deliverance and salvation? In contrast however, Christianity and its tenets have been, and continue to be, used to empower the White race to consistently oppress, enslave, rape, murder, and slaughter millions of indigenous people of color across the globe to date!

The unfortunate result of this comprehensively effective mind control project is that Christianity eventually became the dominant influence of America, the superpower of the world. Like Rome, The U.S. has the largest military might on the planet; just as Rome did when it birthed the Christian Era. Now, the powers that be of America weave this same false doctrine into every nook and cranny of modern American politics, public policy, government and culture; a culture that is the primary influencer of the world stage. Thus, the entire global society is held captive from generation to generation. It is easy to see how believing in and practicing Christianity is not only the norm, but the expected belief and behavior protocol for the modern-day American, and the greater global community. And that, my friends, is how you keep the world under control...with religion and war!

But I didn't know all that back then. I didn't realize the world was a diabolical place with secret agendas and conspiracies. I didn't know the script was chock full of lies masquerading as truth. All I knew was that I was experiencing a tremendous amount of power in the words I was reading. I didn't realize the power of the words was predicated by the power of my belief in the words and the repetition and frequency of the mental programming. I didn't know repetition was/is a weapon in the hands of the oppressor being used against me. The process is called brainwashing. I guess that's why the Catholic liturgical calendar, repeats the entire bible every 3 years! Just think...at that pace you've heard the entire bible 5 times by your Confirmation! Now that is the power of mental programming! Selah

BACK TO MY STORY

Well time kept moving forward. Meanwhile, I received a weekly dosage of Christian therapy via bible study and church on Sunday. I didn't know I was swirling down the rabbit hole of religion and I did not know that so much of what is in scripture is misrepresented as historical fact. To this day, I regret that I did not search far beyond the boundaries of religion to get to the truth of the matter. Even though I didn't believe the bible verbatim, I still interpreted the testaments of the bible as, somewhat true. I didn't know I was cultivating a belief system with very little basis in fact or history. And here, propped up by my own study and the explanations that were imparted to me by my mate and the church, my faith in Christianity began to grow.

The more I learned, the more I believed. The more I sought out the "truth", the more "truth" I found. My innate curiosity and tendency to question everything led me to discover many truths by which I live today and, some I did not expect to find. I am thankful, however, that under the tutelage of my first spiritual mentor, teacher, and friend, Rev. Jerald D. Ford, I was strongly encouraged to study the bible for myself, think for myself, and come to my own conclusions about how to apply this wisdom to my everyday life. I am certain that my passion for study and learning ultimately led me to the spiritual perceptions I hold today.

MY EARLY DAYS OF MINISTRY

Rev. Ford was pastor and founder of Bread of Life Fellowship, a non-denominational church with a strong Charismatic/Pentecostal doctrine rooted deeply in New Testament Pauline theology. Rev. Ford was a dynamic preacher and theologian. His knowledge, oratory delivery, and exegetical application of biblical scripture to everyday life circumstances was powerful and uplifting. For he was a master at bringing the scriptures to brilliant light and relating each passage to a real-life scenario to which these spiritual lessons and revelations could be applied. I soaked up "The Word" during that time and my spiritual understanding grew exponentially. Of all the instruction I received, the most valuable principle I ever learned came from the following scripture:

> *"Study to shew thyself approved unto God, a workman that need not be ashamed, rightly dividing the word of truth".* **2Timothy 2:15**

And study, I did. Once I sunk my teeth into the bible, the wisdom within it spoke to me very personally. Soon, I was driven to absorb, as much of it as I could, into my being and, into my soul. I was driven. I sought salvation from so many heartaches and struggles that lingered from my youth. And yes, I felt empowered as my faith in the God of my understanding grew. I was convinced that if I could learn all that this dynamic book of wisdom could provide, I would satisfy my search for inner peace. In a few years I felt the tug of the Universal Mind of God calling me to serve humanity. As a now practicing evangelical Christian, I of course, interpreted this tug as a call to become a Christian minister. Once I realized my purpose was to heal, love, and minister to the lost and forgotten, I was convinced this biblical knowledge, mixed with spiritual wisdom and faith, would empower me to "save" many people.

After ordination, however, I quickly realized that I was not called to the ministry of organized religion nor the promulgation of religious doctrine. Though I was still a devout Christian, I simply could not figure out how to wiggle my way out of this conundrum. I was too young and inexperienced to understand where the Spirit was leading me, so I persevered in my relationship with church, despite the flaws and disappointments I encountered. I knew full well that the people who sought spiritual help, were coming to the church to find that help. As many Christian pastors believe: *Church is a hospital for the spiritually ill.* Agreeing with that philosophy, I resolved to move forward in ministry so I could continue to help, serve and heal those who came to church seeking comfort, instruction, guidance, inspiration, and ultimately, salvation from the "sins" that ailed them.

As I matured spiritually, however, this mission of saving souls became more and more problematic. That's because my views of sin, forgiveness, and the relationship between mind, body, and spirit had begun to expand with every personal study session. My rather subtle approach to ministry worked for a while, as I dibbled and dabbled with finding creative ways to bypass the patriarchal system of institutional church, despite the limitations and obstacles I faced. Like most women in church leadership, I was discouraged from thinking for myself and questioning the prevailing doctrines, teachings and traditions of the church. Eventually I decided that the politics and rules of church were no place for an inquisitive truth seeker, so I gradually sought opportunities outside of church to take my free and curious spirit to people who were hurting.

During these years of discovery, it was very frustrating to accept that the bible was an inaccurate rendering of inspired spiritual wisdom. I had, after all, amassed a tremendous amount of biblical education and knowledge. In the early years, it was easier to dismiss the dissonance of the contradictions by referencing some scripture or another. I now find it so amusing that most Christians defend the facts of the bible, with the "facts" of the bible! Yet, as I faced the uncomfortable truth of each new revelation, I did just that. That is, until my Spirit pressed me to search beyond the bible and the tenets of organized religion to find my place and purpose in a life of ministry.

The interesting result of my hunger for spiritual truth is that it took me on a journey far beyond the Bible. Eventually, personal research led me to a wide field of study including, metaphysics, quantum physics, anthropology, physiology, sociology, psychology, theology, paleontology and archeology. As time went on, many truths had to be accepted because the "facts" I discovered clearly negated many of my traditionally held Christian beliefs.

This is when ministry began to become problematic. For I found myself gradually modifying my message, publicly and privately, based upon all the new knowledge I had acquired beyond the tenets of Christianity. As life experience became my greatest teacher, I decided to let my Spirit be the judge and jury on what I should accept, reject, believe, and follow. As my spiritual life experiences evolved, so did my religious understanding. I learned that I would simply have to trust the "God" within me in order to inner-stand what is The Mind of the Spirit. This was my approach to Christianity for the next 20 years.

One issue that troubled me tremendously was that biblical history clearly conflicted with actual world history. In fact, very few accounts in the bible corroborate well with reliable, historical facts; except for the dates and names of "pagan" kings like Nebuchadnezzar and Herod. And when I later learned that the true children of Israel and Judah were African people whose legacy and history has been plagiarized, it became impossible to continue preaching and teaching the current Judeo-Christian fairytale. For how do we explain the big, Caucasian, "Jewish" elephant in the room? It's a shame that no one wants to address this historical fact. It doesn't surprise me though, because I had to read many books to piece together the nuggets of truth which exist deep in the interior of historical obscurity!

Nevertheless, the contradictions of biblical "facts" and historical facts begged to be reconciled both intellectually and spiritually. That meant full disclosure of the truth to those I was called to steward, serve and heal along their spiritual journey. Naturally, my evolving belief systems made my ministry increasingly more complicated over time. I made many adjustments; changing lyrics to songs, preaching spiritual concepts rather than scripture-based doctrines I could no longer support. But the more I learned the truth about the historicity of the man they call Jesus, the historical atrocities of The Church, and the long-standing unholy alliance of the Holy See of Rome, the Crown of England, The United States of America Inc., and the Rothchild Empire, I simply had that very necessary moment of clarity which made it impossible to ignore the truth that stared back at me from my research. For how could such a grandiose alliance be kept secret from those I loved and was tasked to shepherd?

JESUS AIN'T REAL

By far the hardest of all pills I had to swallow, is the fact that Jesus (as he has been portrayed to the world through Christianity) is not real. In truth, the entire concept of a White savior coming from a nation and a continent of Black people is the obvious Pink Elephant in the room which cannot be reconciled with logic. In addition, the facts that I shared earlier in this chapter, which laid out a clear understanding of how a White king became a "savior" to the African people of Egypt in the first place, gives one pause to, at the least, challenge the alleged Jesus salvation narrative by doing your own research.

It was at this crossroads, ironically, that I started searching for evidence that would reaffirm my "Jesus-Is-Real" belief paradigm! But the deeper the research, the deeper the rabbit hole of Jesus-Ain't-Real became because, historical evidence for "Jesus-Is-Real" simply could not be found. In fact, almost all the evidence to support the Jesus-As-Savior narrative is found in...you guessed it, The Holy Bible! Even the references to a man called "Jesus" in the writings of Josephus still land in the basket of hearsay, since Josephus admits he was not a witness to the events he referenced.

After I searched and searched for evidence that Jesus was real to no avail, I finally had to accept that I had to let go of the Jesus-Is-Real/Jesus-Is Savior belief paradigm. Soon after, I stopped preaching altogether as my Mind, Heart, Soul and Spirit accepted the very uncomfortable truth of my findings. This final blow to my life of Christian ministry is what brought me to the conclusive reality that the mythology of Jesus, as the God-human savior of the world, simply isn't true.

That is the point of this overview of my spiritual journey; to impress upon you that I know all too well that this chapter, title and all, will be most egregious for Christian-based readers. Some of the impressions could trigger extreme, "negative" or disturbing reactions; especially for those with years of religious conditioning. Such a reaction is to be expected, and I regret whatever discomfort you have had reading this chapter.

TIME OUT!

I don't know about you, but I really need a 10-Minute Moment right about now! Honestly, I had to "step-away-from-the-writing-project!" when I got to this point of the book. So, I realize that the implications of where we're headed does give one pause.

I remember the day I came to the epiphany that... "Jesus ain't real". I was utterly traumatized because there was just no way that I could dismiss the information I'd learned in my research. For, when I began this journey of discovery, I was seeking truth much more than a confirmation of what I already believed. I did not then, nor do I now, wish to be ignorant of any truth, even if that truth shatters my previously held beliefs. For the truth makes us free! But now, I saw the facts, as well as the history, and the processes by which this diabolical plan for a one world rule was administered, just as plain as day!

I kept asking myself how I missed all this information the first time around. I studied the bible and what I thought was biblical history for nearly 30 years. Then I realized that I had not learned this new information because I was looking in the wrong places! For you cannot study any discipline in the vacuum of that discipline alone. The study of modern medicine is a great example of how students are so busy learning medicine that they don't really understand healing. Therefore, they are trained to treat symptoms rather than heal the dis-ease. Likewise, studying the bible and peripheral bible study resources alone will not lead you to an understanding of Christianity outside the vacuum of "biblical history". For there is no biblical history because The Bible, old and new testament, is not a true representation of history. It is, instead, a rather well-constructed tale created for one purpose; to be a tool for a global mind control project administered at the hands of the Roman Empire and the Holy Roman Catholic Church! A lie! A trick!

Your spiritual emancipation, therefore, begins here with "Jesus ain't real" and "the Church ain't holy!" Neither was the bible written by men inspired by God to save the lost. It was, instead, written for the sole purpose of global mind control. Now here we are, 2019 years later, still "stuck on stupid" because we have been conditioned to follow, rather than, lead ourselves to a higher calling of true spiritual inner-standing of our divinity!

REFLECTIONS ON ASCENSION
SOMEONE TO LOVE ME

Once I calmed down from the trauma, (it took a half pint of Hennessy and hours of tears, questions, and regrets), my memories took me back to the original proclamation I made to my family when I was twelve. The day I told my mother that I did not believe in "God". Back then, I was clear about one thing for sure which was, I did not believe in god as god had been presented to me. Neither was I persuaded to do so after the mandatory baptism. Nor was I moved after four years in Catholic high school. It took falling in love with a man whom I loved and trusted completely to bring the message of "God so loved the world..." to me in a way that sounded like just what I needed at the time... someone to love me.

The truth is that at 19 years old, I was quite broken and feeling both unloved and alienated from my immediate family. I felt alone most of my life and now, here is someone saying, I love you so much that I must tell you... God so loves you Michelle that he gave... The rest, as they say, is history!

I am certain my receptivity to the idea of god loving me came from feeling unloved in the first place. I also believe that is the most powerful lure which continues to draw people to Christianity in particular. For, so many of us are broken, despondent, hurting, lonely, poor, ill, or rejected by the world and those who are supposed to love us. Now, out of nowhere, someone loves me enough to die for me. For me? It was such an extreme concept; such a heroic act I thought! For me?

I did not feel loved, nor did I feel worthy of being loved. So, yes, I needed love and even wrote a song with that title! The idea that Jesus, a man I'd never met, loved me filled a deep void within my Soul's Self. Since I believed that if there had been a Jesus, he most certainly was Black, it was easy enough to connect with. Why it was the most miraculous news I had ever heard! So, I latched onto the possibility that somewhere, someway, somehow, there was some super-human Black man "out there" who loved me enough to put my needs before his own. I am just realizing all this as I write these words! And, I am just as surprised as you are that I said that! But I won't lie, there was also a feeling of conscious Black empowerment in believing "God" was Black! (I am laughing so hard right now.) Finding a god who truly cared about me, sacrificed for me, and transformed me, as well as my budding love for my first love, was the beginning of many transformative spiritual experiences along my ascension journey. I know for certain they were necessary.

WHAT THEN, IS FAITH: UNDERSTANDING THE STRENGTH OF YOUR BELIEFS

As I mentioned before, my relationship with the man called Jesus lasted for nearly 30 years. In fact, I lived a life of full service to the church and the people of the god of my understanding. I flourished and matured and grew in my faith. I learned that I can indeed do all things through the power of an ever-growing faith in the divinity that was strengthening me! And I did "do" many things; persevering through numerous trials, tribulations and hardships as well as manifesting many blessings and, what many would call, miracles.

I now inner-stand that it was the strength of my faith that was my true salvation. It was not so much what I believed but, rather, that I believed it completely, that was the catalyst for manifesting more love, peace, joy, and blessings in my life. Do you see the difference? It's the same power that brokers on Wall Street use for success; for their success relies upon the strength of their belief that money is their salvation, and, that they are destined to possess it! The stronger their belief, the more focus they develop, and with more focus they are more likely to succeed. The power of the mind to believe anything resolutely, is the creative power that makes it manifest in the mental reality and the physical world. Do You See? Asé

> *"For as he thinketh in his heart, so is he"* **Proverbs 23:7**

Remember Wall Street with Leonardo Di Caprio? The truth is that faith in and love of anything can empower us to manifest what we desire because that is the nature of faith and belief. A serial killer can have faith that he will pull off crime after crime and never get caught! That faith ignites the creativity to plan crimes with full confidence in what the outcome will be. That is their faith! Therefore, they execute all the creative works necessary to make those plans a reality. If you see the full story of Jeffrey Dahmer or Ted Bundy, you will understand the power of a psychopath's faith in what he/she is doing. The man called Jesus allegedly told us as much when he said... *"according to your faith be it unto you"* (**Matthew 9:29**). And thus, every "thing" that is, was manifest according to the power of the creative faith that caused it to be; regardless of what or whom we have faith in.

For faith is the substance of things imagined. It is the "energy" that your creative Self uses to bring things from the ethereal imagination into the physical world. For without imagination and faith, no "thing", would ever come into being! It was the creative mind and powerful will of the "Divine Creator", (whoever or whatever that is), that imagined everything and nothing; creating all. Who or what supplies this power to create something out of nothing? I prescribe that it is the confidence in the belief, working together with self-determination, which cultivates the ethereal "substance" of faith. For faith is the catalyst for turning beliefs and desires into physical existence; whether the belief you have faith in is harmful or helpful. For faith functions through the energy of the Unseen Heart (Inner-Self). The heart, in turn, prompts the Soul (the Outer Self) to action.

In fact, you will not see "faith" until it is evident as "something" in the physical realm. Before it manifests in the physical, it is just a thought in the mind, an idea, a concept, a feeling, or a belief. As confidence in that thought grows, we inner-stand faith as we experience that thought becoming reality. Do you see? The AMI Principle of Being and Becoming is a powerful tool for understanding this transitional manifestation experience, so be sure to visit the AMI website to access this training module. For now, just remember as you proceed on your ascension journey, that you must choose your thoughts, words, and actions wisely. Choose what you will meditate upon and what possibilities you will entertain for "thoughts are things". What you say and do is the evidence of what you think and believe. It is the intensity of those thoughts, and the frequency with which you entertain them, that determines the power or strength of your faith or belief, in anything. The more you say you hate another race of people, for example, the more you will encounter hateful interactions with that race of people; because your faith will make it so. Thus, on the journey of ascension, you manifest what you think in your Mind, speak with your words, believe in your Heart, and pursue with your Soul.

IN CONCLUSION

"So how am I supposed to process all this Michelle" **You**

Frankly that's an answer I cannot force feed you. I took great care to get you to this moment as gently as one can under the circumstances. It's like...when do you tell your adoptive child that he/she is not really your child and that somewhere, out there, is a true parent who loves them. Someone who has been searching for and yearning to connect with them. Well in this case guess who that someone is? That's right, it's the creator of all things coming forth by day and night expressed through you, as you!

Furthermore, how do you explain that some precious truth is hovering over your make-believe world waiting to show itself and set you free? Or how do you decide the right time to tell little Bobby and Suzy that there is no Santa Clause and no Easter Bunny? So how can I tell you, who believe whatever you believe with the utmost convictions about your religion, that what you have been believing in is a fabricated amalgamation of hodgepodge history remnants evolving from the simplest of beginnings. As I told you in chapter three, I am trying to crack open your mind by compelling you to question everything you think you know. I am asking you to open your mind to the possibility that you have been programmed to believe what you believe and that these beliefs have kept you, and centuries of ancestors before you, blind to the truth of real history. It's a classic case of history being written by the conquerors! The victors' job is to take the fruits and spoils of the victory, by force, in the battle for the control of your mind! What better way to seal the deal than by planting an untruth in you to prevent you from discovering the deepest mystery of all...the mystery of YOU!

My goal in this chapter is not to prove that I am an expert on world history, for I most certainly am not. Instead it is to encourage you to conduct your own research and seek until you find the truth. The Universal Truth is that truth does make you free. This is what the man called Jesus said. But to recognize the truth, you must first question everything you think is true and when you discover that truth to be a lie, you must accept, learn, and apply your new reality to your life moving forward.

That is why I have emphasized that "No One Is Coming to Save You." For the truth is, the only one who can save you is You and that salvation begins with knowing the truth. As you proceed you either see or you don't. So, do just that...see or don't see. Because you're either waking up and smelling the poop or choosing to remain asleep. The choice is yours.

CHAPTER ELEVEN

Time to Save Yourself

INTRODUCTION:

It is tantamount to the process of awakening that we deal with this Christianity and salvation doctrine openly and honestly. If, as a result, you come to similar conclusions, then so be it. If you completely reject the information and my point of view, so be it. But you will never be able to say no one told you. For I more than anyone else know how difficult it is to accept the notion that... "Jesus ain't real!" Because I know how deeply the doctrine of salvation was rooted within my reality after my conversion to Christianity at the ripe age of nineteen.

Even that far back, I recognized that I needed saving from something. It would be almost 30 years before I realized, that the "something" I needed to save myself from was my own misguided beliefs! Imagine my dismay when I finally realized that I had the power to save myself all along! Nevertheless, at 19, I still had many questions about my purpose in the world. Though I was not searching for religion when it found me, I was, nevertheless, searching for answers to some of the biggest questions of life. Fortunately, it was my journey through scripture that led me to many universal truths. Concepts like:

"all things work together for good" **Romans 8:28**

"faith is the substance of things hoped for; the evidence of things not seen" (**Hebrews 11:1**)

"trust in the spirit with all your heart, lean to your spiritual understanding. in all your ways acknowledge the spirit and spirit will direct your path" (paraphrased from **Proverbs 3:5 by Michelle Crenshaw**)

"I can do all things through (my divine spirit) which strengthens me" (paraphrased from **Philippians 4:13 by Michelle Crenshaw**

for example, became words that I learned to live by as I applied them to real life situations, struggles and challenges. As I focused, not so much on the doctrine or the history, but rather, the application of the scriptures to daily life, I learned that much of the wisdom therein was reliable, trustworthy and powerfully true. I did not realize at the time, however, that these words of wisdom had existed long before the Christian Era. Neither did I know that most of the wisdom in the Bible came from ancient truths dating back thousands of years BCE.

I also came to trust the general narrative of what I'll call **John 3:16** Christianity:

For God so loved the world, that he gave his only begotten Son, that whosoever believeth in him should not perish, but have everlasting life. **John 3:16**

For, I believed God loved the world, and inspired many to teach us the ways of righteousness, divinity and faith. I also believed that living a righteous life would ultimately "save me" from despair and trials, preparing me for eternal life. I admit, however, that I had a problem with the "only begotten son" part from the start. For are we not all the children of the divine source? Furthermore, as a Black woman raised in the Black Power movement I knew the truth of my African heritage, such as the fact that the original Hebrew speaking people were Black. So, I decided early on that *"Jesus is real"* is only okay if we admit that the real Jesus, if there ever was one, was most certainly, a Black Man! It was a reasonable conclusion since I learned, early on, that the accomplishments, inventions, and discoveries of many Black men and women had been misrepresented or completely disguised as White folks' achievements for centuries. I figured the system had, quite likely, misrepresented the identity of this man we called Jesus as well. But because, back then, I studied the Bible as though it were historical as well as spiritual, I failed to catch the many clues that would later be identified as plagiarisms and worse, out and out lies.

The uncomfortable truth is that most organized religions are just that...organized! It does not matter which one you pick. You can rest assured that every religion has been organized for a purpose that serves the one(s) who created it in the first place. As you will see in the following pages: the Egyptians, Persians, and Greeks were all conquering nations of antiquity; as were the Romans, the Roman Catholic Church, the Muslims, the Huns, the Mongols, the Khazars, the Aryans, and many others. All these nations had the same agenda: to conquer and control. For whenever you conquer a foreign enemy, you must have a system in place that empowers you to control them. That is one reason many ancient cultures killed all the men when they conquered an enemy. Forcing the conquered to convert to the religion of the conqueror was, therefore, simply a necessity of warring nations.

DO YOUR OWN RESEARCH & THINK FOR YOURSELF

Believe whatever you want, but I'm here to tell you...If you really want to ascend spiritually, you are going to have to let go of your entanglement with organized religions. For organized religion is a device of man, not

God. Furthermore, if you truly want to save yourself, you'll have to accept that, your church experience making you feel good, does not negate the fact that it was originally designed to control and imprison you. I am not speaking here of Father Joe or Reverend Johnson. I am referring to the founding institutions of organized religions around the globe.

This is the true, yet often hidden, agenda of organized religions: *to promulgate a doctrine that will efficiently and effectively guide your thinking toward perpetual dependence upon the organization that is preaching that doctrine.*

The goal being to prevent you from ever growing and experiencing yourself as the complete, independent, infinite spirit being that you are and were always meant to be.

Just think...if we all suddenly realized our individual and collective power and creativity, the world as we know it would instantly become something far too expansive, spectacular and utterly divine for us to comprehend in this current earthly hologram. I hope to be a catalyst for such change in the world. Furthermore, I believe this book sets each reader on a journey of infinite possibilities, creative expressions, and mindful actions for change and collective ascension. I believe we all should, and can, harness the divine energy that is us. For together, we have the power to experience the fullness of One, Divine, Universal Spirit. Or, you can just continue to wait for the "God" of your understanding to come and save you. But before you decide please ask yourself... is this current socio-political religious paradigm working for you?...for us? Then, ask yourself *"are you growing, or are you dying?"* More significantly, "are WE growing, or are WE dying? The saddest part of the "savior" theology plan is that while you are waiting for a savior to return, the very salvation power you seek is already in you and... is You! How ironic?!

PLEASE PAUSE FOR YOUR 10 MINUTE MOMENT

CHAPTER TWELVE

Self-Diagnosis (Part 1): The First Awakening

"Let me tell you why you're here. You're here because you know something. What you know, you can't explain. But you feel it. You've felt it your entire life. That there's something wrong in the world. You don't know what it is but it's there, like a splinter in your mind driving you mad. It is this feeling that brought you to me. Do you know what I'm talking about?"

Morpheus-from the film **The Matrix**; Dir. Lana Wachowski, Andy Wachowski

One of the hardest tasks I've ever undertaken in the awakening process was my attempt at self-diagnosis of my own socio-emotional psychosis. Sure, I understood that the system was messed up. But this awareness also forced me to reconcile with the fact that I was, subsequently, a by-product of that messed up system and therefore also, most likely, messed up. The pill is even harder to swallow if you begin the process of awakening while simultaneously in aggressive hamster wheel pursuit of the success carrot; which I was.

Now since most people in the system are conditioned to function at a rather high level of stress and an underlying presence of low self-esteem, it is simply too paralyzing for most of us to look in the mirror and accept ourselves as being any more messed up than we already perceive we are. It's kind of like hitting rock bottom in an addiction lifestyle. For you've been going full steam ahead with your addiction to the current mental paradigm for so long, you don't even recognize that you've been hurting yourself and others along the way. Coming to this rock bottom awareness, however, is essential to the first awakening.

I liken this experience to being in an awful nightmare in which giant spiders are chasing you. You run and you run, your breathing becomes more and more shallow, your heart rate is accelerated, and you are certain of your eminent demise. Then, somehow, just in the nick of time you realize...hey, I'm dreaming! and then you consciously wake yourself up just before the spiders eat you!

REFLECTIONS ON ASCENSION
HOOKED ON THE SYSTEM

Earlier in Chapter One, I stated that at my first awakening I had to "face the truth that my life was out of control, no longer manageable and self-destructive in nature." This choice of words was purposeful because I wanted to give you a foreshadowing of where the true awakening begins; which is…at rock bottom. Well, that's just more of that 12-Step mumbo jumbo, right? Yes, that's right. I am most certainly likening this journey from mental bondage to self-empowerment to the process which recovering addicts use to start letting go of their addiction. That process begins by first admitting and owning the fact that you are, in fact, hooked; hence the AA introduction: My Name is XYZ and I'm an alcoholic.

The truth is, we are all a product of the sum-total of our "history". Furthermore, we can agree that we didn't just wake up today and realize we were addicted to pushing too much, coveting the success of others too much, running after possessions and shopping too much, eating too much, wasting too much, striving too much, stressing too much, etc., etc. Yes.

Deep down inside we know that we are fully wired to the System in almost every aspect of our lives, though our cognitive dissonance kicks against the prick to deny it. No matter what we do, we cannot seem to break free from the tell-lie vision, the media, the internet, the miseducation and the political side show, just for starters. Visual and aural stimuli blare into our psyche urging us to buy this, eat that, go here, be there, think this way, don't think that way, care about this, pay no attention to that...and on and on in an unending barrage of socio-emotional behavioral conditioning experiences.

Sure, we like our old toilet paper, but we've simply got to get the "new and improved"; never once questioning if the "new" one is any more "improved" than the one we'd come to know and love. Droves of people standing in line, with baited-breath like crack fiends as they anticipate the fix from the next I-Phone #472, is just one of many examples of this Systemic Syndrome running amuck in modern society. As we are in constant pursuit of things that appeal to our senses and emotions, we are caught up in a systemically induced emotional relationship with our stuff, which only drives us harder to pursue more stuff just to satisfy our addictive nature.

I love my better car, my bigger house, my more stylish clothes, my better body and even my richer spouse. Yes, we are all putting our energy into somehow outdoing our next-door neighbor, our colleague, ourselves, and even some unidentifiable persona we endearingly refer to as success. Let's face it... The System has us hooked. Hooked...from genetically modified meals to generationally modified religious and social constructs, we are without exception hooked on the things of this world. If you think you're not "hooked", just look around the room you're sitting in as you read this paragraph. Now ask yourself how much of your stuff you'd be willing to part with today, right now. Could you live without your phone, your computer, your television, your car, your nice clothes, your favorite television show, and all the rest of your stuff? I simply must pause to laugh out loud here LOL.

I remember the feelings of anxiety I experienced when I first decided it was time to break up with my "stuff". You see, I had pondered it for a while, so I believed it would be an easy enough thing to do. After all, I had been in awakening mode for quite some time, I thought. There was no reason I should have anxiety about getting rid of my stuff because I was ascending, right? And in my mind, I understood the need to let go of things and could intellectually pontificate on that subject. It's like the first time an addict tries to quit using their drug of choice. Or better yet, like giving up something for Lent (that's a little easier to identify with if you, like me, have never been an addict).

The first day on the wagon seems easy. "I can do this" you say to yourself. But in a few days, the urge to reconnect with that thing, that feeling… that mocha latte… that helped you find your comfort zone, grows stronger and stronger. And before you know it, you're standing in Starbucks waiting to hear your name called by the barista to satisfy that craving you swore you could fend off for 6 weeks, until Easter! And likewise, as our addiction to our stuff continues over the years, we constantly say... "I don't even need this stuff", knowing full well that you do! And you stay in denial about your addiction until the day you must throw that stuff you've come to know and love in the trash, or the Goodwill bin, etc. Please note that the practice of letting go of our stuff, as well as, identifying and letting go of thoughts which no longer serve us, is strongly encouraged as the first step in spiritual ascension.

For now, it's the addiction issue on which I wish to focus; specifically, the addiction to The System. Once you wake up enough to realize that you are hooked on all these systemic entrapments, i.e. your thought processes, beliefs, values, concepts of reality, social traditions, and addiction to stuff, etc., you then have to come to terms with the fact that your addiction has you by the throat and you are, therefore, not at all in control of your own life nor most of the decisions that you are making. Furthermore, you are most likely acting out of systemic programming that has been in place in your life almost from birth. Now that's an unmanageable state if ever I saw one.

Then, once you accept that this systemic addiction is designed to entrap you in behaviors that tear down rather than build up your mind, spirit, body and soul, the self-destructive nature of the addiction can no longer be denied. This, my friend, is the beginning of the beginning of your healing and your ascension; here, at this junction where you first realize and acknowledge that you need to wake up because you are not in control of your thoughts, your mind and many of your own actions. Here is where the real work to heal yourself begins. Here, you start to understand that you must now *"unlearn what you have learned"*. Yes, you must *"question everything"* that you have been taught, told, and shown; here, at rock bottom. Here, at **The First Awakening.**

AN INTRODUCTION TO THE FIRST AWAKENING

How did you come to believe what you now believe...about life, love, friendship, decency, honor, integrity, sin, miracles, right, wrong, hate, marriage, sex, sexuality, communication, self-esteem, humility, family, values, tradition, culture, and righteousness...and the list goes on? Who told you what it means to be a republican, or democrat, rich or poor, or to be considered a success or failure? Have you ever questioned why you perform tasks the way you do, why you perceive certain people the way you do, and why you fear that which you do not understand or those who appear to be different? How deeply embedded are these beliefs and perceptions? More importantly, are my beliefs and behaviors a product of my choices and true desires or have I been subconsciously conditioned to think, feel, believe, and view the world and others the way I do? These are serious and fundamental questions that any self-aware being should at least ask as life progresses. And these are questions that, once asked and answered, become pivotal in determining our mental, physical, and spiritual awareness.

For if we are at a point of rock bottom, we are most likely at a point of despair. No one who is truly happy is unclear about how they got there. And most people who are struggling emotionally or spiritually, or feeling disappointed or disenfranchised with life, are, in contrast, completely unclear about how they got there…until such questions are asked and ultimately answered. That is why we must first "wake up" the patient! We need to know where you've been, what you've been feeding on, what "addictions" you may have and which "medications" you might be taking. First and foremost, we need to know your vital signs.

So, get ready for a jolt with this next exercise in letting go. It will challenge your self-view and hopefully awaken something within you that quickens your desire to think for yourself for a change. And you won't start thinking for yourself if you don't ask the right questions. Enjoy the following questionnaire. It is imperative that you are 100% honest with yourself. Remember…if you lie to yourself, you are your own worst enemy. If you answer truthfully, you are your own best friend.

JOURNAL EXERCISE

1. Make a list of the five most important elements of your life (in order of most important to least important). Why are each of these life elements important to you? At what age did they become important to you?
2. Complete the Self Awareness Questionnaire provided in the Appendix of this book

CHAPTER THIRTEEN

Self-Diagnosis (Part 2): Check Your Vital Signs

Let's continue our self-diagnosis by examining the vital signs of the patient. Here in the metaphysical ER, the first area of our attention is **The Unseen Heart** (*The Inner Self*), followed closely by **The Mind** (*Ethereal Processor & Storage Center*), **The Will** (*The Transformer of thoughts and emotions into action*) and finally, **The Soul** (*Actions & Behaviors driven by the amalgamated energy of the Mind, Heart, & Will*). We also cannot forget the Spirit; that invisible, ("Divine Energy Life Force") which is present in all creation.

THE UNSEEN HEART (*The Inner Self*)

If your heart is like that of most people, it has been formed by an innumerable host of experiences, thoughts, ideas and choices, which have shaped it into whatever condition it is in today. Most agree that the heart of a person is much more than the physical life pump that keeps the body animated from heartbeat to heartbeat. From a spiritual perspective, the Unseen Heart is that deepest, innermost, part of a person which:

1. commandeers or abandons the thoughts of the mind
2. defines and generates the desires and passions of the will
3. dictates the emotional behaviors of the soul

For the purposes of this exploration in spiritual ascension, the Unseen Heart is defined as: *the amalgamated essence of the individual, or the Self.* As such, the heart is the intangible dwelling place for virtue and vice, guilt and innocence, fear and faith, love and hate, hope and despair, wisdom and folly, understanding and ignorance. The heart houses our self-esteem, self-determination, and self-awareness and in contrast, the lack of same. In the heart, our personal truth and conscience is established. The heart is indeed a vast cauldron of impressions, understandings, questions, conclusions, doubts, fears, concerns, joys, sorrows, loves and so on. As such, it is the most influenced and influential, esoteric part of who we are, and it is as essential to life as the physical heart.

For it is here, in the Unseen Heart, that the true nature of a person is established; consciously or otherwise. The heart seeks and finds, convicts and affirms, imagines and blocks-out, hesitates and forges ahead, lusts and shuns, serves and harms. In this unseen incubator, the cumulative beliefs and values of the individual are processed and formulated into an amalgamated awareness of "Self" which is, our conscience. I define the conscience as: ***"the conscious impression within the Inner Self of all things and experiences, whether tangible or intangible".*** As the finished product of this inner process, the conscience, therefore, rules how we feel and how we see the world.

The intentions and condition of the Unseen Heart of every being is manifest (seen and demonstrated) through the person's Soul, or behavior. As a result, the tendency is that "good-hearted" people usually act with goodness, and "hard-hearted" people generally treat others with harshness. Contrary to some opinions, you are who/what you act like, regardless of your stated good intentions. As the adage goes… *you can make your mouth say anything!*

But, let's face it. No one wants to be viewed as mean, uncompassionate, unforgiving, heartless or spiritually corrupt if they truly believe they are a "good" person. Nevertheless, if you keep saying you're a "good person" yet commit harmful acts, toward yourself or others, I would certainly suggest you take a full diagnostic of your

Spiritual Cardiovascular System (SCS) before dismissing feedback you may be getting from others regarding how you behave in the world. As we all know, there are many people who see themselves in a completely different light than their actions indicate. I suppose it is difficult, at times, to reconcile our intentions with our behavior. Nevertheless, behavior is the barometer of the Self. In other words, if multiple people keep telling you you're an asshole…you are probably behaving like one!

Thus, the Mind feeds thoughts and the interpretation of our personal experiences, through the Unseen Heart for the formation of the conscience. Just as the physical heart pumps blood through the physical body, animating the outer-self, the Unseen Heart pumps consciousness through the inner-Self in the form of beliefs, values, and personal reality. Here, in the Unseen Heart, our fears or strengths, hopes or doubts, disappointments or triumphs, determination or hesitation, self-esteem or self-loathing, self-awareness or disassociation, cognitive dissonance or harmony, anxieties or reassurances, are established as the Inner Self. This Inner Self is then expressed in the physical world through our behaviors and are observed, measured and interpreted as a barometer of who we truly are.

As the conscious or unconscious impression of all things and experiences, the Unseen Heart, like the physical heart, goes on, even when it is fatigued or distressed; because it exists with that person until the Spirit or life-energy leaves the physical body. As the conscience of the Self, the Unseen Heart is also the dwelling place of wisdom or folly, knowledge or ignorance, consciousness or unconsciousness, character and integrity or, deceitfulness and depravity. Since we are clear on the function of the Unseen Heart, we can make a closer examination of The Mind, since it is the place from which all information in the heart originates. Just as we get an annual physical, we should also make a full diagnostic of our ethereal heart health for a more balanced Self.

THE MIND
THE ETHEREAL ENERGY PROCESSOR

> *"I must not fear. Fear is the mind killer. Fear is the little-death that brings total obliteration. I will face my fear. I will permit it to pass over me and through me. And when it has gone past, I will turn the inner eye to see its path. Where the fear has gone there will be nothing. Only I will remain."* From the chronicles of **Dune (Book 1) by Frank Herbert**

The Mind, like the heart, is also an unseen yet very apparent realm wherein we view, choose, process, and create our thoughts and ideas. Through the intangible processes of the mind, we have the potential to access an infinite variety of thoughts and ideas which exist in the Universal Mind of all Creation. These thoughts exist in the infinite energy field of what some call, the Akashic Records or the Akashic Field. In the Akashic Field, every thought that ever was, exists; for it holds the collective mind of all that ever was. As such, the Akashic Field or the Universal Mind as some call it, is also the unseen imagination where all things are infinitely possible. It is the stuff from whence the "substance of things hoped for" (**Hebrews 11:11**) originates. Because the Akashic Field contains all thoughts and ideas, accessing it through the Inner Self can be overwhelming because navigating an ethereal realm of infinite thoughts can be a difficult task to manage. That is why the Heart must assist with helping the Mind choose wisely; choosing which thoughts to entertain and which to discard.

The Mind establishes who we are. As French philosopher **Rene Descartes** (1596-1650) reminds us: *"I think, therefore, I am"*.

> *"But …I observed that, whilst I thus wished to think that all was false, it was absolutely necessary that I, who thus thought, should be somewhat; and as I observed that this truth, I think, therefore I am (cogito ergo sum), was so certain of such evidence that no ground of doubt, however extravagant, could be alleged by the sceptics capable of shaking it, I concluded that I might, without scruple, accept it as the first principle of the philosophy of which I was in search"* **Rene Descartes**

Thus, the ethereal realm of The Universal Mind is where the seeds of our beliefs begin.

Figuratively, I describe the realm of the infinitely Universal Mind as a "train" of thought that carries an infinite array of thoughts, ideas and concepts; which may be perceived in a wide variety of ways. These possibilities will be interpreted as either, good or bad, right or wrong, foolish or wise, useful or harmful; depending on all the other formative factors, which I mentioned earlier, that shape our belief paradigm.

I like the imagery of an infinite train of infinite thoughts because it helps me to remember that the creative imagination of the Mind is infinite and eternal. It is as old and vast and deep as the Universe itself. It also helps me remember that as I peruse the thought train, I have the right to choose my thoughts; whether I exercise that right or not. This imagery also reminds me that it is my responsibility to consciously choose; that is, if I want to avoid adopting thoughts that are harmful or that no longer serve my best interests. This awareness of choice is particularly important when we consider that all our thoughts, whether consciously chosen or not, can and will be influenced by previous thoughts, beliefs, experiences, and understandings that exist in our subconscious awareness. Furthermore, because our subconscious "mind conductors" function behind the scenes, they can and usually will, strongly impede our ability to make conscious choices in opposition to them.

With practice, however, we can train ourselves to consciously choose what we will think and believe. Either way, the thoughts we choose, consciously or otherwise, will be established in our conscience (Unseen Heart), and expressed through our desires (the Will) as well as our actions (the Soul). In this "choice center", the heart and mind converge to make decisions about what we will create in the physical world and most importantly, how we will behave toward others in the material world. If you wish to ascend or change your thinking, you must learn to choose what you will think; for thoughts become things and actions in the physical world. So, the next time you entertain a passing thought, I recommend you refrain from taking possession of it without scrutiny. If you don't, it will take root in your heart, be experienced in your emotions, and become apparent in your expressed behavior.

A perfect example of this process is seen in the mental condition of fear. When a person grasps hold of fear, that fear is deposited into the heart and is experienced in the emotions as anxiety, stress and discomfort. Out of that emotion of discomfort, the behavior of a fearful person can become antagonistic, defensive or even violent; thus, debilitating the person's mental, physical and spiritual health. Yes, fear starts as a harmless thought because before you choose it, fear is as powerless as any other thought passing by on the thought train of life.

ASCENSION AND THE TRAIN OF THOUGHT

As an always awakening spirit, it is imperative that you recognize that your thought train is an external presence in the ethereal realm. I say that it is external from the Inner-Self because, as we exist now, we can neither contain nor comprehend all the energy of all the creative thoughts of I AM from the "beginning", if there be such a thing, to eternity. This train is in constant movement across the "tracks" of the One (Universal Mind). It is only upon choosing and then, mentally interacting with a thought as it passes, that the thought can and may merge with your personal mind to become a part of your collective "Self". This fusion of thought and Self naturally occurs when you choose to entertain a thought. Now this thought, which you are thinking of in your Mind, can and will integrate with the rest of your being; within the Heart, Soul, Body and Spirit. Once again... *"I think, therefore, I am"* **Rene Descartes**

It's sort of like that trip to Disneyland. When you arrive, every form of entertainment the park has to offer is available to you. Nevertheless, it is you who decides which rides or foods or shows you wish to experience. As a single mother, I'm sure I overlooked many of the attractions purely due to the cost I'd have to pay for entertaining three children as well as myself. Each time I visited the theme park, I left knowing that I had not experienced all that it had to offer. In this way, the Disneyland experience is analogous to our interaction with the Thought Train by demonstrating how attraction and choice determine one's personal experience of reality. Some enjoy the food, some the kiddy rides, some the music concerts and others the thrill rides. Like Disneyland, the Thought Train offers thoughts that make us happy, some that give us a thrill, some that scare us half to death and others that just make us plain sick to the stomach!

Ancient texts teach us that wisdom enters the heart when we are receptive to knowledge and, when that knowledge is pleasant to us. Receptivity to new thoughts and ideas, then, is key to spiritual ascension. That's because without openness to new information you are more likely to choose the same, or similar, thoughts that merely reinforce your existing perception of the world. Furthermore, because of this commitment to sameness, you are also more likely to vehemently reject any new information, unfamiliar thoughts, concepts, and ideas which conflict with your established beliefs and values. Once limiting, or even harmful, thoughts and beliefs take hold in your heart as your truth, the mind simply blocks the capacity to choose; as rigid thinking patterns become "normal". If this kind of normal thinking goes unchecked within the Self, we can certainly understand how resolute thinking might hinder us mentally, emotionally, and spiritually.

Such is the case with many who suffer from severe depression or other complex psychological disorders. Here, understanding the operation of what I call the mental stalemate, helps us see why some mental illnesses are so difficult to overcome. In the case of the psychopath, for example, who cannot perceive their own violent or destructive behavior as "wrong", the lack of empathy, which empowers one to see from another person's emotional perspective, impairs their capacity to change the way they think, as well as their desire to do so. There is, after all, nothing wrong with their psychopathic thoughts, and therefore, no need to change them, right? Similarly, the sociopath, who has learned deviant behavior through experiential learning, loses the capacity to change their behavior as the sociopathic mental stalemate keeps them stuck in a loop of destructive behavior toward themselves and others. Both instances provide clear examples of how rigid thinking can be harmful to the Inner and Outer Self.

In another example, Mary, an anorexic, thinks: "*I'm not beautiful because I'm fat*". But Mary is clearly not fat to those observing her from the outside. Nevertheless, she believes she is fat and therefore, any therapy geared toward convincing her that she is not only thin but ill, is ineffective! Thus, for the anorexic, "I'm fat" becomes the norm of her reality, even though that reality is not based in the observable truth. Now Mary's harmful "normal", plays out in the outer world as illness of the mind and body. Mary is living in a mental, spiritual, emotional and behavioral prison where new information is nearly impossible for her to hear or accept. When such crippling thoughts take hold, the ascension process is halted until Mary unlearns what she has learned and chooses to think in a new and very different way.

MORE ON CHOICE

Once you choose a thought and you plant it in your heart, nothing else looks good to you. It's like falling in love with someone who is no good for you. Once you choose that person, no one can tell you to let them go. Eventually, and usually after much trepidation of the soul and emotions, a person may, eventually, see the relationship as harmful. Unfortunately, this revelation often doesn't even arise until the person has endured much sadness, disappointment and sometimes, even physical abuse.

The point here is, our choices, subconscious or conscious, helpful or harmful, feel normal to us. It is particularly true when we review beliefs and world views that are passed down generationally such as: political alliances, religious affiliations or lifestyle practices. These values often become more rigid because they are so deeply imbedded in our hearts that choice seems almost non-existent; I'm a Republican, I'm a Democrat, I'm a Christian, I'm a Muslim, I'm a Mason, I'm a Lakers fan, and the list goes on and on. Yes, many are living with their thoughts, beliefs, values etc. in auto-pilot mode with very little awareness that they are not consciously choosing to be the person they are...they just "are". The challenge of an always ascending mind is to recognize that every belief must be reviewed through the eyes of the Conscious Observer. Furthermore, the lens through which that belief is observed must factor in the variable of pre-existing beliefs, which must be reconciled before any new and/or potentially conflicting thought or idea may be introduced, entertained or considered.

Contrary to what many seem to believe, your thoughts alone are not you. They do become attached to you, however, once you grab hold to them and take them as your own. The thought to hurt someone, for example, may "cross your mind" but it does not become a part of you until you choose that thought, meditate upon it, and allow it to take root within the Unseen Heart.

So here we are at the part of the book where you should be completely honest with yourself about what you think, what you feel, what you believe, and most importantly, how you behave. If your goal is to grow spiritually, you cannot pretend with yourself under any circumstances. You cannot pretend that you've got this part of your inner life under control if you know you are, as they say, a hot mess when the rubber meets the road. If you're a good person…you engage in good deeds. If you know you want to be a compassionate person, for example, but you run from those who need that compassion, you are fooling yourself only; for the Heart knows the Mind of the Spirit. And the heart knows when you are an imposter. And if you engage in one singular act of compassion by feeding the homeless once a year on Thanksgiving, yes, I'm talking to you! How many times have we heard a person who speaks with a mind/heart/soul conflict like Paul? The mantra of these folk sort of goes like this:

EXAMPLE: *"You know I'd really like to volunteer to help the homeless, but I just don't have the time. I know I'm a good person and I want to do those kinds of good things, but I just can't find the time. I feel so bad about it because, as you know, I'm a really good person and in my heart, I really want to do that".*

The truth of the matter is, however, that human beings usually do the things they "really want to do". And when you *really want to do* anything, you usually figure out a way to do it. You really want to eat every day so, most of the time, you will make sure you eat every day. If you want to go out to the club and dance the night away with friends, you will do that as well. Because by nature, we do what we "really want to do", not what we need to do. If the person quoted above is saying she/he wants to help the homeless, but they are not actually doing it, this means they do not really want to do it. A very hard pill to swallow, I know. **Selah**

See the dilemma here is that helping sounds like a good idea on the thought train. But since you haven't chosen this thought as your own and planted it in your heart, your soul cannot manifest that outcome in your behavior.

> *"To manifest any thought, you must choose it and let it take root in your Heart. The Heart, in turn, ignites the Will, which prompts your Soul to action."* **Michelle Crenshaw**

CHOOSING YOUR THOUGHTS

Initially, your thoughts are not you. You must comprehend this because, the thought train is full of thoughts that are both compatible and incompatible with your conscience (heart). When someone hurts you and you think for a moment that you want to hurt them in return, for example, that thought has no power until you choose it and plant it in your heart. Once planted, that thought now has the power to dictate how you feel and, more significantly, how you behave. The key is in the choosing.

But how can one choose what one thinks about? To anyone who does not consciously choose what they think about, this proposition is absurd. This is when Systemic Syndrome kicks in; because we have been conditioned to believe that we cannot control what we think. In truth, the engineers of the Global Control System know very well that we <u>can</u> choose what we decide to think about and meditate upon. Therefore, they made sure to create advertising, marketing and propaganda to control what the masses of people hear, and subsequently, think. Since you're reading this book, you already know that the media is built to implant thoughts in our minds and to condition us to act upon the ideas planted there via this medium.

They also know that if we hear a thought enough times, we will embrace it and act upon it even if it is untrue. That truth really pisses me off to be honest because even though people comprehend this tactic intellectually, most are still manipulated by the barrage of media assault.

> *Blessed is the one who does not walk in the counsel of the wicked, nor stand in the path of sinners, nor sit in the seat of scoffers. But his delight is in the law of God and in that law does s/he meditate day and night"* **Psalms 1:1**

Yes, you choose what you meditate upon; what you ponder. Subsequently, this pondering manifests in our day to day lives. If you are overrun by negative thoughts that take root in your heart, the thoughts can drain you of the "nutrients" needed to keep the Self in balance. Now that you know this, I suggest you begin guarding your mind and questioning your beliefs immediately. The **Self Awareness Questionnaire** (*see Appendix*) will help you get started with this much needed process.

THE SPIRIT-SOUL: LIFE FORCE OF THE SELF

> *"Through pain, joy, sorrow, conscience and perceptions the core of the person is established."* **Michelle Crenshaw**

The Spirit is the life energy of the Universe, expressed as all things. Known in ancient metaphysics as the Chi, Ki or Kundalini, the Universal Spirit (Creation Energy) expresses itself as both the **S**ingular **E**nergy **L**ife **F**orce, or SELF, and, the Universal Life Force that is, was and ever shall be. Thus, there is no Self without the Spirit-Soul and there is no Soul without the Self. Through the Soul we become "individual" persons. Likewise, the SELF, empowered and informed by the Universal Energy of the Spirit-Soul, expresses itself through the duality of universal and singular awareness. What that singular expression looks like is as unique as the individual, inclusive of all the perceptions, choices, beliefs and values which make the Self unique. The presence of the Soul and the Spirit in One, creates individuals who are uniquely different and yet, universally the same.

We can think of the Spirit-Soul as the life force, or the energy plant that empowers and animates the Self to exist in the first place. As such, this life force is the power source for each uniquely different Self. Collectively that same Kundalini energy flows through the entire universal body (or soul) of creation.

I AM SALVATION AND SIN

I now find it interesting that Christians (and other faith traditions) adhere so strongly to the concept of souls needing saving. If anything, it is the Self, or rather, the Mind of the Self, that probably needs to be delivered from the bondage of mental imprisonment. But I suppose, if we perceive good and evil as separate forces in opposition, rather than polar energies working in operational cooperation with each other, the notion that the Soul or the Self needs saving is understandable. If, however, I believe "I AM" is everything that exists and everything that does not exist, simultaneously, there should be no judgement in the universal collective.

I AM is all things, therefore, I AM predator and prey, victor and victim, darkness and light, good and evil, positive and negative, and so on. Scientifically, the Universe is in a constant state of resistant energies (positive & negative) manifested in the ever-expanding galaxies and at the most minute energy level. Quantum physicists have discovered that the cell, the atom and now the quan are all mini universes of resistance within themselves. If this universal resistance is a sin, then the entire Universe is one hell of a sinful place! What a miracle of Creation!

I believe the biblical parable of the Tree of the Knowledge of Good and Evil captures the metaphoric duality of the I AM life force that exists in all things. I also believe that acting in the world without balance, leaning more toward one pole than the other, prevents the Self from inner-standing the power and the peace of the universal duality that dwells within us. Recognizing this dual dynamic as a normal operation of the Universe removes the perception of "sinfulness" which begs the need for "salvation". Our goal, as individual selves is to find balance in this duality, so the Spirit and the Soul can coexist in cooperation to manifest the power of the entire Universe through each individual Self. Once this harmony and balance is reached, the need for salvation of the Soul becomes moot.

The Soul is, therefore, much more than just the seat of the emotions, as it has been called. For the realm of the emotions is as vast as the Universe itself. Therefore, the "seat" would also have to be a limitless vortex of energy! For humanity, experiencing creation through the limitations of time, space and matter has also limited our comprehension of I AM. For when we take an objective view of our outward self-expressions (behavior), we can trace them back to the root causes of our inner dis-ease. In so doing, we are simultaneously empowered to change those outer expressions of our inner thoughts, understandings, and spiritual conscience with a conscious choice rather than a *devil made me do it* approach to living. So, can we really say that a newborn infant enters the world with "original sin"? God Forbid! For it is after conception that the tape starts rolling and external influences begin forming our understanding of Self. I happen to believe all Spirits Being Human arrive in the outer world full of all divine energies. More importantly, I believe we all enter this realm by choice and, we express our Self by choice, eternally.

Furthermore, I would suggest that it is not our divine, universal souls that need saving but rather, our minds and our perception of the purpose of this duality that we must address from day to day. For, we well know that we are not what we hope to be, but rather, what we do. If I say I'm a kind person but I behave unkindly, I am having an experience of cognitive dissonance, and I AM deceiving my own Self. I AM also behaving as though I have a split personality and, more importantly, as if I have no choice in how I behave. Therein lies the dissonance, for I do have a choice. And I know, deep down that either I AM choosing to act in ways which are inconsistent with my intentions or, I AM choosing to deny what I know about myself, which is that: I am not a kind person! If I proceed without that acknowledgement, I AM simply lying to myself and the outer world. Now my Singular Energy Life Force (SELF) is struggling with the Universal Life Force that causes me to exist in the first place.

If there is a sin, it exists not in some mysterious realm of the unknown where "something" is making me do egregious things, but rather, it exists in my unwillingness to change my thinking and behavior. Furthermore, telling myself over and over again that I just "can't get right" by some fault of the unknown, the "devil" or "sin", puts me in a perpetual state of denial about the spiritual condition of my Inner Self and my own culpability in contributing to that condition by denying that my lack of self-discipline is the problem. I think the man referred to as the Apostle Paul articulates this mental condition quite well in his letter to the Romans:

> *"For we know that the law is spiritual: but I am carnal, sold under sin. For that which I do I allow not: for what I would, that do I not; but what I hate, that I do. If then I do that which I would not, I consent unto the law that it is good. Now then it is no more I that do it, but sin that dwelleth in me. For I know that in me (that is, in my flesh,) dwelleth no good thing; for to will is present with me; but how to perform that which is good I find not. For the good that I would I do not: but the evil which I would not, that I do. Now if I do that I would not, it is no more I that do it, but sin that dwelleth in me. I find then a law, that, when I would do good, evil is present with me. For I delight in the law of God after the inward man: But I see another law in my members, warring against the law of my mind, and bringing me into captivity to the law of sin which is in my members. O wretched man that I am! Who shall deliver me from the body of this death? I thank God through Jesus Christ our Lord. So then with the mind I myself serve the law of God; but with the flesh the law of sin."* **Romans 7:14 - 7:25**

Paul's description here is a clear indication of mental illness by today's standard and yet most Christians interpret these statements with a sense of familiarity that says: *Hey Paul, I can identify with your struggle!*. The sheer fact that he emphasizes this disconnect between himself and his actions (sin) is enough to diagnose a case of mental disassociation. Paul states: *"then it is no more I that do it, but sin that dwelleth in me"*. Sin in this context may as well be capitalized, as he describes "sin" as having a mind and a will of its own. Who is this Sin? My goodness! Now he has a split personality to boot! The reality, however, is that what you're really saying is *I'm mentally ill just like you Paul so I must be normal!* Sure, we can fluff it all up and add some religious exegesis and say that Paul was being very deep and insightful about the dichotomy of human nature. But the truth is that Paul himself is admitting that he cannot find harmony and balance between his thinking, his conscience, and his actions.

The problem I have with accepting this train of thought as normal is that it forever gives Christians an excuse for bad behavior. Sin made me do it or "the devil" made me do it is a common place reason given when we miss the mark for good behavior. The result is a weak-minded approach to Christianity that placates the Christian's failure to manifest intentions of goodness, peace, and compassion into actions that are the same. Moreover, the idea of sinful beings trapped in sinful behavior does a huge disservice to the power of the Creator Spirit living in, and as, all of us. All of us in theory at least, should have the innate ability to summon that Creator Spirit energy to manifest the good, as Spirit-Beings having a human experience. It's a hard pill to swallow but as I've said throughout the book, No One is Coming to Save You! Therefore, I suggest you get busy coming to an inner-standing of balance and harmony between You, your Self, and your divine, eternal, Spirit! Selah

AGREEMENT OF THE INNER AND OUTER SELF

Herein lies the conundrum of the battle of the Inner Self (the Unseen Heart) and the Outer Self (the Soul) as well as the seemingly, perpetual disconnect between these two forces. The confusion begins with the arduous task of training the Mind, the Heart, and the Soul to function in a cohesive and complimentary fashion to express the inner-Self in the outer-world. Unlike Paul, I believe the disassociated mental condition he describes is neither normal, nor acceptable behavior for the Always Ascending Mind. This book is about saving yourself. I am of the belief that far too many people have used this passage of scripture and many others to explain, condone, or justify why they can't, or won't, deal with the inner resistance that causes this behavioral confusion. Paul's perspective is that we cannot help this condition because the Spirit and the flesh are at war and that's just how we are made. I do not believe our Divine Source creates in this manner of confusion. For everything in the Universe has an order to it...right down to the smallest un-observably observable unit! Nor, do I believe we must accept this inner conflict as a normal, and unavoidable, condition of being human. For all is one with the Universe and all is well in the Universe. It would take a very cruel Creator to deliberately make us with such an inner and outer conflict!

I believe the "flesh" Paul references is the outward evidence of the influence of the Divine Spirit, or absence thereof, upon the Mind, Heart, and Self, expressed by the Soul. I also believe that influence is subject to the choices we make and not the evidence of some law of nature that cannot be subdued. For what Paul refers to as carnal sin is predicated by choice, not law. We all have the choice and responsibility to decide what we will think and what we will do. Once we recognize that our Spirit is a singular extension of all creation energy, we have a sharper image of the potential that is in us and, is us! Just as one strand of hair (The Self) exists, as One, within the totality of what we would call our "hair", (The Universe).

Because that collective life force is in all of us and, is us, simultaneously, we are always empowered to live as our truest and purest Divine Self. This means we don't have to be a prisoner of "sin" nor prisoners of collective dis-ease. In addition, I believe the Spirit is who and what we were before our singular energy was injected into this physical dimension. Thus, the Universal Soul of the Spirit exists within us as a power unencumbered by the limitations of the human condition. It is my belief and goal that through implementing the Ascending Mind™ spiritual practices, you will come to experience the freedom of Self-Awareness and Choice. With freedom and choice also comes an internal peace which keeps the Heart, Mind, Soul and Spirit working in full agreement and harmony in your inner & outer life. The Ascending Mind Principle of "Spirit Being Human", found on the Ascending Mind website, addresses this relationship in more detail.

CHAPTER FOURTEEN

Change is Good

> *"Revolution…Complete, Constructive, Change!"* **Khalid Muhammad**

INTRODUCTION

As I ascend, I notice that Spirit emphasizes the need to expect, welcome, and embrace change. There was a time when I, like most, found the idea of change an unwelcomed interruption of my emotional and intellectual comfort. Accordingly, the abhorrence of change, because of what change requires of us, is quite common among most people. As one who has struggled with weight for most of my life, I understand how difficult the pursuit of complete, constructive, change, as Mr. Muhammad put it, can be. Truth be told, controlling my weight has been the biggest change-challenge of my life (besides accepting that "Jesus ain't real").

For my relationship with food was the Achilles heel of my personal journey of self-empowerment. It was like trying to break up with a boyfriend who is no good for you, but you love him intensely anyway. As in any abusive relationship, I finally realized I had to *"break up"* with food and lack of consistent exercise, for good!. I think that was the most difficult part of the journey. Because I "loved" food, I refused to see or admit that I had a real problem. I didn't recognize that one should not have a "love relationship" with food in the first place. But being an "attractive" chubby girl, I told myself that my weight wasn't really an issue; though deep inside I knew that was just an excuse and moreover, an illusion. Thus, the first jolt needed to spark a change in my behavior was recognizing that I must face the truth.

With mindful attention to introspection and research, I came to understand that I am an emotional eater. Therefore, as an emotional person; I had a tendency toward eating far beyond the point of hunger satisfaction. Thus, my unhealthy relationship with food resulted in a body that experienced my poor eating habits as "normal". To maintain that unhealthy but "normal" condition, my body and mind craved the diet it had become addicted to; an unhealthy one chock full of sugar, carbs, and fat! I can't blame my body for that but, I can blame my mind. I didn't realize that at first. As I scrutinized these subtle intricacies, I concluded that I must unlearn (change) eating in unhealthy ways and learn (more change) the behavioral pathways to a healthier lifestyle. Sounds obvious, right? Just think of how many times you have recognized the barriers to change and yet, complete, constructive change continued to elude you!

The big purple elephant in the room was that, without addressing the mental and emotional reasons for my dysfunctional relationship with food, I simply could not change my behavior. I tried and tried, but with little or minimal results. But as I stopped resisting change, (and staying the course of my objective), my healthier thinking emerged as healthier behaviors. I started scrutinizing my choices; what I was eating and more importantly, why. It was at this point that I realized that I was often eating because of how I was feeling (bored, stressed, sad, happy, lonely, frustrated, etc.). Well imagine my dismay when I realized that I would have to change not one thing, but many things on the inside…thoughts, beliefs, and behaviors…before I would be able to change this one thing (my body) on the outside!

Yes! I've had to change the way I think about food. I also addressed the origins of self-defeating feelings and beliefs I had/have about myself. Keep in mind here that habitual behaviors were processed and stored in my emotional history from birth. Only after addressing my emotional memory was I able to change why I was eating, what I was eating, when I was eating, and how that overall tendency toward inconsistency showed up in other areas of my life. Whew! That's when I realized that the project of reprogramming my brain to think in new and different ways is the ultimate challenge! It is a big deal and it is a huge step. I commend you for staying the ascension course as we proceed.

> If your intention is to grow, ascend, and manifest your Divine, Creative Self in this world, **YOU MUST INNER-STAND, ACCEPT, AND BELIEVE THAT CHANGE IS GOOD**

The very presence of change presents infinite possibilities in your life! Reminding myself of that has helped me "break-up" with food and improve my health and eating habits considerably over the years. As I write this book, I am still a work in progress; learning to change my emotional relationship with food from harmful to healing and healthy. It has sparked a lifestyle demonstrative of more willpower, self-discipline, and yes… acceptance of change as a beneficial necessity of life!

CHANGE IS WORK

I don't want to make it seem like changing is something that you just do like changing your socks or your hair color. No. The work that goes into internal change, change in the way you think, is a process of unlearning what you have learned and then, learning what you must learn in order to move forward in the reality of that desired change. For example: if I were petrified of swimming but wanted to learn to swim, I would first have to get rid of the fear of water, the fear of drowning, the fear of helplessness... and of course, the fear of swimming. Then, and only then, would I be capable of learning how to swim. In fact, in order to become a confident swimmer, I would have to become fearless. It's the same thing in your spiritual growth. In every instance, you must first change the way you think to change behavior. And in most instances, the fear of something is almost always at the core of the undesirable thoughts we have, the choices we make, and the behaviors we engage in that are harmful to our spirit, mind and body.

Let's use the example of weight loss. If, in my mind, I have all kinds of misconceived beliefs that I am holding onto, my actions will affirm those beliefs and perpetuate the outcomes that those beliefs generate.

EXAMPLE:

I used to tell myself: *"I really don't eat so badly that I should be this fat...why, I'm the healthiest eating fat person you'll ever meet"!* Believe it or not, I operated with that belief for a long time. Ironically, those around me supported me in that insanity saying things like, "yeah... you really don't".

But deep within my Inner Self, I know how many times I have failed at having disciplined eating habits. Though others might witness me eating healthily, I know how often I'm messing up and falling off the healthy food wagon! I know when I've missed the gym for a whole week! I know all the places where I'm dropping the ball. So, I can tell myself *"I'm the healthiest fat person you'll ever meet"* all I want. But the reality is that I am most certainly not the healthiest fat person you're ever going to meet because there's no such thing as a "healthy" fat person! In truth, none of us are meant to be fat, for the presence of fat in the body is a clear indication of acidic toxicity. Thus, for me to flippantly make a statement like *"I'm the healthiest fat person you'll ever meet"* is concrete evidence of my own cognitive dissonance trying to justify-away why I weighed nearly 270 pounds!

If you really want to change, you must first recognize the behaviors that no longer serve you. Then, you must take personal responsibility for those behaviors. After all, ascending minds know that we are all ultimately responsible for our actions, right? Next, you look for the limiting beliefs that influence these behaviors. Finally, you must accept and sincerely believe that you need to change. I emphasize that you must <u>feel the need</u> to change because most often, we act out of our feelings rather than our intellect. Obviously, if you really think you've got it all together, you will not see a need to change. Sort of like how I convinced myself that my emotional eating habits were okay! So, if you are a selfish person and you want to become an unselfish person, you must first believe that being selfish is an undesirable characteristic that is, therefore, worth changing. Then, you own it by accepting that you are indeed, a selfish person. Now you are motivated and empowered for change.

Yes, owing your "ish" as they call it, is a crucial first step on your personal journey of ascension. For let's face it, owning your flaws is not the trend of our modern times, therefore, we can't assume that everyone has a problem with being selfish. Afterall, some people like being selfish...just ask the 1% of the 1%! In the meantime, I encourage you to begin the practice of routinely checking in with yourself and asking the questions...

What kind of life am I living anyway?

Am I living the best version of myself?

Can I do better?

Remember, ascending minds question everything! If you really want to grow into your highest spiritual self in this lifetime, you must perpetually ask yourself the question why. Why am I happy? Why am I sad? Why am I loving? Why am I rude? Why am I impatient? Why do I feel unloved? Why am I selfish? Why am I anxious? Why am I worrying? Why am I a pushover? Why do I eat too much? Why do I lie? Why do I hate? Why do I love? Why do I procrastinate? Why don't I take better care of my health (emotional & physical)? Why do I take better care of others? Why am I so angry? Why don't I know my purpose? Why am I inconsistent? Why can't I concentrate? ...and on and on. Often, this type of self-questioning and assessment will lead you to discover a past event or experience which birthed a psychological response (belief) into your reality. For your own mental health I recommend you focus on one question and one clearing process at a time.

These responses have helped your mind and heart cope with tragedy, confusion, abuse, neglect or disappointments from the past; all the way back to conception! Fortunately, you don't have to worry about changing the cumulative total of destructive thoughts and beliefs simultaneously. For now, just trust that if you engage in perpetual self-review and assessment, you will begin to identify those beliefs and thoughts which no longer serve you.

The purpose of this chapter is to help you discover that change is an inevitable aspect of life because the universe is not static, but rather, constantly evolving. Therefore, like everything else in creation, we, too, must evolve. In fact, it is only when we fail to evolve (change) that our mind and our experience of reality becomes stagnant, oppressive, uncreative and self-destructive. Thus, an ascending mind is an evolving mind, a changing mind, and an expanding mind. My commission is to prepare you for that process of change, which begins with recognizing that a need for change exists. I believe as you read on, you will be excited about all the possibilities that lay before you on this journey. When you are ready, the AMI Principle of Change is Good will help you become more comfortable with your personal ascension experience, thereby facilitating positive change in your life.

> *"Proper Planning and Preparation Prevents Piss Poor Performance"* **The 7 P's-A British Army Adage**

A PLAN FOR CHANGE

As this adage reminds us...If you fail to plan, you might as well go ahead and expect failure. For no intentional change occurs without a plan and the action needed to make that plan unfold favorably. As I mentioned earlier, change begins with first recognizing the need for it. Only then can we make a conscious decision to think and act in new and different ways. But how does one transform a decision into an actual experience of personal transformation? First, a full inventory of oneself is required to be truly effective. No building was built in a day. Neither was it built without a plan.

INNER-STANDING

Ascension is, first and foremost, a by-product of a life of purposeful intention to become your highest Self. It involves a process of perpetually being and becoming; a process of constant change. That is why you must perceive and embrace all change as good. Because, the willingness to change is a resource that will serve you often on this very important spiritual journey of discovery, growth and expansion. Transformation requires purpose, clarity, organization, and tenacity, as well as strategic use of creativity and objectivity. Ascension (change) is a comprehensive experience of transformation and evolution. If you are serious about personal transformation, you should start with a plan.

LIFE LESSONS ON ASCENSION

Making A Comprehensive Plan to Plan

If I decide I want to lose weight, I must organize my entire life accordingly. First, I must consider my weaknesses, my strengths, my history with food, my current eating patterns verses my desired ones, and my lifestyle. I must look at all the intersections where food comes into play in my daily life (at work, at home, in social settings, etc.) and plan accordingly. I must anticipate hunger, schedule my meals, research healthy menus, and shop for the most nutritious foods. I must put myself on an exercise schedule that is practical and attainable. Most importantly, I must design a plan to which I can adhere. Then, I must shop correctly. In my case, I must make sure that there is no forbidden food in my kitchen because I know that sometimes, I just don't have the will power to say no to ice cream calling me from the freezer!

In addition, I will have to take a full inventory of the triggers that cause my emotional eating. Next, research the origins of those emotions. Then, I construct a plan for responding to those triggers in new and healthy ways that don't involve eating! After that, I can begin integrating these new, planned responses into my daily life. Ultimately, this process of research, scrutiny and deductive reasoning empowers me to construct a comprehensive plan for changing my mind. If I stay the course, I will surely experience a type of transformation that helps me manage and even eliminate the emotional triggers which once had such a hold on me.

Now, this is where dealing with past issues and emotions or, as my mother calls it, history, becomes of crucial importance. How will I speak about food as I let go of this comforting, yet dysfunctional, relationship? I can't go back... not if I want to manifest complete, constructive, change in my inner-self and my outer-life. Surely, there is no point in making a temporary change in thinking. So...how in the world can/will I change what I think about food permanently? How will I unlearn over 50 years of unhealthy food relationship programming? Though such an endeavor seems like a recipe for failure, I choose to press on with this agenda for change because I am convinced that change is good, and necessary.

Let me encourage you here. You are correct. Change is not usually easy, especially not at first. Truthfully, the changes we need to make most are usually the hardest to implement. Drugs or not, we all become addicted to our thoughts and behaviors. That's because our thoughts, emotions, feelings, perceptions, beliefs, etc. trigger the same neurotransmitters which are activated in drug addiction. Change originates in our thoughts after all and these thoughts and beliefs, exist a vast wilderness of emotional weeds, resistant thoughts, and seeds of pain and heartache and yes…history.

If we try to change our behavior without addressing the origins of our thoughts, emotions, and beliefs, we are simply chasing our tail and might as well give up the pursuit of change altogether! Therefore, because our behavior is a by-product of our beliefs, thoughts, and feelings, we must consistently scrutinize them. These behavioral triggers manifest in our lives as expressions of love, hate, joy, sorrow, peace, chaos, beauty, anger, inner-standing, ignorance, patience, anxiety, confusion, and health or dis-ease in the body. Practicing regular introspection, contemplation, self-monitoring and evaluation helps you identify and address thoughts and behaviors that no longer serve you. This approach to personal growth is essential if you truly want to "save yourself before normal kills you"!

Once again, let me encourage you. Even if this information is new to you, be assured that you can create a plan for change if you try. I have complete confidence that you can. Spirit impressed upon me the urgency of writing this book and this chapter. People are hurting all over the world because they cannot gain control over their thoughts and feelings. Just think of all the times you've heard someone say:

"I would change, but I don't have the will power."

I would argue here that they don't have the will power and they don't have an action plan for change either. Just remember, the plan begins with the pursuit of one step; one goal at a time.

> *"Good intentions sure ain't enough, if you can't keep them when the going gets rough. Good intentions won't get you by. They'll just become, another thing undone, in your life"*
>
> ***Patti Labelle and the Bluebells: Music & Lyrics by Nona Hendryx***

Keep in mind, even though they are intricately interwoven, the tasks of changing your thinking and changing your actions are two very different and separate projects. In the former, your true Self is transformed as your thoughts are transformed and, in the latter, your life is transformed into an outward expression of your inner-standing. If you try to change undesirable behavior without addressing the emotional source of that behavior first, your good intentions won't be enough to sustain you through the process of change. That's why you need a plan to support your intentions: i.e., a schedule, a list of do's and don'ts, affirmations, rituals, etc. to help you keep those intentions when times get rough.

For your actions are the mirror of who you truly are inside. Your actions are the physical representations of your Heart, Mind, Soul & Will. Thus, changes in behavior are the evidence of changes in thinking. Remember, good intentions do not change anything. Actions do that. Once again, as the old folks say… *you can make your mouth say anything.* Which is why it is easier to succeed at a short-term diet plan than it is to change your eating habits for a lifetime. Trust me…I know! LOL. But I assure you. If I can change, so can you. This book is here to spark the idea that it is time for change in your life and to reinforce the belief that: Change is Good.

SELF-AWARENESS AND INNER-STANDING

As we all know, undesirable habits are generally very hard to break. That is because habits are connected to an unseen, and in some cases, an unexplored mind. If you really want to see change in your life, commit yourself to a life of self-awareness, introspection, reflection, meditation, and personal evolution. Pay attention to your choices, your attitude, your inner-dialogue, your Outer Self-talk and, yes, the feedback you get from others regarding your behavior. Remember to take a regular inventory of the thoughts and beliefs that live in the invisible world of your mind. Keep a written journal, record your thoughts, then, scrutinize them from the view of the Objective Observer.

I often recommend that my clients create video journals when they are trying to get to the bottom of their feelings or if they need to objectively see and experience themselves as they really are. Now that we have cell phones, making a video selfie is easy. Your video journal is also a very useful tool for creating an objective observer point of view. Just remember to express how you really feel and think; using this exercise as an opportunity to be vulnerable and honest with yourself. If you feel like you want to cry, cry. If you want to scream, scream. And if you want to blame everyone for your current condition, blame them. But I can assure you when you play that recording back and look at yourself for who you really are, you will come to know that the only one judging you, is you. For there is no one else to judge or critique you. There is no one else to blame.

Now, you can observe your own humanity; for better or for worse. Now, you can see and more importantly, inner-stand many of the underlying emotions that are behind your thoughts, beliefs, disappointments, opinions, values, and behaviors that no longer serve you. Don't get me wrong. I understand that approaching life in this way may seem like a daunting task. If, however, you apply this approach consistently, you will find that this practice of objective review gets easier and more useful over time. That is why I recommend all ascending minds practice a lifestyle of self-evaluation, introspection, reflection, dissection, and creation.

THE SUBCONSCIOUS CONDUCTOR

Most of what we do is a product of habit, without conscious thought. As we go through the day, we aren't even aware that our subconscious mind is navigating our conscious mental train. We are also probably not aware that our subconscious thoughts are driving our behaviors. It's like driving and talking on the phone. You're driving the car, but your conscious attention is on the call more than it is on the road. Though your attention is split, you can effectively multitask as your conscious mind is engaged in conversation and your subconscious mind is helping you safely drive the car. We can do this because these two minds work in concert to synergize the functionality and efficiency of the brain, body, and mind. The evidence of both minds at work is also intricately woven within the neurological pathways of the brain. Concurrently, that mental activity is apparent in the cumulative thoughts, beliefs, values and behaviors that make up the totality of the Self.

Inherently, you know you can rely upon this relationship between your conscious and subconscious mind because your brain has been functioning this way since birth! You also feel confident because you know you can trust the Subconscious Conductor to help you safely drive the car as you talk. In the process of personal change, however, you must reprogram the conscious mind and simultaneously reprogram the muscle memory of the subconscious mind if you want to experience a mental and behavioral revolution! Ultimately, as you begin to isolate both the conscious and subconscious influencers of your thoughts, emotions and behavioral habits, you can change how you feel, what you think, and how you behave in daily life.

TIME FOR A REVOLUTION!

In order to facilitate true and lasting change in any area of life, you must start with a mental revolution. **Merriam Webster** defines revolution as "***a sudden, radical, or complete change***". When it comes to mental operations, revolution can be defined as: *fundamental change in the way of thinking about or visualizing something; a change of paradigm.*

Let's first deal with this concept of a paradigm. We always hear corporate executives, marketing professionals, news reporters and the like throw this term around. The word paradigm is often used to describe changing trends in politics, economics, fashion and music. When analysts use it, the word always sounds a bit technically official. Maybe that's why people don't usually use it when speaking of making personal life changes. In its simplest definition, however, a paradigm is nothing more than *a pattern*. For the purposes of this chapter, paradigm refers specifically to a pattern of behavior. Thus, a personal paradigm shift refers to a change in your personal patterns of behavior.

Can you identify and describe the patterns of your own behavior? Do you know why you do things in the way that you do them? Do you know why you respond to others in specific and predictable ways? Do you know why you prefer a certain side of the bed, why you laugh at familiar jokes or why you always cry when you see movies you've seen many times before? I always cry at the same places of the movie Meet Joe Black. Though I know Brad Pitt is going to get hit by that car, I still jump as if it is as unexpected as it was the first time I saw the movie. And I still tear up in the scene where he makes love for the first time.

Following are personal survey questions that may help you start thinking about changing your Personal Paradigm. My hope is that after you answer the questions, you will recognize areas of thought and emotion that are begging for a revolution. Even if you are saying, "I'm not ready to change yet; I've got too much going on in my life right now" I admonish you to work through the Survey questions. In fact, I deliberately placed the survey in the chapter instead of the Appendix because I know how easy it is to put off till tomorrow what you can do today. So, if this chapter has sparked some desire within you to move toward personal change and growth, please proceed. What have you got to lose?

....

PERSONAL PARADIGM SURVEY

Your pathway to personal ascension begins here, with introspection, observation, and honesty. I commend you for taking part in this survey and I encourage you to make a commitment to yourself to integrate a life of perpetual change and evolution. You deserve it!

Do you know your paradigms, or rather, patterns of behavior? **YES___ NO___**

Please answer the following questions as honestly as possible. I recommend you start a new journal and write **"My Plan for Change"** on the cover. Please write as much detail as you can. Be specific about your moods, feelings, choices, influences, behaviors, opinions of yourselves and others, etc.

Describe your behavioral paradigms (patterns) in the following situations: Be sure to ask and answer why you behave the way you do.

(1) When you are with strangers.
(2) When you are with friends.

(3) When you are with people of other races.
(4) When you are with people of other ages (older/younger)
(5) When you are alone.

These are your unique, personal paradigms, or patterns, of thinking and behaving. They provide a roadmap to your inner-standing of your Self. What do these behaviors tell you about your inner thoughts, feelings, values, and/or beliefs?

MY DREAM PLAN FOR PERSONAL CHANGE

If you could design the world however you wanted it to be, what kind of world would you create? Describe what this new world would look like.

____

____

If you could design your life within that world however you wanted it to be, what kind of life would you create? Describe what your new life would look like.

____

____

If this new world and new life started today, what would you change first about your old life?

____

____

Select one aspect of yourself, your personality, thinking, beliefs, etc., that you think needs to change.

____

____

Why do you think this trait or behavior needs to change?

What new paradigm will you create to replace the old paradigm?

How will this change in behavior, self-perception, etc. improve the quality of your life?

What specific actions will you take to facilitate this change in your personality? This is the "plan" we discussed earlier in the chapter.

What will you sacrifice (let go of) for your plan work successfully?

What new experiences will result from this paradigm shift? And, how will you feel once this change is fully realized in your life?

PERSONAL SACRIFICE

Christians believe that the man they call Jesus paid for your salvation with his life. They believe that he made the ultimate sacrifice by dying for our "sins." Now I ask you…Will You die for You? Will you let your old ways of thinking and doing die, in order to experience new life with a mind free of guilt and full of love for yourself and others? Perhaps you would prefer to just exist, rather than live a life of expanding inner-standing, purpose and personal fulfillment? Time will tell. I am a living witness that this outcome is what a life of ascension (being and becoming) does for you…it sets you free and empowers you to evolve into the best version of your Self. Living a life of perpetual evolution (change) also teaches us something profound over time which is: all things work together for our good and the universe is, indeed, unfolding as it should! So, will you take a knife to the gut? Will you die for you? How much are you willing to sacrifice to live a happier life of more peace, joy, insight, and inner-standing?

The best thing that ever happened to me was having my children. Raising them taught me how to sacrifice. I learned how to put someone else's needs in front of my own. And I learned to prioritize what was most important over what I could set aside or eliminate in order to give my children the best life experience I could provide. Now, in my ascending mind journey, I understand that the sacrifices I make empower me to expand my Mind and liberate my Spirit. That is a sacrifice worth making! Writing this book was a sacrifice. It made me summon my personal discipline, fortitude, faith in myself, and faith in the belief that the book is necessary to help others, so I could stay the course to achieve the goal.

Isn't it ironic that we are willing to sacrifice for others more than we are willing to sacrifice for ourselves? This phenomenon speaks to a mental condition that most of us have which is low self-esteem. And low self-esteem is at the core of almost ever mental illness, neurosis, psychosis, deviant social behavior, and other mental dis-eases that people encounter. Let's face it. Most of us don't really think we're worthy to be loved. Nor do we think we're worthy for someone else to make a sacrifice for us. Unless, of course, we put our full salvation responsibility upon the man they call Jesus; a man we've never met and a man that only the Christian narrative presumes to verify ever existed.

MORE ON SELF-ESTEEM

When I speak of self-esteem, I'm not talking about egotism. Heaven knows the world does not need any more narcissists flexing their muscles and inflating their egos so they can devour the world. That too, is, an indicator of low self-esteem. But rather, I am shooting for you to have the kind of healthy self-view that enables you to look in the mirror and say…

> *I'm alright. I'm doing good things in the world. I believe in my ability to learn, grow and improve (change) myself and the world around me. I have confidence in my decisions. I lovingly take care of my Mind, Soul, Body and Spirit and my positive, personal view is evident in the loving, creative, productive life I live daily.*

I know that was a mouthful! I do recommend, however, that you recite this profession of your inner-standing as a starting place for reprogramming your Self-view. For the personal view you have is a very influential factor in your quest for change and spiritual ascension. For your Spirit will not override your emotions, nor your thoughts. If it did, we'd all be walking around in our fullest divine Self! For the Mind of the Spirit knows that we are one with a vast, eternal Universe of love, joy, peace, creativity, and expansion which we only experience if, we take the time to consciously observe it. My prayer is that each of us comes to experience that kind of reality more and more with each passing day!

May you know your Self as the wonderful creation you are! Asé

PLEASE PAUSE FOR YOUR 10 MINUTE MOMENT

CHAPTER FIFTEEN

The First Principle of the Ascending Mind: Love Yourself Enough

"Love thy neighbor as thyself" **(Matthew 22:39)**

INTRODUCTION:

It is no wonder that most people are simply not good at the execution of consistently loving their neighbor. That statement might seem negative or pessimistic to some. For there are many people who still do a good job of taking their neighbors into consideration as they proceed throughout the day. And yes, many people volunteer and help those in need or recognize, at the very least, that they should try to help those less fortunate than themselves. Nevertheless, I think most would still agree that today's global society is neither promoting nor encouraging a world where an individual's capacity for, and understanding of, neighborly conduct is cultivated.

Everyone is so rushed; both the young and the old. Moreover, most people are driven, consciously or otherwise, by a quest to finish first in their own self-induced drag race of life. In every major city of the world we hustle and bustle with our focus aimed squarely on our individual destinations. As a result, many common courtesies of old such as saying please, thank you, and excuse me, for example, have been replaced with impatience, lack of tolerance and oversight of the needs of our fellow man or woman. We do not hold the door for another because we have somewhere to go. We do not usually put ourselves in the shoes of others because we convince ourselves that bad choices put them in their unfortunate shoes in the first place. Many don't even try to see the world or each other through compassionate eyes anymore. I think that is because we judge ourselves and others so harshly. As a result, we find it difficult to deal compassionately with ourselves and others. How often have you ignored, stepped over, or been rude to someone on the street who needed your help? Yes, from the checkout line at the grocer to the communion line at church, we are often impatient, discourteous or oblivious to the needs of those around us.

So, when the dust settles on our busy lives, we usually find that the needs of the one, outweigh the needs of the many for most individuals. Our neighbor is the guy who lives next door, not the guy who processes our packages at the Post Office. This kind of thinking also plays out on a global scale; where the needs of the strongest military powers always outweigh the needs of the militarily inferior countries who struggle to protect their traditions and resource rich lands. Such was the case in the 2019 burning of the Amazon Rain Forest.

Similarly, the incessant wars and rumors of wars over the centuries in pursuit of gold, oil, diamonds, food and other natural commodities has created a crisis-level depletion of the earth's resources. In the name of profit and progress, products touting bigger, faster, better mean more and more money in the pockets of those who have the power to take these resources from their weaker counterparts. Likewise, our societal culture turns a blind eye to these atrocities for the sake of convenience and more stuff. All the while, we enjoy the fruits of these screw-your-neighbor behaviors, turning a blind eye to the impact that our need for the bigger-better has on our global neighbors.

The American people's blind eye to the personal colonization and rape of the world's resources, has also created a fracture in the delicate balance of the earth. Many cultures and ancient ways of life have been destroyed. Still we continue unconcerned with the long-term effects that our needs impose upon our fellow man, as we refuse to do without the latest convenience. Furthermore, in all endeavors, we must be first at whoever's expense. From our career goals to our position in the never-ending lanes of traffic on the freeway, we want to get there and get there first! Yet, we continue to assume that regardless of this constant air of competition, we will somehow have a culture that fosters our capacity to treat each other with mutual respect. It's sort of like expecting your garden to bloom when you know you, nor anyone else, has planted seeds in the first place.

Yes, we have all witnessed man's inhumanity to man played out on stages small and large across the ages. In contrast, we have also seen great feats of love and compassion even in the worst of times. Nevertheless, the consistent prevalence of man's inhumanity to man, stands alone as the prevailing barrier to world peace and global unity. As I write these words, the world is on edge as wars and rumors of world wars prevail in the news. Here at home, controversy and disagreement loom from the kitchen table to the conference table; while the hells of skid row are chock full of unfortunate souls who have been forgotten.

The streets of every major city bear witness to the demise of neighbors who have been left behind due to vast socio-economic disparities between the haves and the have nots. Consumerism and I-ism, that noble pursuit of self over the greater good, leaves an aftermath of destruction and lack world-wide. We now live in a global culture where inequality is the norm, the poor are forgotten, and the remainder are to live in a vacuum of singular and collective lack or privilege. As such, most are simply not consciously aware that they are no longer "loving their neighbors" let alone, themselves, as they pursue the economic dream that most have come to cherish more than life itself. Such a culture of mass conditioning leaves little room for learning how to love others and more damaging, how to love ourselves.

Unfortunately, amid all this hustle and bustle, we fail to recognize that the one who suffers most from this way of life and thinking is the collective whole of humanity. It's ironic really, that we don't realize there is a grace within the divine exchange between creatures, be they man or beast. When you pause for that moment, as you swiftly pass through an office door, to hold the door for the person behind you, there is a grace that is shared between you and that person, if only for a moment, which says, *"I care"*. Likewise, a quick, *"thank you"* affirms in reply, *"I appreciate your sacrifice"*. It is in that moment that grace is bestowed upon both parties and the reward is an affirmation that an act of love or at least mutual respect, has been shared. Moments like these tell you that you are worthy of love and respect. Moreover, taking the time to initiate this act, instills in the giver, a sense of purposeful awareness of his/her own capacity to love him/herself enough to create such a moment of mutual benefit in the first place.

In this chapter we will explore the AMI Principle: Love Yourself Enough. The concepts presented provide a pathway to inner-standing:

- What self-love is and what it isn't
- Which behaviors and beliefs prevent us from experiencing self-love
- Why the absence of self-love blocks our creative energy, diminishes self-esteem, blocks us from receiving love from others, and affects our overall mental, physical, emotional and spiritual health
- How self-love empowers us to love others more sincerely and demonstratively

YOU ARE WORTHY OF LOVE

Many experiences can contribute to a person feeling and believing they are worthy of love. I have already mentioned how feelings of love, care, concern, protection, tenderness, etc. can be transmitted to the unborn child of a pregnant woman. Plenty of scientific evidence supports this belief and many studies have verified the effect that the state of mind of the mother, has on the emotional and physical development of the fetus. Physically, metaphysically, emotionally, and spiritually, the mother and the child are interconnected, from conception forward. And this mother/child connection is usually the first human experience of what love is. So, whatever love message the mother is sending, establishes a blueprint for what love will look like as the infant becomes a child, an adolescent, a teenager, and ultimately an adult. Similarly, the interaction of the father with the mother and the child also contributes to the child's long-term mental and emotional love programming.

As the child grows, the experiences of life kick in as more contributing elements come into play. These experiences either reinforce the child's love blueprint with loving acts from parents, grandparents, siblings, classmates, etc. or they will distort the child's understanding of love, and expression of love for him/herself and others. Ultimately, the more positive, or negative, expressions of love the child is exposed to, the more the child's love bank is built into a design that evolves uniquely throughout the person's lifetime. That is why I strongly advise taking a full inventory of your love relationship with your parents if you struggle with self-love. Doing so may help you understand your unique "love blueprint" with more objective eyes. If you are a victim of parental abuse or neglect, however, I strongly advise that you only explore this process of discovery under the counsel of a mental health professional.

> *"...it is more blessed to give than to receive"*
>
> **Acts 20:35, The Apostle Paul**

IS IT MORE BLESSED TO GIVE THAN TO RECEIVE?

I don't know about you, but I can still come up with a significant list of things I should/would/could do differently, if I was truly committed to loving myself enough to do them. But when it comes to performing acts of loving sacrifice for others, it suddenly becomes much easier for me to commit to them. When I think of my capacity to sacrifice and persevere for the sake of others, all in the name of love, I am profoundly perplexed as to why I cannot or do not, consistently make those same sacrifices for myself. I suspect that somehow, I have subconsciously misinterpreted *"it is better to give than to receive"* to mean that receiving is somehow a less desirable condition to be pursued. However, when I ponder the ways in which I have shared mutual love with others, where I was both the giver and receiver of love, I am overwhelmed with grace and gratitude.

I teach that it is in giving and receiving, not just one or the other, that we witness the kind of creation love that the artist experiences through creative expression. For out of the depths of the artist's inner love energy, beauty is created and expressed. In return, the artist also becomes the receiver of that loving beauty that s/he experienced within and brought forth without. This is the divine cycle of the Universal Creator, who, being love, incarnated a loving creation that responds to that life-giving love as inexplicably divine beauty in all life. The Divine Creator is thus inspired to, and inspiring us to, repeat this loving cycle of giving and receiving with each new inner prompting to impart that creative, indwelling love to others.

Likewise, as we live as both the giver of love (*through creative expression*) and the receiver of love, (*through divine inspiration*) we reap and sow a loving harvest of our own design. In so doing, we learn to honor the divine beauty of the Universal Creator dwelling within us and every person we encounter. **The Principle of Loving Yourself Enough**, grounded in the practice of lovingly acknowledging the divinity in ourselves, as well as others, encourages us to seek and find this creative nature of **I AM**, the Creator who is and is in, each of us. *Namaste!*

I do not take this mutual exchange of love for granted because all love is energy that is shared, sacred and divine. For love is the energy from which life comes. What a miracle! Yet, I can also identify with times when giving love backfired and resulted in injury, emotional and otherwise. In the aftermath, all that was left was a garden runover with disappointments, emptiness, sadness, and regret. It took many years of personal repair to let go of the emotions attached to some of those memories. For there is truly nothing as painful as loving someone who does not love you back.

The *"loving"* I'm referring to here is the conscious, intentional, reciprocal exchange of intimacy (*physical, emotional & spiritual*) between two people. It is this particular *"mingling of the waters"* which ignites the Kundalini energy (*creation power*) of **I AM**; the creator and recreator of all life. But love unrequited, disrespected, overlooked, negated, abused, etc. creates an energy reaction that can function like a black hole; drawing into its dense vacuum, the emotional and spiritual debris of our cumulative life experiences. But as the loving nature of the Creator yearns within us, we confidently trust that finding these co-creative love experiences will once again, manifest life, wisdom, peace, joy, contentment, benevolence and insight into our own love-creating nature. With each new act of love, we are "born again" from the ashes of the seemingly destructive cosmic energy of the creative life force. Once again, what a miracle!

Knowing that the cyclical order of Creation is always one of birth, death and rebirth, I have trained myself to process the unfortunate love-hurt-recover-love again cycle as a much needed and efficient cleanse-and-purge necessity of life while still in the body; a function of the spirit-human growth paradigm. Moreover, I have trained myself to view my cyclical journey from the point of view of the conscious observer, which fosters an ability to see both sides of the coin, so to speak, in more perfect synchronicity.

CALLED TO SERVE
A Brief Reflection

As one who has a life vocation in service to others, there have been many times when I chose "being there" for another person over "being there" for myself; with disastrous emotional results I might add. Specifically, I am referring to the resentment and anger I felt when that person took my sacrifice for granted. Though I chose to ignore my needs in that moment and was not acting with a conscious need for acknowledgment, the hurt was still there; and with it, the revelation and regret that I had neglected myself in the process. This is a very common experience for people who have trained themselves to put others first. For we make the sacrifice, to put the needs of others before our own, with noble intentions.

But we do not realize that in setting aside the self-love that is needed to keep us "loved-up" for the masses, we, in fact, offer to others only a portion of our full capacity to love because we are not actually "loving" on a full tank. If you ask me for a ride in my car and I fail to put enough fuel in the tank, for example, I have done us both a disservice when we end up stranded on the side of the road with nothing but my good intentions to keep us safe and warm.

IS YOUR OXYGEN MASK ON?

I am reminded, here, of the first time I flew in an airplane with my three children. You all know the instructions that go something like this: *in the event of an emergency the oxygen masks will drop down... and if you are traveling with a child, please put the mask on yourself first before assisting the child.* Well, being a mother, this just didn't sit right with me at first. But when I considered the true purpose of this instruction, I had to appreciate the wisdom therein. For how can I save my child if I'm passed out for lack of oxygen? Now the child and me are facing our demise.

But if I am strong and thinking clearly with oxygen through the mask, my judgment is better and my ability to save my child is, most certainly, improved. Likewise, when I attentively address my fundamental need for self-love, I am empowering myself to love others with confident, capable assurance that the love I am giving is fueled with grace and complete commitment; without the potential for resentment. Thus, the first step for assessing whether I am loving myself enough begins with the question:

"Is my oxygen mask on?"

Consider the biblical reference to the "*breath of life*" mentioned in **Genesis 2:7.** According to that scripture, that breath of life caused man to transform into a living being... *"and man became a living soul"*; meaning without that breath of life, man was just a clump of clay! Metaphysically speaking, the breath of life is that same Kundalini "lifeforce" which was in the beginning and is all that ever was or shall be in the perceived future. Creation Energy; moving in and out of matter until that matter can no longer sustain the ever-expanding life force! And where does this breath of life go when the body can no longer contain it? Only THE ONE can say for sure. Our job is to be one with that life force as it expands and expresses us to our fullest potential, which is eternal and unlimited!

Take all this a step further and ask yourself why the airlines felt the need to include this in the safety instructions for all airlines? Surely it is because they recognized that a person's first reaction, because of their overwhelming love for their child would be to put the child's need before his own and save the child. We, as loving parents are groomed to put the needs of the child first. It is instinctual. Likewise, the more you love others first, the more automatic your response to the needs of others you love will condition you to put others' needs ahead of your own. It's usually way after the fact, perhaps when that love has been met with a lack of appreciation, that one thinks, *"I should have taken care of myself first!"*

There exists a certain social conditioning that also reinforces the tendency to put the needs of others first. And I am not at all saying that this is a bad thing. To the contrary, I am merely chipping away at some of the presumptions that make us put the needs of others first to such an extent that it occurs at the expense of our own well-being. Once this is happening, mind chatter that fosters envy, resentment, and anger, as well as, low self-esteem, self-loathing, and self-abuse can lead to a level of despair that would best be described by the various forms of mental illness that are so prevalent in the world today.

FREE TO LOVE

Walk the streets of any major city and you will witness the vast disparities in socio-economic wealth & opportunity. In fact, whether they know it or not, most global citizens are merely slaves to their jobs; regardless of the amount of money they earn. Homeowners are slaves to exorbitant property taxes and the middle class is buried in debt, while we all pay top dollar for organically grown food and health care products just to stay alive. Concurrently, the working poor, the largest segment of the workforce, live without equal access to quality education, a living wage, safe and affordable housing and quality healthcare.

Finally, the poorest and destitute must exist on the *"kindness of strangers"* (**Blanche-From A Streetcar Named Desire by Tennessee Williams**), both public and private. Yes, the reality is that in America, the "greatest country in the world", no one is truly free to live a life of economic or personal freedom. Even the wealthiest of citizens can affirm that money makes one neither happy, nor free. As the old hip hop adage suggests… *"more money, more problems"*.

Living under such oppressive conditions, it is no surprise that *"an estimated one in four Americans will experience a mental health disorder such as depression or anxiety"* according to the **National Alliance on Mental Illness.** When we factor in the skyrocketing opioid epidemic, *"on average, 130 Americans die every day from an opioid overdose"* according to the CDC as of December 2018, there is plenty of evidence to explain the cloud of despair, pain, hopelessness, and stress that looms over our modern-day society.

With all that pain, it is only logical that we do not consciously consider our neighbor's needs until the pastor announces the holiday food /toy drive at Thanksgiving and Christmas! For many, this seasonal approach to neighborly love does provide a feeling of community. But what happens to our neighbors in the in-between time? I'm not criticizing the seasonal givers. I am merely demonstrating how easy it is for one to sum up one's experience of neighborly love in one or two acts of sacrifice per year. But with this kind of thinking, living a life that consistently demonstrates a sincere love and concern for others becomes quite challenging. At the root of this dilemma, however, is the reality that most people cannot love others fully because they have not learned to love themselves enough.

REFLECTIONS ON ASCENSION
PRISONERS OF LOVE

Love is an act of our free will. Thus, in order to give love freely, one must be truly free. But in a world where we are conditioned to follow like sheep who have gone astray, where is the freedom? In a hamster wheel existence of work, eat, sleep…work, eat, sleep, who has the freedom to stop and smell the roses or help another? When I was a prisoner of systemic thinking, I was so busy doing for others that loving myself wasn't even a part of my thinking.

Because I believed doing for others was better than doing for myself, I made that my priority. You see, I wanted to do the right thing before "God" and man. I wanted to do right by my parents, teachers, spouse and children. And somewhere, during that pursuit, I became a prisoner to a cycle where my need for self-love was overridden by my need for demonstrating love toward others. More importantly, I came to realize that this mentality was driven by my need to feel loved by the people I loved…my parents, my spouse, my children and so on.

But I realize now that this decision was out of fear; fear of appearing selfish, fear of being a bad daughter or bad student or bad wife or bad mother, and yes, fear of not being loved by others! What a crazy existence it was. But now I know that fear of anything is the opposite of freedom. Because the one thing that makes love so divine, so fulfilling and so wonderful is that love is only love when it's given freely and without condition. That's what makes it love! Wow! I can't tell you how freeing it was to come to that revelation.

Discovering a pathway to self-love, as well as the love of others, requires a conscious and deliberate act of one's will. Society says give to the toy drive and you've done your duty to those less fortunate. Society even says, feed, clothe and shelter your children and you've done your duty to them. But as anyone who has ever raised children knows, there is much more to raising children than food, clothing and shelter. For it is the element of love that makes the most difference in a child's emotional and spiritual growth and development. But in order to give love freely, one must first be free, because love is an act of understanding, free will, and intention. If you are not experiencing freedom in your life, most likely, you are not experiencing your fullest capacity to love in the joy and abundance of free will.

WHAT IS LOVE ANYWAY?

Let us now look at love as a new concept to be explored and learned. Let us not comprehend love through the social norms of societies, religions, or feelings. Instead, let's examine the meaning, as well as the origins of the word itself so that we can create and define a pathway which leads us to this new and exciting experience called self-love.

So, what is love anyway? Is it an emotion? Is it a feeling or knowing that cannot be described? Is love an experience of euphoric joy, aroused by the presence of a special person? Is love a mysterious state of passion that we can neither explain nor define? How do we define love? And finally, what are the dangers of assuming we all mean the same thing when we speak of love, give love or receive love? The truth is, because people define love differently, they show it and experience it differently. These differences are diverse and from an outside view, can even be perverse and/or destructive. Likewise, our expectations of what love is supposed to look like differ just as drastically. The good news is that once you have decided for yourself what love is, you can then define what love should look like toward and from others. More importantly, you can then define what your plan for self-love should look like.

PERCEPTIONS AS BARRIERS TO SELF-LOVE

In my interactions with people who are hurting, I have observed certain patterns of thinking and self-destructive behaviors that are surely manifest as a byproduct of an underlying dis-ease of low self-esteem. As one who has counseled, taught, coached and directed others, I hear a certain reoccurring mantra time and again in response to the question:

Q: Why don't you just do what would be best for you?
Overwhelming Answer from Most:
A: I don't know. I guess I just feel like if I do that, I'm being selfish

Well that's an interesting response, to say the least! Mostly because it establishes a boundary in thinking, believing and faith by equating doing what's "best for you" with the negative connotation of the familiar word "selfish". Everyone knows that it's a bad thing to be selfish. Yet in reality, "attaching your oxygen mask first" clearly empowers you to be more supportive to others and, at the least, provides a calming effect on the mind, body, soul and spirit for better responsiveness in an emergency.

These four, Spirit, Soul, Body & Mind, are the essential elements of all souls vibrating within this realm of space and time we call life on Earth. Any imbalance in these four elements, mixed with environmental and socio-economic factors, can easily result in the disharmony we describe as low self-esteem.

WHAT IS SELF-ESTEEM?

According to the **Oxford Dictionary**, self-esteem is defined as: *"confidence in one's own worth or abilities; self-respect"*. Synonyms include: pride, dignity, self-regard, faith in oneself, morale, self-confidence, and self-assurance. Low self-esteem, in contrast, *"is characterized by a lack of confidence and/or feeling badly about oneself"*. People with low self-esteem also tend to feel unlovable, awkward or incompetent. In addition, *"people with low self-esteem tend to be hypersensitive, fragile and easily wounded by others."* **From: psychalive.org; Low Self-Esteem: What Does it Mean to Lack Self-Esteem?**

Let's focus for a moment on the terms "self-regard", "unlovable", and "self-assurance".

SELF-REGARD

REGARD:

To have regard for something or someone, is to consider, view, judge, or think of someone or something in a specified way. Your regard or view of that person or thing can be high or low, positive or negative, and/or helpful or destructive to your relationship with that person.

Since this chapter is all about loving oneself first, (not loving oneself only), we must remember here that how we regard another person plays a huge role in how we interact with that person and how much we allow our feelings and opinions, positive or negative, about that person to form our behavior toward them. If we have a high regard for another, say a supervisor at work, a public figure, or a famous entertainer, for example, we tend to hold that person in high esteem and treat them with respect, admiration, appreciation, and sometimes even reverence for the qualities they possess and/or the work they do.

We recognize their talents and abilities and we will even go as far as to defend them, even when we here news that they have perhaps done something unfavorable. Just think of all the times a celebrity has been caught doing something egregious, and how quickly a fan will defend their actions because of the high regard that fan has for them. Sometimes the fan's confidence in the person's integrity abides even when the facts are clearly displayed for all the public to see. I used this example because it shows to what degree a person's adoration may remain, even when that admiration is tainted by verifiable proof of a person's wrongdoing.

Now flip the script and think of yourself. How often do you beat yourself up because of some mistake you may have made? Or just think of how quick we are to criticize the unique traits that make us who we are; such as our facial features, our hair or our bodies. Yes, the pattern of self-critique runs rampant in human nature and often results in a self-view ranging from a slight oversensitivity about one feature to a comprehensive view of self-loathing. Subsequently, self-criticism can also lead to self-abuse, as in the case of addictions, or even suicide. Thus, when we perceive ourselves as inferior to others or to our own expectations, or, when we have a self-view that is always in search of what's wrong with us, we are fostering an atmosphere where self-loathing can easily develop.

But what if you decided one day to search for what's right about yourself instead of what's wrong? What if, upon review of the list of what's right about us, we decided to become our biggest fan. In so doing, we begin to recognize our talents and abilities, to hold ourselves in high esteem and to treat ourselves with respect, admiration, appreciation and yes, love. In so doing, we develop confidence in our own integrity and courage to defend our decision to love ourselves unconditionally.

I'm sure that sounds like quite a commission to someone who is suffocating in the quagmire of low-self-esteem; a condition that is difficult to rectify in this current age of media reminding you that you must look younger, feel stronger, run faster, work harder and live according to the paradigm of self-worship over collective appreciation of difference and diversity.

It would be naïve to think that this process of self-criticism rests solely on the media. Children are often compared to other students in class or siblings at home. *Why can't you be like Bobby and finish your peas Sheldon?"* Or, *"this 'B' on your report card is unacceptable, you should be making straight A's like Tiffany next door!"* The external critiques go on and on. Subtle statements from peers, teachers, parents, siblings, etc., contribute subconsciously or otherwise to our personal self-view. For some, the flaws that others point out far outweigh the positive messages we receive. Before too long, that child who felt inadequate becomes an adult with lots of issues that must now be removed from their suitcase of personal self-regard.

This discussion on self-love encourages you to take a full inventory of what has been said to you about you. How do others regard you? How do you regard yourself? Make a list and be surprised at how quickly the what's-wrong-with-me-list grows in comparison to the what's-right-with-me-list. As we move forward with this road trip on the "Free Way" of thinking, we will continue to visit our assessment of personal self-regard and how it, or the lack of it, plays a key role in our capacity to treat ourselves with consideration, self-respect, self-admiration, and self-appreciation.

SELF-ASSURANCE

ASSURANCE:

"A positive declaration intended to give confidence; a promise"

Synonyms: word of honor, promise, pledge, vow, oath, bond, undertaking, guarantee, commitment

Oxford Dictionary

Whenever I make a promise to someone, I am at least 90% certain to keep it unless some unavoidable circumstance arises to prevent me from doing so. If I pledge allegiance to a cause, the same applies. If I give someone my word of honor, I'd better be telling the truth or else I will be overwhelmed with an ocean of guilt for lying. And if I get a guarantee on a refrigerator purchase, that fridge sure as hell better work for the full term of that guarantee. If not, the seller has an obligation to repair it, replace it, or refund my purchase.

In other words, the seller has a commitment to fix the problem to my satisfaction or at the least, in accord with all stipulations of that guarantee. For the guarantee establishes a relationship of assurance between the two because the seller makes a promise, pledge, vow, and commitment to compensate the buyer if the product fails during the term of the guarantee agreement. But how does this type of relationship apply to our journey toward self-love?

Tis a lesson you should heed, if at first you don't succeed,
Try, try, again
Then your courage should appear, for if you will persevere
You will conquer, never fear
Try, try, again
Once or twice, though you should fail, if you would at last prevail,
Try, try again
If we strive, tis no disgrace, though we do not win the race;
What should you do in the case?
Try, try, again
If you find your task is hard, time will bring you your reward,
Try, try, again
All that other folks can do, why, with patience, should not you?
Only keep this rule in view:
Try, Try Again
By T. H. Palmer

How many times have you made a commitment to yourself that you failed to keep? If you're like most people, you probably can't come up with an actual number because you've broken promises to yourself many times over, and over again. This recurring pattern is both a cause and an effect of low self-esteem. I can't tell you how many people I have counseled who openly admit that they struggle with keeping the commitments they've made to themselves.

According to an article by Dan Diamond; Forbes, Jan 1, 2013 Edition; "*more than 40% of Americans make New Year's resolutions*" while "*just 8% of people achieve their New Year's goals*". Though these vows are made with the best of intentions, the reality is that most people simply do not make good on these annual promises they make to themselves. So, the good news is, you're not alone when it comes to the challenge at hand and the bad news is, there is no bad news if you... (you've got it), "*try, try again*"!

Unfortunately, many fail once and do not try again. Others, more sadly, do not even try the first time because they've been conditioned for failure from an early age. While others will try, and try, and try, and try without ever defining (or adapting) the game plan by which the goal may be attained. And yet, do you make, and break, promises to your loved ones? Not if you can help it...right? When you pledge your allegiance to a sorority or fraternity or a football team, how quick are you to forsake that bond?

As a die-hard St. Louis Cardinal Baseball fan, I wouldn't be caught dead in a jersey brandishing the Cubs or the Yankees. Closer to home, I would never put the needs of someone else's family over the needs of my own. Nor would I give up on one of my children who needed my support...emotional, financial or otherwise. Still, in most cases, when it comes to the man or woman in the mirror, it suddenly becomes easier to break a commitment made to oneself, even when that personal commitment is established in one's own best interests.

When I finally realized what I was doing, I couldn't help but wonder why I was giving up on myself so easily. I would try, fail, and then my self-talk kicked in to tell me... I'm not smart enough or I'm not equipped with the tools that I need to be successful. But did I do anything about these barriers, or did I cave in? I must be honest and say, yes, in the past, I quit many times.

In contrast, I am reminded, here, of Christmas' when my children were very young. It's right after that bewitching hour of the children's bedtime that we waited impatiently for them to go to sleep so we could start assembling the toys we'd purchased. It did not matter how much time it took, or how many instructions we had to read, or how many tools we had to scurry about to find in order to get the job done. Because those toys had to be ready before sunrise! Those children were counting on us to wow them as we did the year before. Every year we were determined to give them "the best Christmas ever" by any means possible.

Though I don't celebrate Christmas anymore, the point here is, we didn't want to disappoint them. We wanted to see them smiling and laughing and playing and happy. We wanted to keep all the promises we made throughout the year as we reassuringly said with each request for new toys; *"Just wait till Christmas"*. We wanted to give them our very best and disappointment was not an option. Yet, we disappoint ourselves all the time by breaking the promises we've made to lose weight, be more disciplined, achieve a goal or change a behavior. When we succumb to this pattern, we keep ourselves from enjoying life to the fullest and from experiencing the feelings of accomplishment, gratitude, joy, self-worth, and happiness that is our guarantee from our loving Creator. What's even worse is that in a state of low self-esteem, we break promises to ourselves again and again. And in doing so, we reinforce feelings of inadequacy, self-loathing, faithlessness, hopelessness and despair.

I believe that these indicators are the barometer of our capacity to love ourselves enough to make personal commitments, create plans to achieve our goals, make the necessary sacrifices, and yes… to "try, try, again" if at first, we don't succeed.

One Christmas we assembled, and reassembled, one of the toys 3 times before we got it right! And yet, though frustrated, my husband did not give up because he refused to disappoint our son. I contest that we all need to push through the frustrations that make self-love so challenging, just as we would if we were acting for the happiness of another. To do this, we must begin to make ourselves the object of our own affection when these times of "failure to commit" come upon us. We must love ourselves enough to want to see a smile on our own face, to refuse to disappoint ourselves, and to push through to give ourselves the best life ever! So, the next time you let yourself down...love yourself enough to try, try, again. Then, continue to do so until you reach the outcome that makes you love and appreciate yourself for a change. This reinforces your commitment to manifest this same outcome in the future. Just as we did not give up on that toy assembly project for the sake of our son's joy, you should, likewise, never give up on your ascension project for the sake of Your Joy! By doing this consistently and repeatedly, you ensure the success of your personal Ascension Project as you set and reach love-infused goals for yourself. This is how we manifest happiness...through conscious, persistent acts of self-love!.

For example, if you say you're going to start going to the gym, make that goal a reality by making the steps progressively attainable and realistic. A perfect example of the effectiveness of this progressive approach to change was revealed to me when I received a Fitbit last Christmas. I wanted the device because I knew in order to be successful, I would need accountability and feedback (another essential Ascending Mind Principle that is discussed on my website). The device proved a pivotal factor to my journey of weight loss, self-improvement and discovery.

The first day I walked a couple of thousand steps. I was exhausted, and, I also experienced intense pain in my lower back since I hadn't been walking much before I started the Fitbit fitness project. I was a bit discouraged at first. I remember thinking, man how am I ever going to get my fat, out of shape ass, up to the goal of 10,000 steps per day. Nevertheless, the next day pain and all, I walked again. But this time, I walked a shorter distance. When the back pain kicked in, I stopped, sat down, and rested until the discomfort subsided. When it did, I decided to try, try, again and walked a little further. Each day I pushed myself just enough…enough to keep my commitment at first and gradually, enough to exceed the number of steps I completed the previous day. And each day, after my walking was completed, I looked in the mirror and said… "you did it"!

Now, one year and thirty pounds later, I have a goal of 13,000 steps per day and find myself often walking as much as 20,000 steps or more when it gets good to me! Now, I have the self-assurance that I can stick to an exercise plan, after years of starting and stopping, trying and giving up on myself too soon. Now I am proud to tell others of my accomplishments and let them share that joy with me. These accomplishments have become outward indicators of my inner commitment. Now that's self-love! Remember, in order to break the cycle of self-sabotage and disappointment, you must give yourself the assurance that you will try, try again and never give up. You must be willing to do this for yourself, just as you would if a loved one's life depended on you doing it. Because a loved one's life does depend on it. That loved one is YOU! Asé

LOVABILITY

After searching in several source searches I finally concluded that lovability simply means you have charisma; that Je'ne sais quoi (translated as that "I don't know what") which makes a person want to kiss, hug, squeeze, and shower you with acts of affection. Babies are lovable, puppies are lovable, and the elderly are lovable. Even people who are notorious for bad behavior have been deemed lovable by those who love them. Selfish people must be lovable, for many times we find ourselves loving someone who fails to reciprocate that love in return while still receiving the abundant love we desire to give. That is, after all, how many hearts are broken. If one is lovable, therefore, it simply means that you are-able-to be loved. When you think of all the things people love, including toxic people, toxic food, and toxic behaviors, it is easy to see how the concept of lovability is truly in the eyes of the beholder.

In working with women who were victims of domestic violence, I learned how complex the concept of lovability truly manifests in our lives. For it's easy, from the outside looking in, to question how a person can love someone who is abusing them. And it's just as complex to understand how someone who is clearly lovable in the eyes of another, can perceive themselves as being unlovable based on their own self-regard (consideration or view) of themselves.

LOVE IS...MORE THAN AN EMOTION: MAKING THE DECISION TO LOVE

It is my position that love is much more than a feeling of affection, attraction, tenderness, admiration, benevolence and devotion for another. For if love were just a feeling or emotion, relationships grounded in love would not be able to endure once that feeling leaves. We have all continued to love someone who was hurting us emotionally or causing some great trauma in our lives. Women who "love" abusive husbands, for example, usually continue to love the perpetrator even though they are not consistently experiencing feelings of assurance, affection or benevolence in that relationship. Parents can love their children but still abuse or neglect them for a multitude of reasons and circumstances. If you were to ask a neglectful parent if they love their child, however, they will insist that they do. And even when abused children feel physical and emotional pain at the hands of their abusive parents, most of them, oddly enough, will usually continue to state that they do love their parents regardless.

Likewise, any couple who has been married more than 20 years can surely testify that if love were just a feeling of affection or adoration for another, their marriages would have crumbled years ago. For though we do not always feel like we love the person who is the object of our love, we can continue to honor the decision to love that person and still demonstrate the behaviors associated with love such as self-sacrifice, kindness, charity, compassion, or benevolence. So, when we pay attention, maturity teaches us that love must involve much more than an emotional feeling.

Unlike Merriam Webster, real life gives us a much more complex and panoramic view of love that dispels this misconception that love feels good! To the contrary, it is evident in circumstances of prolonged love relationships that the range of emotions have more than likely spanned every aspect of the human emotional spectrum from profound love, affection and admiration to the most extreme hatred, despair, or desolation; and every feeling in between. Such extremes are evident in the frequency of tragic crimes of passion wherein someone takes the life of the one they supposedly love because of jealousy or unrequited love.

I don't mean to sound morbid here but the point I'm trying to make is: if you walk through life believing love is a feeling only, you may miss out on the vastly profound revelation that love is also an experience of personal decisions that are made in relationships, regardless of the feeling one may have for that loved one at any given moment in time within the full span of that relationship. As a wife and mother, I can certainly say there were many days when I performed acts of love despite how I may have been feeling about my family on any given day. Anyone who has had a husband or wife, a daughter or son, a mother or father should be able to relate to this phenomenon. That being, it is quite possible to perform acts of love without feeling emotional affection for the recipient of that love while performing said acts.

So, then, there must be some other contributing factor that prompts us to behave outside of our emotions for those we love; something beyond the feeling of the moment. For true love, true affection, true admiration, attachment, devotion and unselfish concern and sacrifice for our loved ones requires a commitment, sacrifice and dedication that is not necessarily always based in an emotional response to another human being. It is that commitment and dedication that empowers one to choose to act with loving intention, despite the absence of the emotions needed to fuel our intentions toward the ones we love.

I believe we certainly need to revisit the definitions provided by antiquity on the meaning and function of the action noun LOVE. For in my experience, love was/is much more a function of a mental decision than it is an emotional inspiration. Not that feelings or emotions are somehow less relevant, god forbid. But the element of decision, a key factor in every loving choice made, is part of what makes love such an ethereal anomaly within the realm of the human experience. People do great things for love. Wars have been fought and countries toppled for the sake of love. Families have persevered through addictions, financial hardships, infidelities and other broken trusts, for love. And, it is that decision to love that has trumped the emotion of love every time.

Because I loved my parents, I was committed to doing what was expected by, and pleasing to, them. But my obedience had much more to do with wanting their approval than it did with a feeling of love. I realize now that it was getting their approval that gave me a feeling of acceptance, connection and belonging which I instinctively craved! Now that's a real hot potato to toss! If you are honest with yourself, you'll have to admit that seeking someone's approval is most likely not a desire that is rooted in love so much as it is a need for validation. And the need for 3rd party validation is directly linked to our universal tendency toward…that's right…low self-esteem. For it is this approval of others that feeds our human tendency to measure and compare our value to the value we perceive others to have. A perfect example of this is the social phenomenon of *keeping up with the Jones'* wherein my car is fine if it's better than my neighbor's car. But if my neighbor gets a better car, my car quickly pales by comparison;

making it no longer nice but below par. I believe that this tendency to make these comparisons to others activates our craving for attention and acceptance from outside of ourselves. This craving for outside approval is a tremendous contributing factor that directs our decision making and internal motivations. I would love to elaborate fully on this train of thought, but I have so much for you to consider.

For the purposes of this chapter, simply keep in mind that it is essential to your understanding of the Love Yourself Enough Principle to recognize and distinguish the source of your love motivators, which trigger your decision to act in loving ways toward others.

LOVE AND SCIENCE

The miracle of the human body is a divinely wonderful creation; a merging of cosmic, organic, matter synergized into an energy command center that repairs, regulates, destroys and rebuilds in response to the ever-evolving inner and outer experiences of the human mind, heart, body and spirit. Though we think we know much, modern science and medicine is still learning how the brain & glands function. Most scholars in these fields admit however, that there is still so much more to explore. It is only recently that modern man has even acknowledged the existence of the 360 cosmic energy centers of the body, which work together to operate the complex spiritual temple we call the human body. Most western doctors do not understand the unseen, yet apparent influence that metaphysics has on the physical world. They cannot, therefore, fully comprehend the energy potential that the human body possesses. Though the ancients, had a deep understanding and respect for these universal physical and supernatural relationships before the modern age, these teachings have become mysteries and secrets held captive by an elite class who understand the power of the Eternal Spirit.

In our current age, however, where the universe is expanding at an accelerated rate that opens spiritual seekers to the wonderment of possibilities, we find more and more spirits-being-human discovering the miraculous power of the human mind, body and spirit. This awareness will also be cultivated through the empowerment process. For now, simply know that this journey to self-love and the subsequent freedom that arises from that love, is eternally tied to functions in the metaphysical realm; in dimensions unseen or unrecognizable by the average person. These energy impulses can be activated by your heightened awareness of certain practices and disciplines that will connect you to a love of self, a love of others, and a love of all creation!

LOVE AND THE BRAIN

One phenomenal discovery of modern physiological psychology, however, has emerged from research in the field of child abuse. The question in a series of research initiatives sought to determine why children of abusive parents were able to retain a feeling of love for their parents, despite the abuse. In testing certain neurological centers in the brain, scientists discovered an attachment control center that is active in an infant's brain at birth. According to **Dr. Regina Sullivan, Ph.D.**, negative early experiences can cause long-term genetic, brain, behavioral, and hormonal changes that can affect not only the abuse victim but also the victim's descendants. These changes can create a biological formation of bio-chemical reactions that are remembered and repeated within the infant's brain. **Dr. Sullivan** explains that:

> *"once a newborn knows its mother, it will do its best to remain with her. That's because the infant's brain is wired from birth to attach to the caregiver. This attachment, regardless of who the initial caregiver is, will remain in that child through its lifetime."* **Dr. Regina Sullivan, Ph.D.**

Thus, the initial wiring remains in the electro-chemical bio-circuits of that child throughout their lifetime. Likewise, any triggers associated with this initial attachment experience, will continue to actively influence that person's response to abusive stimuli far beyond the relationship with the initial caregiver.

The long-term influence of this bio-chemical attachment center is one reason why low self-esteem, once branded in the human organic matter, becomes one of the largest barriers to self-love and self-empowerment. I believe this feeling of attachment is vital to our understanding of love and how we express it to others and ourselves. If, for example, you are a victim of abuse from a loved one, you may find yourself unconsciously playing out this same pattern of caregiver attachment to the next lover who comes your way.

My objective here is to help you consider the many influencers that may play a part in your ability to cultivate your own personally induced self-esteem project. And since I have already addressed how self-esteem, or the lack thereof, plays such a key role in your self-love project, I want you to know that I realize some of us have a much harder barrier to breakdown and rebuild than others. The good news is you're not in competition with anyone here…not even yourself! The most important thing to remember is that building self-esteem is a process and more than that, a journey of discovery that you will come to appreciate on the AMI Free-Way approach to life and personal happiness. A **Personal Empowerment Plan** is essential to helping you reprogram your organic brain matter, your emotional memory centers and your cosmic balance. For you must remember that all is connected, all is divine, and all is working in concert toward the manifestation of this great existence.

WHAT WOULD BE BEST FOR ME?

Conscious reprogramming not only helps you to engage in active self-love, it also trains the mind to remember to ask this question with consistent repetition: *What would be best for me?* Keep in mind that asking the question does not mean you plan to disregard the needs of others or that you will even decide to put your needs first. Moreover, it would be naïve to assume that asking that question will make you disregard, or worse, mistreat others just because you took yourself and your needs and feelings into consideration too; unless you are already a person of such degraded spirit and character. The fact is, a conscious choice, a fully informed choice, always has a better outcome that a haphazard one. Considering your needs and feelings and bests should happen before you act.

Remember, the Always Ascending way is all about making conscious, informed choices; springing forth from your awareness that you are one with all things and all people. I tend to believe that people who stop to ask themselves... *"wait a minute, is that what I really want to do...?"* or, *"would this action or that choice be best for me?"* are much less likely to experience resentment or regret about the decisions they make. You can't get mad at everybody else because you didn't take the time to show love for yourself by taking your feelings and needs into consideration! Oh...but people do it every day.

If you make a list of half the things you do for others to show them that you love them, then do just half of those things for yourself, you will be amazed at how your mood, your sleep and your state of mind will improve. When did you last buy yourself a beautiful bouquet of flowers or take yourself to the spa for a me-cation: that's a vacation for just me, with me. These acts of love bring a certain energy into our inner and outer space that says... *"I'm worthy of being treated lovingly"* or *"I love me enough to do nice things for myself just as I would for another."* And no, I haven't forgotten my introduction because all of this must be discussed if you're going to develop the ability to love others well. Love thy neighbor as thyself. Love they neighbor in the same way that you love yourself. Treat yourself poorly and you are likely to treat others poorly too. For without self-love, what quality of love are you giving to others? On the flip side, how can you expect others to love you if you do not see yourself as being lovable? If you will not cultivate the discipline to make loving choices for your own wellbeing and wholeness, how can you possibly cultivate the self-discipline needed to treat others with the care, consideration and respect that is so vital to neighborly awareness?

The AMI Principle of **Love Yourself Enough** teaches that our ability and desire to love others is directly correlated to our capacity for loving ourselves. That is because loving ourselves first, through intentional acts of self-care and self-awareness, causes us to exude love and self-confidence. In turn, our self-assured energy attracts others who are also self-loving, and who also bestow loving acts upon us. Have you ever wondered why some public figures are so adored by their fans? It is that air of self-love and confidence which draws loving fans like magnets to their charisma, and, outer appearance of confidence and self-assurance. The truth, however, is that most people, struggle with some degree of low self-esteem...even celebrities! Many of them have simply learned how to "act" as if they "love" themselves and others. In all walks of life, therefore, we will discover that many are struggling behind the scenes with low self-esteem, depression, insecurity and even, self-loathing. Sometimes, this inner distress manifests as anger, aggression, dominance, arrogance, or violence toward themselves or others.

The AMI Principle of **Love Yourself Enough** is, therefore, essential to the process of personal ascension. Mastering this principle also keeps us in alignment with the evolutionary nature of all of creation. For everything is infused with the Kundalini energy of creation, which is powered by love and intention. Yes, purposeful intention is the action that brings forth reaction! It takes intention to stop and pick up a bouquet of flowers for your mate on your anniversary. It takes deliberate acts of intention, sacrifice and stamina to purposefully love and raise your children. Yes, it takes fortitude and courage to encourage them to grow and learn and keep going even when the going gets tough, etc. And because all of nature is designed with such clarity and specificity, I am convinced that all living things on Earth are here intentionally. Therefore, I believe we are not an accident and, most assuredly, are here, right now, for a divine, creative, purpose.

For true love of others is manifest in the things we do to express our intention to sacrifice for the good and betterment of another. This sacrifice may or may not be evident to the one who receives that love in all its forms and expressions. But when we express love to others and that love is acknowledged by the recipient, we are filled with the same joy and feeling of love that we have just expressed. More profoundly, when we express love for/to ourselves, we become both the giver and receiver, experiencing a double dose of love that nurtures our spirit, mind, body and soul. So, when we love ourselves first, we connect ourselves to the greater energy of love that is all naturally created life. It is this connection to all creation that begins our journey of personal empowerment.

CONCLUSION

Where do We go from Here?

I did not start this journey with the intention of writing a book. I just started out with questions. The answers to which, begat more questions and more answers than I could ever have anticipated. For I was looking for information and information found me. As seeking and finding became my way of life, curiosity and deductive reasoning led me on a path of personal discovery and spiritual ascension. With each new revelation I applied myself to unlearning what I had learned; as old belief systems fell on fertile soil, birthing new seeds of growth and personal awareness. The more truth I experienced, the more persistent my search for the truth became. I did not fall down a rabbit hole. Instead, I dug my way through of tunnel of modern lies and ancient truths as I crumbled away the dirt and uncovered gem after gem of brilliant revelation. With each gem I added to my collection, the doors to my mental prison eased open until I finally realized I was free! That is what I want for you today. That is why I wrote the book. To help you set yourself FREE!

For my journey to freedom led me to more self-love, better self-care, conscious-collective awareness, deeper inner-standing, clarity, motivation, productivity, connectivity, spiritual and mental ascension, and yes, personal power, than I could have ever hoped for. I have learned to say no to illusion, to create pathways to purposeful outcomes, to manifest joy, peace, contentment, happiness and blessings, and, to overcome barriers to hopelessness. Now, every day, I find myself waking up with expectation, gratitude and joy. I celebrate me, because I know I will always be there for me. I will always love me, and I will always know and live truth, because I AM TRUTH. Yes, I AM a divine spark of the One, a micro-quan in the universal energy of Creation…and I matter. Moreover, I have a job to do that no one else can do…because I am uniquely ME and FREE! That is what I hope you get out of this book…a feeling of hope in the possibility that you, too, can experience authenticity and freedom. Yes, I'm believing that you will leave this book knowing that the answer to all your "problems" lies within you and is YOU! For only you can know YOU. And yet, WE are also known, in ONE. Do you see? Do you know? Can you imagine infinite possibilities?

Your final assignment for this book is to take a 10-Minute moment right now; before you forget to remember that you can and must Save Yourself. Before you settle into that moment, however, I want you to set aside a piece of paper or your favorite journal. In this 10-Minute Moment, do your very best to think of nothing at all. No questions, no answers, no promises, no emotions, no conclusions. If you need 20 or even 30 minutes to settle down to peace and stillness, take the time. For the process of making soup starts with an empty pot. When your quiet time is up, just turn to the next page of this book and answer the question presented there. Do not cheat and turn the page now. If you do, you are cheating yourself out of a divine opportunity for a spiritual awakening that will forever change the trajectory of your life. For you are, indeed, the savior that you seek, and, no one else is coming to save you! But do not despair because you are saving yourself right now! For you are made of the stuff of the universe, an ever-expanding energy ordered by divine love, creative energy, and synchronicity. All is one and one is all, and so, you cannot fail. This is just the beginning!

In love and faith!
Michelle "*Mama*" Crenshaw!

THE END

FINAL EXERCISE

> *"It matters not how strait the gate, how charged with punishments the scroll,*
>
> *I am the master of my fate,*
>
> *I am the captain of my soul.*
>
> From the poem **Invictus** by **William Ernest Henley**

PLEASE RESPOND TO THE FOLLOWING QUESTIONS IN YOUR JOURNAL ENTRY

1. What are your initial thoughts on this quote?
2. Is this statement consistent with your current self-view? Why or why not?
3. Would you like to be the master of your own fate? Why or why not?
4. Would you like to be the captain of your soul? Why or why not?
5. How would your life be different if you were the master and captain of it?
6. Does your current belief system compete or conflict with Mr. Henley's statement?
7. What can you do to make this statement true in your life?

8. What thoughts or beliefs must you overcome to make this statement a reality in your life?
9. Who are you?
10. What kind of life are you living anyway?

THE AMI PERSONAL AWARENESS QUESTIONAIRE

True or False

______ 1). I work at my present job because I need the money.
______ 2). I usually do what others ask me to do.
______ 3). I feel that I have many options and choices in my life.
______ 4). People always come to me for help.
______ 5). My job is the most important thing in my life.
______ 6). I don't have time for vacations.
______ 7). If I had more money I would be happier.
______ 8). I enjoy spending time alone.
______ 9). Meditation is a waste of time.
______ 10). I look forward to tomorrow with expectation.
______ 11). Life's a bitch and then you die.
______ 12). I am comfortable trying new things.
______ 13). My energy is usually low.
______ 14). I try to enjoy myself when I can.
______ 15). I never have enough time.
______ 16). I feel bad when I tell loved ones no.
______ 17). I am the strong one in my family.
______ 18). My work is very creative.
______ 19). I wish I knew my true purpose.
______ 20). I experience peace often.
______ 21). Sometimes I feel like nothing will ever change.
______ 22). I love the work I do and would gladly do it for free.
______ 23). If I could live my life over, I wouldn't change a thing.

______ 24). I have made a lot of mistakes in life, but, I have learned from most of them.

______ 25). I feel I have control over my life.

______ 26). When I set goals for myself, I usually achieve them.

______ 27). Money is very important to me.

______ 28). I would describe myself as a happy person

______ 29). People give me help when I ask for it.

______ 30). My family/friends are a great support group for me.

______ 31). I know how to do many things well.

______ 32). I have at least one hobby.

______ 33). I usually put the needs of others before my own.

______ 34). I know how to make a plan and stick to it.

______ 35). I work better with a team.

______ 36). I do not feel I have a "special" gift.

______ 37). If I have a gift, I don't know what it is.

______ 38). I always have lots of energy.

______ 39). I look forward to tomorrow.

______ 40). My life is hard.

______ 41). I depend a lot on other people.

______ 42). I find it hard to make difficult decisions on my own.

______ 43). I feel isolated from others.

______ 44). I want my life to stay the same.

______ 45). I usually speak my mind.

______ 46). No one is ever truly free.

______ 47). I think outside the box.

______ 48). I consider myself to be of average intelligence.

______ 49). I am very smart.

______ 50). I wish I was smarter.

______ 51). I love the work I do.

______ 52). I don't like to be alone.

______ 53). I am usually tired.

______ 54). I hate my job.

______ 55). I often get in a rut

______ 56). Change makes me nervous.

______ 57). I usually go along with the majority.
______ 58). It's better to follow the rules.
______ 59). Other people get all the breaks.
______ 60). I hope my life will change someday.
______ 61). I don't want to be different.
______ 62). I like being different.
______ 63). I am a leader.
______ 64). I follow the crowd.
______ 65). Things never goes my way.
______ 66). I make my own decisions.
______ 67). I don't care about the future.
______ 68). You can't change the world.
______ 69). People are basically evil.
______ 70). People are basically kind.
______ 71). I have a mentor.
______ 72). I do not have everything I need.
______ 73). I often help others solve their problems
______ 74). I believe in the tenets of religion.
______ 75). My life is exactly how it should be.
______ 76). My past mistakes keep influencing my future.
______ 77). I am afraid sometimes.
______ 78). I sometimes feel depressed.
______ 79). I think for myself.
______ 80). I have many choices.
______ 81). Other people seem to have all the luck.
______ 82). I never win.
______ 83). I don't have the resources I need to pursue my dreams.
______ 84). Dreams and plans are the same.
______ 85). I could achieve my goals if I had help.
______ 86). There is never enough money.
______ 87). I love myself just the way I am.
______ 88). I don't need to change anything about myself.
______ 89). There is not enough time in the day
______ 90). I am smart.

______ 91). I am intelligent.
______ 92). I am interesting.
______ 93). I am likeable.
______ 94). I am different.
______ 95). I make my own decisions, regardless of social norms.
______ 96). I am easy to get along with.
______ 97). Self-love is the same as selfishness.
______ 98). Happiness eludes me.
______ 99). I love other unconditionally

100). Please fill in the blank. Then complete the writing exercise

(Please complete the following sentence. Be specific and include all the wishes you may have): "I wish I had..."

____

____

____

WRITING EXERCISE

THE ROAD MAP: ***My Life Without Limitations***

Describe what your life would be like if you had no obstacles or limitations in your life... starting today! What would you do differently? How would you live? How would you change? How would you grow? Who would you help? Where would you live? What kind of work would you choose? How would you feel about yourself?... your life?... and others? Remember: Money, or the lack thereof, is not an issue in this exercise. You can pursue any life path(s) you desire. I recommend you take a 10-Minute Moment before you begin, and, spend at least 30-60 minutes on this exercise. Be sure to ignore, or creatively solve any perceived limitations. Also, avoid the temptation to think of this exercise within "normal" parameters. If you encounter any perceived obstacles, think creatively and out of the box if necessary. For the sky is the limit. Do not be concerned with the opinions of others. You do not have to follow any existing "norms" for this exercise because ALL THINGS ARE POSSIBLE. ENJOY!

____

____

____

____

____

____

____

____

____

____

BIBLIOGRAPHY

Taggert,	L.	*The Field: The Quest for the Secret Force of the Universe*	HarperCollins Publishers Inc.,	2002
Toynbee,	A. J.	*A Study of History: Abridgement of Volumes I-VI by D.C. Somervell*	Oxford University Press	1974
Talbot,	M.	*The Holographic Universe*	HarperCollins Publishers Inc.,	1991
Goswami,	A. J.	*The Self-Aware Universe: How Consciousness Creates the Material World*	J.P. Tarcher	1993
Hawking,	S. W.	*A Brief History of Time: From the Big Bang to Black Holes*	Bantam Books	1988
Hawking,	S. W.	*The Theory of Everything: The Origin and Fate of the Universe*	Jaico Publishing House	2006
Laszlo,	E.	*Science and the Akashic Field: An Integral Theory of Everything*	Inner Traditions	2004
Sertima,	I. V.	*They Came Before Columbus: The African Presence in Ancient America*	Random House	1976
Clarke,	J. H.	*Christopher Columbus and the Afrikan Holocaust: Slavery and the Rise of European Capitalism*	Eworld Inc.	1994
Conway,	D.J.	*The Ancient & Shining Ones: World Myth, Magick & Religion*	Llewellyn Publications	1993

Papadopoulos	R. K.	***The Handbook of Jungian Psychology: Theory, Practice and Applications 1st Edition***	Routledge	2006
Sitchin	Z.	***Genesis Revisited: Is Modern Science Catching Up with Ancient Knowledge?***	Bear & Company	1991
Jaroszkiewicz	G.	***Images of Time: Mind, Science, Reality***	Oxford University Press Inc.	2016
Stenger,	V. J.,	***Timeless Reality: Symmetry, Simplicity, and Multiple Universes***	Prometheus Books	2000
Icke,	D.J.	***Children of the Matrix: How an Interdimensional Race Has Controlled the World for thousands of Years-- And Still Does***	Icke, David Books	2001
Darwin	C.	***The Origin of Species***	New York : P. F. Collier	1909
Leakey	R.	***The Origin of Humankind***	Phoenix/Orion Books LTD.	1994

Printed in the United States
By Bookmasters